Gender and Work

SUNY Series in the Sociology of Work
Judith R. Blau, Editor

Gender and Work:
A Comparative Analysis of Industrial Societies

Patricia A. Roos

State University of New York Press

Published by
State University of New York Press, Albany

©1985 State University of New York

Printed in the United States of America

For information, address State University of New York
Press, State University Plaza, Albany, N.Y., 12246

Library of Congress Cataloging-in-Publication Data

Roos, Patricia A.
    Gender and work.

    Bibliography: p.
    Includes index.
    1. Sexual division of labor. I. Title.
HD6060.6.R66 1985   305.4′3   85-10078
ISBN 0-88706-031-5
ISBN 0-88706-032-3 (pbk.)

For my parents

Contents

Figures and Tables

APPENDIXES

Acknowledgments

This work benefited substantially from the insights, comments, and criticisms of many friends and colleagues. My greatest intellectual debt is to Donald Treiman, whose high standards and editorial skills made this book much richer than it would have otherwise been. Several other colleagues generously provided criticism and advice on earlier drafts of the manuscript, including Valerie Oppenheimer, David Lopez, John Czajka, David McFarland, Jonathan McLeod, Bernice Pescosolido, Robert Robinson, Michael Sobel, Linda Waite, Finis Welch, and Wendy Wolf. I also benefited from discussions with Pamela Cain, Robert Erikson, Katharine Gaskin, Heidi Hartmann, Jonathan Kelley, Vered Kraus, Barbara Reskin, Georges Sabagh, and Ronnie Steinberg. Katharine Donato, Sue Eddy, Joyce Hennessy, and Roberta Karant provided valuable assistance during the final revision and editorial process. I would also like to thank Marianne Roos for her diligence in compiling the index. Through their editorial assistance, Bill Eastman and Peggy Gifford at SUNY Press ably facilitated the completion of the manuscript. Finally, I wish to thank Lee Clarke for his continued support, intellectual and otherwise.

I gratefully acknowledge research support from several sources, including an NIMH grant to Donald Treiman and Jonathan Kelley (#RO1 MH 26606-01), a U.S. Department of Labor grant (#DD–06–80–003), and a faculty research fellowship from SUNY Stony Brook (#431–7531–A). A much revised version of Chapter 6 was published earlier in the *American Sociological Review* (Volume 48:852–64, 1983).

The data used in this book were made available by Donald Treiman and the Inter-University Consortium for Political and Social Research

(ICPSR). Neither are responsible for the analyses or interpretations presented here.

Finally, I would like to express my appreciation to my parents, to whom I dedicate this book. Their support over the years has been invaluable.

Port Jefferson, N.Y.
January, 1985

CHAPTER ONE

Industrial Society and the Division of Labor by Sex

INTRODUCTION

The American occupational structure, like that of other industrial societies, is highly segregated by sex. This gender division of labor was characteristic of the industrializing United States economy and, despite important social changes over the last century, persists today at similar levels (Gross 1968; Oppenheimer 1970; Blau and Hendricks 1979). Since 1970, women have made modest progress integrating jobs held traditionally by men, and men have moved into some traditionally female jobs. However, most women and men continue to work in sex-typical jobs with coworkers of the same sex (Bianchi and Rytina 1984; Bielby and Baron 1984; for an overview, see Reskin and Hartmann 1985).

In this study, I use comparative data to investigate gender differences in occupational location in twelve industrial societies. I have two major purposes. First, I describe crosscultural patterns of occupational sex segregation, and the attainment processes of men and women that help to produce these patterns; and, second, I investigate the extent to which occupational sex segregation is attributable to gender differences in family responsibilities. The explanation that makes this claim—human-capital theory—is based on the premise that, unlike men, married women who work outside the home contend with two distinct sets of responsibilities, those of wife/ mother and worker.

1

The comparative method is useful in discerning whether current patterns of sex segregation emerged from historical circumstances of particular countries or whether they reflect structural features common to all industrial societies. To the extent that similar levels of occupational sex segregation exist across industrial societies, historical, cultural, and political traditions unique to the United States cannot account for observed gender differences in occupational stratification.

Limitations in the availability of variables necessarily require a certain simplicity in analysis and presentation of results. The level of sophistication found in recent gender comparisons in the United States is not possible here. In the absence of fully adequate data, however, the appropriate strategy is not to abandon crosscultural comparisons but to carry the analysis as far as possible, making what valid partial tests and generalizations are possible on the data available. The sacrifice of a certain measure of precision is worth the gain in knowledge regarding the uniqueness, universality, or systematic covariation of particular social phenomena.

Explanation for Occupational Sex Segregation

There are two major explanations for occupational sex segregation: (1) human-capital explanations—those theories that attribute women's concentration in low-paying employment to their marital and child-rearing responsibilities; and (2) institutional explanations—those theories suggesting that men's and women's differing occupational concentrations result more from institutionalized features of the organization of work. In the present study, I evaluate the explanatory power of human-capital theory for sex differences in occupational location. Although the data do not permit an explicit test of the institutionalist view, the inability of human-capital theory to account for differential occupational locations increases the plausibility of this perspective as an explanation for sex segregation.

Industrial economies provide the best possible test case for investigating the efficacy of human-capital theory, for three major reasons (which I outline in greater detail in subsequent sections). First, the historical shift to an industrial economy changed the traditional productive role of women within the family. The location of the workplace moved out of the home to modern factories and shops. As a consequence, women had a harder time reconciling work and domestic roles. Second, due in part to decreasing levels of fertility and a lowering of the average age at which women complete childbearing, more married women have entered the paid work force in recent years. Thus the difficulty of reconciling work and domestic roles is now felt by a larger proportion of all women workers. Notably, the greatest increase in participation in recent years has been among married women with small children—the group most susceptible to the dual demands of work and family (Sweet 1975; OECD 1975). Third, time-use studies show that wives bear the primary responsibility for childrearing and home work, regardless of whether or not they work outside the home. Husbands, on the other hand, are freer to pursue their work unencumbered by time-consuming family responsibilities.

Human-capital theory. The human-capital explanation for occupational sex segregation postulates that the dual demands on women's time make it difficult for them to compete with men in labor markets (Mincer and Polachek 1974; Polachek 1975; Smith 1980; Becker 1981). Relying on assumptions of maximizing behavior, stable preferences, and the making of investment and time allocation decisions at the family level, human-capital theorists expect differences in the kinds of work men and women do and in the remuneration they receive for employment. Actual (or in the case of single women, anticipated) family responsibilities are presumed to affect the kinds of jobs women choose to (or can) enter, by influencing the amount of time they invest in educational and/or on-the-job training, the number of hours they work, the continuity of their labor-force attachment, and their ability to pursue opportunities for advancement.

Thus, the human-capital perspective uses the characteristics and behaviors of workers to account for gender differences in occupational concentration. These sex-correlated characteristics derive from three factors: gender differences in socialization, differential accumulation of human capital and hence productivity on the job, and household responsibilities [for a fuller exposition of human-capital theory as it relates to occupational segregation and wage discrimination, see Kahne and Kohen (1975); Lloyd (1975); Blau and Jusenius (1976); Treiman and Hartmann (1981); Reskin and Hartmann (1985)].

First, sex differences in *socialization* are the most elusive of the concepts used by human-capital theorists, and the most difficult to measure in empirical tests of the theory. People learn others' expectations as to what constitutes appropriate adult behavior from the socialization they receive as children [for example, through the role models of their own parents or other adults with whom they come in contact, the media, and their school textbooks; for a review of the evidence, see Marini and Brinton (1984)]. Women's roles, according to this view, are those of wife and mother and any career or occupational aspirations are clearly secondary. Men, on the other hand, are expected to provide the primary financial support for the family. To the extent that these expectations operate in the lives of particular individuals, socialization determines the educational and occupational choices of men and women. If women's primary roles are those of wife and mother, it is economically irrational for them to invest in lengthy and costly education or on-the-job training, since they would be investing in useless skills that would depreciate during their years out of the labor force. For men, the opposite is true. Since they are responsible for ensuring their family's financial security, it is economically rational for them to invest in training, both prior to employment and on the job. The consequence is that they enhance their occupational options and maximize expected income.

Human-capital theorists thus view women's participation in the labor force as dependent on their family life cycle, and hence likely to be discontinuous. As a result, it is unlikely that women will make substantial investments in human capital, but likely that they will choose occupations that do not penalize workers for intermittent attachment—that is, jobs that are easy to reenter after childbearing and rearing. There is, however, a price to be paid for this flexibility—jobs that are easy to exit and enter offer little or no economic reward for continuous labor-force attachment. Human-capital theory applies a similar logic to explain why employers are hesitant to invest in costly on-the-job training for women, whom they see as dropping out of the labor force before the employers' investment is realized (Blau and Jusenius 1976; 186).

Second, sex differences in socialization lead directly to sex differences in the *accumulation of human capital*. These differing amounts of human capital are hypothesized to affect the productivity of individual women and men on the job, which in turn gives rise to what are viewed as legitimate sex differences in occupational distribution and economic remuneration. Productivity is thus a key concept in human capital theory, linking sex differences in socialization with sex differences in occupational distribution and economic rewards. The concept is difficult to measure, however, and human capital theorists generally estimate it using education and labor-force experience.

Third, sex differences in amount of *household responsibility*, as a theoretical concept, overlaps considerably with those factors already discussed. Sex differences in socialization affect acceptance or rejection of the traditional division of household labor. It is also true that women's roles as wife and mother are seen as limiting the total amount of experience they are able to accumulate, and then bring to the marketplace, which may then affect their productivity on the job. There are several ways in which family responsibilities are proposed to affect women's productivity and advancement in employment, including (1) limiting the number of hours women can contribute to the job, (2) reducing their ability to travel or geographically relocate, and (3) encouraging them to maximize job characteristics other than earnings or status (for example, flexible working hours or convenient job location). Such limitations are bound to affect the relative speed and size of promotions and pay increases women receive, relative to those of men.

Institutional explanations. Human-capital theory is limited insofar as it assumes that men and women have equivalent access to occupational opportunities. Alternative theories, which I label "institutional" explanations, posit that worker productivity is determined not only by their own characteristics and behaviors, but also by (1) the "tastes for discrimination" of employers, other workers, or consumers; (2) the lack of a perfectly competitive market; and (3) the organization of work that structures access to job or promotional opportunities. Although limitations of data do not permit a test of these alternative theories, some inferences regarding their applicability for occupational sex segregation are appropriate.

The institutional theory most central for the purposes of this study, is the internal labor market approach (see for example, Doeringer and Piore 1971; Piore 1971; Wachter 1974). This theory explicitly addresses the division of the labor market into different sets of occupations and investigates the implications of this division for sex differences in occupational distribution and earnings. According to this view, the external labor market, like the traditional neoclassical competitive market, sets wages by reference to the forces of supply and demand. The competitive market, however, operates at only a few selected entry-level positions. Once entry is accomplished, the internal market, theoretically free of the influence of the external market, takes precedence in the allocation of jobs and the determination of wages. A key element in this theory is that statistical discrimination—discrimination against a particular class of persons because of their group, rather than individual, characteristics—operates at ports of entry. Theoretically, this discrimination in access has long-lasting implications, since once entry is made into the internal or external labor market it is difficult, if not impossible, to transfer between them.

Applying this model to sex differences in occupational distribution, institutional theorists propose that women are denied access to high-paying jobs (or, more correctly, to entry-level career-ladder positions that eventually lead them to high-paying jobs) because of statistical discrimination. For example, since women are on average more likely than men to be intermittently attached to the work force, individual women may be denied access to career-ladder positions solely because of their sex (even though as individuals they may anticipate uninterrupted labor-force attachment). Even with labor-force continuity, women can thus remain concentrated in low-paying jobs throughout their work life, with little opportunity for occupational advancement.

Internal labor-market theory is an advance over human-capital theory in two ways: it recognizes that (1) various classes of workers have differential access to occupational opportunities, and (2) the productivity of individual workers is a function not only of their personal characteristics (such as, amount of labor force experience), but also of the characteristics of the occupations and firms in which they labor.

THE NATURE OF INDUSTRIAL SOCIETY: WOMEN'S CHANGING ECONOMIC ROLE

In the remaining sections of this chapter, I set the context for the assertion that women in industrial societies are particularly susceptible to the negative effects of marriage and childrearing responsibilities on occupational choice and advancement. First, I describe how women's productive role changed with the Industrial Revolution, thereby making the simultaneous balancing of home and work roles more difficult than had been true prior to that time. Second, I describe the increase in women's labor-force participation (especially since 1940), the transformation in the composition of the female workforce, and the implications of both these changes for women's occupational options. Third, I review time-budget studies that verify the time-consuming home responsibilities women bear, regardless of whether or not they work outside the home.

Family Work and Wage Work: Women's Changing Economic Role During the Industrial Revolution

To understand how marriage and family responsibilities affect working women in industrial society, it is imperative to view the historic economic role of women. The present section traces the changing nature of women's economic role since the advent of industrialization.[1] This historical shift changed women's productive role in large measure because the location of the workplace gradually moved out of the home, where women were more easily able to contribute to the household income, and into factories and shops situated away from the household. Women's lesser mobility due to childbearing and rearing affected their access to jobs outside the home and, as a result, women's economic role changed. In industrializing countries, married women became supplementary workers who entered the labor force when economic need was pressing. Single women contributed to the productive effort of their family of origin before they married; widows carried on in the occupations of their self-employed husbands; and working-class women labored in factories and at home in cottage industries as family needs required.

In my overview of women's changing productive role, I focus on the historic process of industrialization which occurred in European and American societies during the eighteenth, nineteenth, and early twentieth centuries. The situation facing most countries industrializing today—that of rapid development in an already industrialized world— is different from that faced by Western Europe and the United States, where changes in productive capacity occurred at a somewhat slower pace, thereby allowing gradual adaptation to changing modes of production.

Integral to the Industrial Revolution of the nineteenth century were a fundamental restructuring of the technology of production and a reshaping of the way work was organized. As the scale of production increased, machinery multiplied the productivity of individual workers and changes in the organization of work increased the differentiation of occupational tasks. Another fundamental feature of the Industrial Revolution was that it reflected a shift from an agricultural mode of production to manufacturing and service jobs. Most important for married women, however, was the fact that factories eventually all but replaced households as the site of the production effort.

In my description of the historical transformation of women's productive role, I draw on the work of Tilly and Scott (1978), who investigated the relationship between women's economic and family roles during the industrialization of England and France from the eighteenth through the twentieth centuries. Smuts (1959) and Degler (1980) provide valuable and comparable portraits of industrialization in the nineteenth and twentieth century United States. In addition, my conceptual framework is informed by recent insights of Friedl (1975) and Huber and Spitze (1983), who developed several principles of crosscultural stratification by sex. Drawing on Friedl, Huber and Spitze argued that the producers of goods exercise more power than those who merely consume those goods. Moreover, they argued that the highest prestige is accorded to those who control the distribution of valued goods beyond the family unit (Huber and Spitze, 1983, xv). Women's access to valued jobs is thus viewed as dependent on the interaction between their childbearing and rearing roles and the kind of (especially subsistence) technology existing at given levels of development. For the purposes of the present study, Huber and Spitze's theory implies that women were more easily able to accommodate family and work roles, and hence gain access to valued work, at some stages of development than at others.

In their exposition, Tilly and Scott (1978) delineated three phases in the transformation of women's economic role. In the first phase, work was located in the household and all family members contributed to the sufficiency of the family unit and the production of goods for exchange. Next was the family wage economy, in which family members still constituted an economic unit even though they were not always working at the same location. Finally, there was the family consumer economy, in which the function of the family unit evolved into that of a consumer.

In describing these three phases in the transformation of women's economic role, three factors are of major significance. First, these economic changes were, in part, a response to changing demographic trends in fertility, mortality, and marriage, factors that interacted with concomitant changes in the mode of production. However, changes in economic structure also affected social and demographic trends (such as, changing levels of fertility and rates of marriage). Second, the types of work performed changed along with the economic structure. The economic roles, and access to valued jobs, of single and married women differed from those of men in each of the three types of economies. Third, since the antecedents of modern-day occupational segregation may well be found in the economic and demographic forces that acted on women's occupational choices during industrialization, I investigate why women historically entered the occupations they did, when they did.

Household economy. In the household (or domestic) economy, the scale of production was small and the economic unit normally overlapped with the domestic unit. As a result, the production of goods was usually centered within or near the family home. The primary purpose of household production was to provide for the subsistence of the family, and secondarily to produce goods for exchange. In such households, men and women were responsible for different tasks. Women, in Tilly's and Scott's (1978, 3) view, contributed mostly to the production of "use" value and men to "exchange" value. As Huber and Spitze (1983) suggested, men's domination in exchange functions afforded them greater status than women. However, both women and men were equally productive and necessary for the family's survival. The differentiation of tasks in the preindustrial household was dependent for the most part on biological differences between men and women. The effect of women's reproductive role was an important one, given the high levels of fertility common at the time.

The primary production good in the domestic economy was agricultural or piecework produced in the home. Economically remunerative work was thus relatively compatible, and even overlapped considerably, with women's domestic responsibilities. Providing evidence that such a production unit was common for the United States, Smuts (1959, 4) reported that as late as 1890 two-thirds of the United States still lived in rural areas and nearly half of United States families worked in agriculture. Women in these agricultural societies were thus linked more directly to the production-consumption process than they would be with the onset of industrialization. In urban areas, family members in the domestic economy often engaged in cottage industries, such as wool and cotton weaving. While urban merchants brought raw material to the household and distributed the finished product, the production process involved family members working together in the home.

With respect to the kinds of work men and women performed, single women followed in the footsteps of their mothers, learning agricultural and domestic skills such as spinning and sewing. Because each additional mouth to feed increased the total household burden, daughters were frequently sent to the homes of others where they earned their keep as domestic servants or spinners (Tilly and Scott 1978, 33). When married, women's activities were dictated by the needs of their families. While men performed the heavy, more burdensome tasks and those that required travel away from home, women's responsibilities were a combination of reproductive and family tasks. Degler (1980, 363) portrayed the work of married women in the United States domestic economy:

> As far as women were concerned, their tasks were not only diverse but almost endless. Over the long term of a lifetime they were probably more arduous and demanding than those of men. . . . Looking after the house was itself a heavy task, since that included not only cleaning the physical interior but the washing and mending of the family's clothes, preparing meals under the handicaps of an open fireplace and no running water, preserving various kinds of foods, making all the soaps, candles, and most of the medicines used by the family, as well as all the clothes for the family . . . the woman had to be ready at planting or harvest time to help in the fields. On top of all this, of course, was the bearing and rearing of children . . . when families of at least six children were common.

The types of activities in which married women worked differed depending on whether they lived in rural or urban areas. Women in cities were free from some of the more time-consuming and burdensome agricultural chores, such as hauling and carrying, and hence concentrated more on textile work in the home. Some of these women assisted, or when widowed succeeded, their husbands in skilled crafts or retail trades.

Family wage economy. As landless men and women moved to the cities in search of employment, and as the means of production was concentrated more in factories, individuals had few options but to sell their labor for wages. The domestic economy gradually evolved into a family wage economy. In this mode of production, families remained highly interdependent economic units. Significantly, the wife managed the family's wages and supervised family workers. Although the location of the workplace had long since moved outside the home, the allocation of work roles to men, women, and children was still dependent on the household's need for money to buy food and pay the rent. Yet, within these parameters, women's economic role had clearly changed. As Tilly and Scott (1978, 124) noted:

> Industrial jobs required specialization and a full-time commitment to work, usually in a specific location away from home. While under the domestic mode of production women combined market-oriented activities and domestic work, the industrial model of production precluded an easy reconciliation of married women's activities.

Because reconciling domestic and market tasks was not easy, married women worked outside the home only intermittently, when it was demanded by their family's economic position. Thus, a woman's economic role depended more heavily on the family life cycle than had previously been the case. For example, a woman often worked (preferably at home, but often in factories) until her children were old enough to replace her. Frequently too, a woman returned to wage labor when her children left home or when the death or illness of an aging husband threatened the family's economic security (Mason et al. 1978; Hareven 1975).

Married women thus became members of a large reserve army of labor. Their principal contribution to the family wage was through cottage-industry production, especially sewing and garment making (Smuts 1959, 15). Although these types of industries continued to flourish for some time after the shift to factory production, competition from more efficient factories, an ever-reduced piece rate, and the development of a new consumer culture based on ready-made items gradually drove small home-based production out of business, further removing women from the economic process (Smuts 1959, 26). Another way women contributed to the family income without leaving home was by taking in boarders, an activity often prompted by their withdrawal from the active wage-earning category (Tilly and Scott 1978, 125; Degler 1980, 394).

Some wives ventured outside the home to find employment in the industrial arena, most notably in the textile mills. This was due in part to the heavy representation of women in the nonmechanized textile and clothing industries that flourished in the preindustrial economy (Tilly and Scott 1978, 68). Hareven (1975, 380) attributed married women's relatively greater representation in textile work to the close proximity of the mills to the home, a factor that helped women to reconcile home and market tasks. Factory work in the textile towns, in fact, was sometimes a family endeavor, with entire families and kin groups working as a unit in the factory (Hareven 1975, 365; Tilly and Scott 1978, 112).

Single women, however, constituted a larger source of labor to the mills than married women. The relocation to the cities of large numbers of single women lessened their economic dependence on their family of origin. Until they married, however, single women often continued to send all or part of their wages to their families. They also worked as domestic servants, farm laborers, unskilled and semiskilled factory workers, and school teachers (Smuts 1959, 24).

Family consumer economy. The family gradually evolved from an economically productive unit to a consumptive one. The nature of women's employment was both shaped by and, in turn, affected economic, demographic, and social trends. Partly as a result of declines in infant mortality rates, and death rates in general, people were living longer and children were more likely to survive infancy. High levels of fertility threatened the working family's ability to benefit from the rise in real wages occurring during this period (Tilly and Scott 1978, 170). In addition, the effect of compulsory school attendance laws and legislation limiting or prohibiting child labor reduced the contribution children could make to the family wage. Each additional child was now an economic liability rather than a potential contributor to the family wage.

Reflecting the changing function of the family, the role of women evolved from that of a producer to a consumer. Their job now involved investing time and energy in the training and development of children, rather than in producing saleable commodities. Degler (1980, 9) argued that the role of women in the twentieth century United States was dependent, in large measure, on the changing concept of childhood:

> The attention, energy, and resources of parents [in the person
> of the wife/mother] in the emerging modern family were
> increasingly centered upon the rearing of their offspring.
> Children were now perceived as being different from adults
> and deserving not only of material care but of solicitude and
> love as well. Childhood was deemed a valuable period in the
> life of every person and to be sharply distinguished in
> character and purpose from adulthood. Parenthood thus
> became a major personal responsibility, perhaps even a
> burden.

As Huber and Spitze (1983) argued, the changed status of women
to that of consumer lowered their prestige and power in the marketplace. Since men maintained their status as the major producers
and exchangers of goods, their power and prestige were relatively
undiminished.

There were other factors at work that combined to affect women's
shifting economic function. As the scale of production magnified, the
preeminence of the textile and clothing industries gave way to the
heavier metallurgy, mining, and engineering industries in which
women were seldom hired. As the industries traditionally hiring
females contracted, a new source of employment—white-collar occupations—opened up for women. Men were able to find work in
the emerging, higher-paying heavy industries, thus decreasing competition with women for white-collar employment. The growing
administrative and commercial bureaucracies actively recruited women,
mainly for clerical work (Tilly and Scott 1978, 150). While clerical
employment had previously been a male occupation, the work was
deskilled at the same time the economy was expanding. Thus, there
was a widening range of employment opportunities, albeit low in
status, for working-class women who had previously been domestic
servants or factory workers, and for the few middle-class women
who ventured into the work force. Tilly and Scott (1978, 157) described the process this way.

> Indeed, during the twentieth century, the profession of clerk
> became a female one. Dicken's Bob Cratchit or Stendhal's
> Julien Sorel represented a now extinct breed—the educated
> aspiring young man, more than a servant, not quite an equal,
> the right arm of a wealthy gentleman. By the twentieth
> century the job of clerk involved little of the opportunity for
> advancement it had in the past. Office work was now
> organized according to narrow specialties: some workers filed,
> others typed, still others folded letters or ran errands. A
> number of clerks replaced the lone figure of the past. The low

skill required and the number of positions to fill made women good recruits.

Similar growth in other occupations, including telephone, telegraphic, and postal services, also attracted women workers. In addition, elementary school teaching employed a large number of (especially middle-class) women during this period, precisely because they provided a cheap source of educated labor (Oppenheimer 1970, 80). The unprecedented movement of women into formerly male-dominated employment sectors during the early twentieth century can thus be viewed as a combination of the increasing demand for low-skill workers and the availability of large numbers of (mostly single) women forced out of changing industries.

This then was what the industrializing economies of Western Europe and the United States looked like during the early twentieth century. One product of these changing demographic, economic, and social factors was a segregated occupational structure. Men and single women worked outside the home, but with very different access to valued jobs. Men were more likely than women to hold positions in the higher-paid industrial sectors of the economy. Single women were concentrated in low-paid industrial jobs, but also increasingly in white-collar employment. Married women remained in the home, where their primary task was to raise children. These women entered the wage-labor force only intermittently. The industrial economy remained essentially unchanged until approximately 1940, when, in response to a domestic labor shortage occasioned by World War II, women began to enter the labor force in unprecedented numbers, and the composition of the female work force changed dramatically.

Recent Changes in Women's Labor-Force Participation and in the Composition of the Female Work Force

Since 1940 women have entered the United States labor force in ever-increasing numbers. The percentage of the United States female population employed increased from 20 percent in 1900, to 26, 29, and 34 percent in 1940, 1950, and 1960, respectively (Oppenheimer 1970, 8). As of 1981, 52 percent of United States women sixteen and over were in the labor force (U.S. Bureau of the Census 1982, 383). The Organisation for Economic Cooperation and Development has collected data documenting a similar increase in women's labor-force participation in most other industrialized countries (OECD 1975, 13–24; 1979, 19–27; ILO 1984, Table 2.8).

The composition of the female labor force has also radically changed, in the United States as well as in most other industrial societies (OECD 1975, Figure 1). What had in 1900 been a young, unmarried female labor force, became an employed population of both young and older returning women by 1960. During those sixty years, the age pattern of female participation changed from an early peak, suggesting that women permanently left their jobs when they married, to a double peak pattern, suggesting that women were returning to the labor force when their children were older (Oppenheimer 1970, 9). More recently cohorts of United States women are remaining in the labor force during their childrearing years (Kreps and Leaper 1976), resulting in a single peak pattern similar to that of men.

Oppenheimer (1970, Chapter 5) argued that these changes for the United States are a consequence of the interaction of two factors: (1) an increasing *demand* for workers in the traditional female occupations (for example in the growing service sector), and (2) a decrease in the *supply* of young single women (due to a decrease in the average age at marriage, the postwar baby boom, and increasing school enrollments). In order to fill the growing numbers of jobs in the clerical and service sectors, employers hired older, married women. The consequence was a radical transformation of the female labor force: whereas between 1890 and 1940, about half of the female labor force were single, by 1960 that proportion had decreased to 24 percent. In 1940, 30 percent of the female labor force were married and living with their husbands; by 1960 the comparable figure was 55 percent (Oppenheimer 1970, Table 1.9; Grossman 1979, 46). By 1981, 25 percent of the female labor force were single, and 59 percent were married (U.S. Bureau of the Census 1982, 383).

The modal female worker in the United States today is married and living with her husband and, by implication, faces dual responsibilities of work and family. Available data for other industrial societies suggest similar patterns: well over half of the women workers in each of the member countries of the Organisation for Economic Cooperation and Development are married (OECD 1975, 10). Similarly, Boulding (1978, Table 1.2) estimated that 62 percent of the world's female workers over age fifteen are married.

A detailed explanation of the dramatic growth of female labor-force participation in most industrial societies is beyond the scope of the present analysis, and, for the United States at least, already well-documented (Oppenheimer 1970; Treiman and Terrell 1975c; Waite 1976). It is important to note, however, that the women exhibiting the greatest increases in labor-force participation in recent years are those traditionally least likely to work—married women with young children (Sweet 1975). In 1960, 19 percent of married United States women with children younger than six years were employed; by 1981 that percentage had increased to 48 (U.S. Bureau of the Census 1982, 382). There is strong evidence that this phenomenon also exists in other industrial societies (Vogel 1976, 18; OECD 1979).

I have noted the effects of demographic trends on women's participation in the work force. In most industrialized countries, life expectancy has increased and fertility rates have fallen sharply (Smith 1979, 6; Newland 1980, 17). As a result, women now have fewer children and complete their childbearing at earlier ages. Women thus have a longer period of their lives that they can devote to paid employment. Decreasing birth rates, and hence decreased childrearing resonsibilities, are thus a compelling explanation for why women have been entering the work force in increasing numbers. However, these trends are also compatible with a causal relationship between fertility and labor-force participation that is opposite in direction— that women's entry into the labor force has further reduced their expected fertility, and hence their expected level of family responsibilities. In Chapter 6 I further discuss the implications of the interaction between these factors.

The decreasing labor-force participation of women in Japan. A notable exception to the general patterns already described is Japan, where women's labor-force participation has decreased, from 60 percent in 1960 to 55 percent in 1980 (ILO 1984, Table 2.8). It is useful to investigate this anomaly at the outset, since the way in which Japan differs from other industrialized countries has implications for the outcomes of the analyses performed in this volume.

The existence of a large agricultural segment among employed Japanese females is the key to understanding the modest but notable decrease in overall female labor-force participation in recent years (recent data indicate this pattern may be in the process of reversing; Martin 1980; ILO 1984, Table 2.8). The decrease is primarily due to a shift away from agricultural production, a shift that occurred much later in Japan than in other industrialized countries (Singelmann 1978). In 1960, 37 percent of the female labor force worked in agriculture. By 1972, that figure had decreased to 19 percent (OECD 1975, 21), and by 1978 to 15 percent (calculated from ILO 1979b, Table 2B). The loss of the large number of family farm workers from the employed female population due to industrialization was not sufficiently offset by the increase of women into the tertiary sector of the economy, and hence an overall decrease occurred in the proportion of all women counted as employed.

A careful investigation of Japanese data on female labor-force participation clearly shows that the decline in economic participation occurred only for married women (OECD 1979, 27). The participation of single women has remained essentially constant, at least from

1965 to 1972 (OECD 1975, 16). With the decrease in the number of female farm workers, married Japanese women, who were previously able to balance home and work responsibilities (because the work was located within the household unit), were not as readily able as single women to pursue an economic role outside the home.

Finally Cook and Hayashi (1980, 101) and the ILO (1984, 54) argued that the decrease in women's labor-force participation in Japan is attributable to an increase in the availability of schooling to younger women. Contrary to the overall trend, labor-force participation of women in all but the youngest age cohort increased from 1973 to 1978. A final explanation for women's decreasing labor-force rates is that women have less access than men to the system of lifetime employment in the larger enterprises (Martin 1980; ILO 1984, 54).

Market Work, Family Work, and Leisure: Gender Differences in the Allocation of Time

In the United States and elsewhere, there is convincing evidence that married women, whether or not they work outside the home, spend a substantially greater part of their day on family chores than their husbands (Szalai 1972; Walker and Woods 1976; Geerken and Gove 1983; Pleck, 1983). Interestingly, this generalization applies equally well to socialist countries, although the impact of women's home responsibilities on their employment options may be lessened somewhat by state-provided facilities (for example, childcare centers or centralized food preparation; Dodge 1971; Boulding 1976; Soko- lowska 1977).

The definitive United States data addressing this issue are part of a long-term research program on the household production of goods and services that began at Cornell University in the 1920s (Walker and Woods 1976). The major focus of the most recent phase of the research (the data were collected in 1967 to 1968) was on measuring the time required to produce household goods and services.[2] The most important finding from these data is that the number of hours per day spent on household responsibilities differs markedly by sex of respondent and employment status of wife: on average, nonem- ployed wives spend 8 hours per day on household chores; employed wives (working full or part time at least 15 hours per week) spend 5.3 hours per day; husbands, regardless of their wives' employment status, average only 1.6 hours per day (Walker and Woods 1976, Table 3.4).[3] Presented as a percentage of total housework hours, nonemployed wives perform 72 percent of the total household work, while the comparable figure for employed wives is 62 percent. In contrast, husbands with nonworking wives contribute 14 percent of the total, while husbands of working wives contribute 18 percent. Interestingly, this 4 percent difference is mainly due to a decrease in the total number of hours devoted to housework in households with working wives, and not to an increase in the total number of hours worked by husbands, other household members, or paid employees (p. 41). These results indicate that even when they work, women are still responsible for the larger part of the household chores, and their husbands do not correspondingly increase their share of the housework.

Married men perform different and less time-consuming tasks than do married women. Husbands' contributions are more likely to be in the areas of marketing and nonphysical care of family members (and secondarily in yard, car, and special house care), while wives are the principal workers in more time-consuming activities (such as, regular meal preparation, regular house care, physical care of family members, and after-meal cleanup). Moreover, men do most of their household work on weekends, so that time devoted to household responsibilities during the weekday, when it conflicts with paid work responsibilities, is actually less than the 1.6 hours per day indicated.

These average figures vary somewhat by family composition. As noted, employed women spend an average of 2.7 hours less per day on household chores than nonemployed women, mainly due to a lesser amount of time spent on the physical care of family members. In addition, a married woman's time allocation to household production also varies by the number and ages of her children. Whether employed or not, time spent on household chores increases with number of children and decreases as the age of the youngest child increases. Notably, number and ages of children, as well as the employment status of wife, have virtually no effect on the number of hours husbands devote to household responsibilities—only husbands with employed wives and a baby or toddler as their youngest child increase the total amount of time they spend on household-related activities (Walker and Woods 1976, 36).

This pattern is international in scope (Szalai 1972).[4] As described by Robinson and his coauthors (1972), the focus of the research was on how individual societal members (employed women, housewives, and employed males) allocated their time among market work, home work, and other (such as leisure) activities. A major finding (p. 118) is that the respective work patterns of employed women, housewives, and employed men show clear and parallel differences across all the survey sites.

Robinson and his coauthors found that employed women spend about half as much time on household activities as housewives, and the total time spent on household-related chores by employed men is much lower: housewives spend an average of 7 hours per day on household activities (ranging from a low of 5.8 in Jackson, Michigan, to a high of 9.5 in Maribor, Yugoslavia); employed women spend 3.7 hours (from a low of 2.5 in Lima, Peru, to 4.7 in Hoyerswerda, East Germany); and employed men spend .6 hours (from .3 in several of the countries to 1.3 in Pskov, the Soviet Union) (averages calculated from Robinson et al. 1972, Table 5). These averages change somewhat when number and ages of children are controlled, but the overall picture remains the same. For example, housewives with two to three children (with one under four) spend an average of 6.8 hours on housework, while employed women with a similar family composition spend 4.3 hours (p. 126).

The similarity of the patterns is striking, given the wide variation in political ideology, economic structure, and cultural tradition across the survey sites. Adding the hours women spend working on household chores to the time they are engaged in paid employment clearly shows that employed women face dual responsibilities—these women typically have from one to two hours per day less leisure than either employed men or housewives. Szalai (1972) showed that employed women adapt to this time pressure by using weekends to catch up on their household chores. Housewives and employed men, in contrast, spend a greater portion of their weekend hours engaged in leisure activities. As in the United States , women in these countries are engaged in different kinds of household activities from those of men, spending most of their time on food preparation, housecleaning, washing dishes, and doing laundry. Men are involved in less time-consuming kinds of household care activities (such as, gardening, care of animals, nonfood shopping).

In sum, data from the United States and other countries provide compelling documentation that women who work outside the home face dual responsibilities. Women's family activities decrease the time they have available for leisure. Contrary to what one might expect, technological innovations have not substantially altered the amount of time women allocate to household activities. While there has been a decrease of thirty minutes in the time spent in food preparation and after-meal cleanup, the half-hour increase in marketing, record keeping, and management has offset this reduction (Szalai 1972, 125; Walker and Woods 1976, 33).

Working women in socialist countries, too, are faced with tremendous time pressures because of their dual responsibilities (Dodge 1971; Boulding 1976); and Sokolowska 1977). Boulding (1976, 110) suggested that despite an ideological orientation to the contrary, socialist countries cannot ultimately afford to take over the household activities traditionally performed by women. She argued that with no fundamental change in the structure of family responsibilities, it was inevitable that household activities would shift back to wives when ideology conflicted with productivity demands.

No industrial society has successfully provided sustained relief for the household burdens of working women. As Boulding suggested, government assumption of the responsibility for selected household activities (such as childcare) will not solve the problem. Instead, there must be a fundamental restructuring of household responsibilities.

ORGANIZATION OF THE VOLUME

As previously noted, this study has two major purposes: (1) the use of comparable data from twelve industrial societies to provide a descriptive, crosscultural overview of occupational sex segregation, and the attainment patterns of men and women that help to produce these patterns; and (2) an investigation of the extent to which sex differences in occupational location are attributable to gender differences in family responsibilities. Chapter 2 presents a detailed description of the data employed in the study, the quality of the sample surveys used, and the methods used to enhance the crosscultural comparability of the data sets and variables.

Chapter 3 presents a descriptive overview of crosscultural differences in labor-force participation, employment status, and occupational composition for the twelve countries examined. These data provide evidence that similar structures of occupational sex segregation exist across industrial society. Chapter 3 also documents the crosscultural similarity in the sextyping of occupations and describes the characteristics of jobs mainly held by men and those mainly held by women.

Chapter 4 further investigates occupational sex segregation by describing gender differences in intergenerational occupational mobility. By investigating gender differences in supply and recruitment to occupational positions, and gender differences in intergenerational mobility within countries (via log-linear analysis), I examine how differences in the process of mobility might lead to occupational sex segregation.

Working within the framework of status attainment analysis, Chapter 5 focuses on the effects of determinants of occupational attainment other than social origins. In particular, I test the efficacy of the human-capital explanation for occupational sex segregation by examining the effect of marital status on occupational attainment for women and men, net of other factors. In this chapter I also propose a new method to measure occupational achievement, one that takes into account differences in the wage rates of men's and women's work.

It is not sufficient, however, to show that men and women have different processes of occupational attainment. In order to test human-capital theory adequately, it is necessary to document that differences in occupational attainment result directly from differential family responsibilities. In Chapter 6 I extend my analyses by comparing the labor-force behavior, occupational distributions, and attainment patterns of ever- and never-married women. Given their more continuous labor-force attachment, never-married women should be more likely than ever-married women to pursue nontraditional work options and to optimize income-producing activities, that is, to be more like men in their occupational choice and orientation toward advancement.

Chapter 7 concludes by presenting a summary of the findings and assessing their relevance for United States public policy.

CHAPTER TWO

Data and Methods

In this study I consider three separate levels of comparison: gender, marital, and country differences in occupational behavior. The first two comparisons are straightforward and require little explanation, especially since I restrict the analyses to *within-society* comparisons. The last level of comparison, however, is more problematic. Comparative studies, especially those based on secondary analysis, are beset with problems regarding the comparability of the samples and variables used, and achieving comparability is a difficult task. Researchers, however, choose comparative analysis, even with its difficulties, because it provides insight into the universality or uniqueness of interesting social phenomena.

Comparative analysis informs the researcher as to whether an observed social pattern is universal (that is, generalizable to other cultural, political, and economic contexts), or whether it is unique to a particular country. Since social phenomena are frequently neither universal nor unique, but instead lie somewhere between these two extremes, one of the major motivations for conducting comparative research is to better understand how various social patterns (for example, age patterns of female labor-force participation or sex differences in occupational mobility) systematically covary across countries. To identify universal, idiosyncratic, and covarying phenomena, however, requires that one have comparable data and variable measurement. There are, therefore, two aspects of comparability that are addressed in the present chapter: the comparability of the survey samples and the comparability of the variables used in the analyses.

DATA

The data used in this study are a subset of a larger number of sample surveys obtained in conjunction with a comparative study of social mobility and status attainment (Treiman and Kelley 1974, 1978). Several of the data sets were originally obtained from the Inter-University Consortium for Political and Social Research (ICPSR) at the University of Michigan, including Japan (principal investigators: Robert E. Ward and Akira Kubota), Northern Ireland (Richard Rose), and the United States (James Davis). Since the present study involves reanalysis of data originally collected for other purposes, considerable preparatory work was required to make the data sets and variables comparable, a task described in the current and subsequent sections of this chapter.

Restriction to Industrialized Countries

As described in Chapter 1, I selected only industrialized countries for inclusion in the study, since it is in such societies that reconciling family and work responsibilities is most difficult for women. As a consequence, the effect of women's dual responsibilities on their occupational options (if it exists) should be strongest in these societies. Selecting only industrialized countries in turn tends to minimize the noncomparabilities arising from varying definitions and measurements of the economically active population, a factor that affects the enumeration of female more than male workers. The International Labour Office (ILO 1979b, 4) specifically cautions that the activity rates of women are not comparable internationally since:

> in many countries relatively large numbers of women assist on farms or in other family enterprises without pay and there are differences from one country to another in the criteria adopted for determining the extent to which such workers are to be counted among the economically active.

One of the major reasons for noncomparability across societies in the enumeration of female workers is that unpaid family workers are more likely to be counted as economically active in preindustrial than in industrial societies. In addition to the likely overcount of female workers in preindustrial societies,[1] the number of family workers is greater than in industrialized countries, since in preindustrial societies agricultural workers constitute a sizable fraction of the labor force. Restricting the sample to industrial societies should thus minimize the noncomparability deriving from differing definitions of the employed population, and minimize the inclusion of countries with large agricultural components. Several of the societies in the present analysis, most notably Japan, had large numbers of agricultural employees at the time of their survey. As shall be seen, the existence of a large agricultural sector does produce cross-country variation in the occupational behavior of men and women.

A Culturally Controlled Comparison

I chose for inclusion in this study those industrialized countries with good data on women, in the sense that an adequate number of females were interviewed and a reasonable selection of variables of interest to a gender comparison of occupational behavior was included. Table 2.1 details the sample characteristics of the surveys, all of which are national representative samples of the adult population. The only idiosyncratic feature that should be mentioned at the outset, since it affects the comparability of the samples, is that the West German survey includes only West German citizens. This sampling decision on the part of Z.U.M.A., the West German survey organization, effectively eliminates from consideration the large number of migrant laborers currently living in that country. This is a serious omission considering that in 1972 2.4 million, or 11 percent, of those employed in West Germany were guest workers (German Federal Institute for Population Research 1974, 32).

Among the twelve countries included in the analysis are societies in North America (the United States); Western Europe (Austria, Denmark, Finland, West Germany, Great Britain, the Netherlands, Northern Ireland, Norway, and Sweden); and Asia (Israel and Japan). The large number of countries from Western Europe is due in part to the lack of adequate data for women in the other countries for which survey data were available. Although excellent data existed for several other countries, they were either restricted to men, were not national samples, or had poor quality data on women.

A critic might argue that the included countries are not sufficiently culturally variable to test for cross-country variation in gender and marital differences in occupational behavior. It could be argued that in spite of the somewhat arbitrary nature of the selection process, the resulting cultural similarity of the included countries (with the possible exceptions of Japan and Israel) should be viewed positively rather than negatively, since such similarity allows for a relatively more controlled comparison. At this early stage of research in this area, it is most important to present comparable data in a systematic manner for a variety of countries so that the basic patterns and anomalies will be evident. The present study is designed to lay the groundwork for establishing the extent of crosscultural similarity in sex differences in occupational distribution and attainment. If this

Table 2.1 Sample Characteristics of Survey Data

Country and survey date	Unweighted sample size total (and weighted number of employed males and females)[a]	Sample characteristics
1. Austria, 1974 (Political Action: An Eight-Nation Study)	1,585 (M=546; F=352)	National multistage probability sample of the adult population, 16 years and older
2. Denmark, 1972 (Comparative Scandinavian Welfare Survey)	1,000 (M=412; F=316)	National probability sample of the 15–64 year old population
3. Finland, 1972 (Comparative Scandinavian Welfare Survey)	994 (M=413; F=363)	National probability sample of the 15–64 year old population
4. Germany (Fed. Rep.), 1976 (West Germany ZUMABUS Survey)	2,036 (M=678; F=442)	Representative population sample based on the total number of persons aged 18 and over, with German citizenship, living in private households in the Federal Republic of Germany (including West Berlin)
5. Great Britain, 1974 (Political Action: An Eight-Nation Study)	1,787 (M=554; F=314)	National multistage probability sample of the adult population, 16 years and older
6. Israel, 1974 (Israel Labor Force Survey)	15,060 (M=8,911; F=4,437)	Representative sample of the noninstitutional population of Israel, except for persons living in kibbutzim and the Bedouin population in the south; respondents are age 14 and over
7. Japan, 1967 (Japanese National Election Study)	1,973 (M=762; F=476)	Multistage stratified nationwide probability sample of adults of voting age, 20 years and above, supplementary sample of youths 15 to 19 drawn

8.	Netherlands, 1974 (Political Action: An Eight-Nation Study)	1,201 (M=466; F=161)	National multistage probability sample of the adult population, 16 years and older
9.	Northern Ireland, 1968 (Northern Ireland Loyalty Study)	1,291 (M=478; F=221)	Multistage stratified random sample of 1500 households, drawn from the Annual Electoral Register; respondents are age 21 and over
10.	Norway, 1972 (Comparative Scandinavian Welfare Survey)	1,005 (M=452; F=199)	National probability sample of the 15–64 year old population
11.	Sweden, 1972 (Comparative Scandinavian Welfare Survey)	1,005 (M=431; F=364)	National probability sample of the 15–64 year old population
12.	United States, 1974–1977 (National Opinion Research Center General Social Surveys)	6,003 (M=1,975; F=1,295)	Four merged representative samples of English-speaking persons 18 years of age and over, living in non-institutional arrangements within the continental United States

[a] Sample was weighted so that the survey data would equal the male-female proportion in the labor force as a whole, as estimated from published data. This weighting recreated the total sample size for which data were available, but altered the proportions of men and women (see text for details).

similarity does not exist in culturally similar countries, it will most assuredly not exist in countries that are more ideologically, politically, and culturally disparate. By establishing a basic similarity, future analyses can more easily document possible points of difference and propose explanations for divergence (for example, political ideology or central planning, as in socialist countries or sexual caste systems, as in the Middle East).

Selection of the Employed Population

Table 2.2 presents a detailed description of the derivation of the employment variable for each country. In addition to listing the survey questions on which the employment variable was derived, the last three columns describe the coding of sampled individuals as "full time," "part time," or "not at work." No full-time/part-time distinction was available for Japan or Northern Ireland.

The employment variables are of two types: (1) those that ask the respondent's present occupation, and (2) those that ask the respondent's primary activity during a specified year period. Eight of the countries are of the first type, called the "labor-force approach," which allows one to determine whether the respondent was at work at the time of the survey. In the four Scandinavian countries, however, a "gainful worker" definition of the economically active population was used (Standing 1978, 25). The consequence of using the second, or gainful worker, definition is that larger proportions of the populations of these countries are enumerated as employed, since those who worked part time at any time during the year were counted as economically active. Where possible (in West Germany and Israel), persons identified as currently unemployed but having worked during the survey year were coded as working part time. These differences in the derivation of the employment variable should be kept in mind throughout the analysis when interpreting cross-country variation in occupational behavior.

Throughout the analysis, I make use of an employed/not at work distinction or select only employed persons. In those analyses, I include all full-time and part-time workers (of any age) as comprising the *employed* population. For other analyses, notably in Chapters 5 and 6, I restrict the sample further to the most economically active portion of the population—employed persons aged twenty to sixty-four working full or part time. This restriction was necessary due to crosscultural variability in the age cutoffs used in the samples as well as in the ages at which people generally start work.

Weighting the Survey Samples

In several analyses, I estimate the characteristics of occupations rather than persons (for example, to determine if they are mainly held by women or mainly by men). To accomplish this it is necessary to have an accurate assessment of the proportion of the labor force that is male and the proportion female. The problem with using representative samples of the populations is that, due to differential response rates, working women and men may be sampled at different rates (relative to each other and to nonworking women and men). This problem may lead to an inaccurate estimation of how male or female a country's labor force is. To rectify this situation and create a truly representative sample of the adult labor force, I used estimates of the proportions male and female in each country's labor force (from published census data) to reweight each sample so that the proportions male and female in the survey sample corresponded to the published data. Care was taken to use, as a standard, census data for a year close to that of the survey date.[2]

An example will clarify how this reweighting was accomplished. The Austrian survey data were collected in 1974 and the estimated proportions male and female in the labor force deriving from these data were .47 and .53, respectively. Census data for 1971 (ILO 1977, Table 1), however, indicated that the respective proportions male and female in the Austrian labor force were .61 and .39, respectively. With no adjustment, the survey data would thus incorrectly give greater weight to the characteristics of women in describing the Austrian labor force. To correct for this, Austrian males (and females) were weighted by the ratio of the expected number of males (females) in the labor force (based on the published census figures) to the number of males (females) in the survey's estimate of the labor force. Note that this weighting recreates the total sample size in the surveys, altering only the proportions male and female. This correction implicitly assumes that differential response by sex is the same for each occupational category. Since most of the study uses separate analyses by sex, the weighting procedure affects only the results in Tables 3.4 and 3.5.

Reliability of the Sample Surveys

The weighting and other adjustments described were undertaken so that the sample surveys might more closely approximate representative national samples of the countries' working populations. The weighting, by definition, equalizes the proportions male and female in the survey data with those in published census volumes. To determine the reliability of the survey data, I computed indexes of

Table 2.2 Derivation of Employment Status Variable

		Definitions of:			
		Employed population			
Country and survey date	Survey question	Full time	Part time	Not at work	
1. Austria, 1974	"Now a few questions about your work. We are interested in your employment status. Are you primarily working, unemployed, retired, a housewife, a student or what?"	Presently working full time	Presently working part time	Former workers, housewives, retired or disabled, looking for work, students, military	
2. Denmark, 1972	What was major activity of respondent in 1971?	Full time 9 or more months during 1971	Part-time work all year or full-time work less than 9 months during 1971	No work at all during 1971, students, pensioners, housewives, persons under institutional care	
3. Finland, 1972	What was major activity of respondent in 1971?	Full time 9 or more months during 1971	Part-time work all year or full-time work less than 9 months during 1971	No work at all during 1971, students, pensioners, housewives, persons under institutional care	
4. Germany (Fed. Rep.), 1976	"Are you at the present time gainfully employed as your main occupation either full time or half time? Are you only incidentally gainfully employed or not at all?"	Gainful employment full-day	Gainful employment half-day or incidentally gainfully employed	Not gainfully employed	
5. Great Britain, 1974	"Now a few questions about your work. We are interested in your employment status. Are you primarily working, unemployed, retired, a housewife, a student or what?"	Presently working full time	Presently working part time	Former workers, housewives, retired or disabled, looking for work, students, military	

		Employed full time last week	Employed part time or temporarily absent last week; unemployed last week but worked during year	No work during year, not in civilian labor force, unpaid family workers, institutional population, working less than 15 hours per week
6.	Israel, 1974	"Last week were you working full time or part time?"	Employed full time last week	Employed part time or temporarily absent last week; unemployed last week but worked during year	No work during year, not in civilian labor force, unpaid family workers, institutional population, working less than 15 hours per week
7.	Japan, 1967	Is the respondent (or head) unemployed, a farmer, or employed in other than agriculture?	Employed in agriculture, nonagriculture, or combination of the two (no full-time vs. part-time distinction available)		Not employed in agriculture, nonagriculture, or combination of the two
8.	Netherlands, 1974	"Now a few questions about your work. We are interested in your employment status. Are you primarily working, unemployed, retired, a housewife, a student or what?"	Presently working full time	Presently working part time	Former workers, housewives, retired or disabled, looking for work, students, military
9.	Northern Ireland, 1968	"What kind of job do you have now?"	Employed (no full-time/part-time distinction available)		Unemployed, dependent, housework or no work outside home, retired
10.	Norway, 1972	What was major activity of respondent in 1971?	Full time 9 or more months during 1971	Part-time work all year or full-time work less than 9 months during 1971	No work at all during 1971, students, pensioners, housewives, persons under institutional care
11.	Sweden, 1972	What was major activity of respondent in 1971?	Full time 9 or more months during 1971	Part-time work all year or full-time work less than 9 months during 1971	No work at all during 1971, students, pensioners, housewives, persons under institutional care
12.	United States, 1974–1977	"Last week were you working full time, part time, going to school, keeping house, or what?"	Working full time	Working part time or with a job but not at work because of temporary illness, vacation, strike	Unemployed, laid off, looking for work, retired, in school, keeping house

dissimilarity comparing the age and occupational distributions of the surveys' employed populations with those from published census or labor-force sample surveys, available from the ILO (1975c, 1977, 1979b) and the United Nations (1973, 1974). The indexes for age were derived by comparing the age distributions of the economically active twenty to sixty-four year old survey population with those from census data. The occupational indexes were derived by comparing the occupational distributions of the employed survey population (all ages) with that from census data. The occupational category used was the seven-category International Standard Classification of Occupations (ISCO), available in both the surveys and the reference volumes. Unfortunately, it was not always possible to find census or labor-force sample survey data for the exact year of the survey. Whenever this occurred, I used data for the closest year available as the standard (see sources for Table 2.3).

The indexes presented in Table 2.3 are reassuring in some cases but troubling in others, reminding us again of the difficulties of comparative research. In interpreting the table, the smaller the indexes, the greater the similarity between the survey and census data; conversely, the larger the indexes, the greater the difference. In the present comparison I employ a criterion of 10 to indicate the maximum level of acceptable differences. An index of dissimilarity of 10 for age, for example, would indicate that 10 percent of the survey's economically active population would have to be in a different age group to make the survey population correspond to that of the census population. The age results indicate that, for the most part, only small differences between the survey and census data exist. All the male indexes are less than 10. The female indexes, in contrast, are usually somewhat higher than the male, and two are greater than the minimum acceptable level. The 12.6 index for Austrian women is due in large measure to an undersampling of young women workers aged twenty to thirty. Similarly, the 13.4 index for Norwegian women derives from an undersampling of young women workers aged twenty to twenty-four.

Turning to the occupational indexes, the results are more troubling. Half the male and female indexes are greater than the acceptable level. A review of the two sets of occupational distributions suggests one possible systematic error: in each country where the index exceeds 10, the proportion of men or women in production work is substantially underestimated in the survey data. In many but not all cases, this underrepresentation in production employment was balanced by an overestimation in either agricultural or, less likely, in some form of white-collar employment.

Table 2.3 Indexes of Dissimilarity Between Survey and Census Data[a]

Country and date of sample survey	Age			Occupation		
	Men	Women	Census date	Men	Women	Census date
Austria, 1974	9.0	12.6	1971 Census	11.6	7.8	1971 Census
Denmark, 1972	4.8	7.0	1970 Census	14.6	15.6	1970 Census
Finland, 1972	2.1	5.6	1970 Census	6.6	14.6	1970 Census
Germany (Fed. Rep.), 1976	6.4	3.2	1976 LFSS	10.4	14.0	1978 LFSS
Great Britain, 1974	6.8	9.6	1971 Census[b]	3.4	3.2	1971 Census[b]
Israel, 1974	2.6	5.4	1972 Census	3.8	3.6	1976 LFSS
Japan, 1967	6.6	6.2	1965 Census	10.6	8.2	1965 Census
Netherlands, 1974	3.9	8.8	1971 Census	13.4	10.2	1971 Census
Northern Ireland, 1968[c]	2.6	6.3	1966 Census	—	—	—
Norway, 1972	4.8	13.4	1970 Census	17.8	12.4	1970 Census
Sweden, 1972	1.9	9.0	1970 Census	7.6	10.4	1970 Census
United States, 1974–1977	4.2	5.8	1976 LFSS	8.4	7.0	1976 LFSS

[a] Indexes of dissimilarity based on comparisons between survey and published census or labor force sample survey (LFSS) data. Age indexes were derived by comparing the age distributions of the economically active 20 to 64 year old populations; occupation indexes were derived by comparing International Standard Classification of Occupations (ISCO) major group scores of the economically active populations.

[b] Survey distributions for Great Britain were compared with 1971 Census figures for England and Wales.

[c] Published occupational data by International Standard Classification of Occupations (ISCO) major group scores not available for Northern Ireland.

Sources: Austria (age: ILO 1977, Table 1; occupation: ILO 1977, Table 2B); Denmark (age: ILO 1975c, Table 1; occupation: ILO 1977, Table 2B); Finland (age: United Nations 1973, Table 8; occupation: ILO 1975c, Table 2B); Germany (age: ILO 1977, Table 1; occupation: ILO 1979b, Table 2B); Great Britian (age: United Nations 1973, Table 8; occupation: United Nations 1973, Table 14); Israel (age: ILO 1979b, Table 1; occupation: ILO 1977, Table 2B); Japan (age: United Nations 1973, Table 8; occupation: United Nations 1973, Table 14); Netherlands (age: ILO 1977, Table 1; occupation: United Nations 1973, Table 8); Northern Ireland (age: United Nations 1973, Table 8); Norway (age: ILO 1977, Table 1; occupation: ILO 1977, Table 2B); Sweden (age: United Nations 1974, Table 38; occupation: ILO 1977, Table 2B); United States (age: ILO 1977, Table 1; occupation: ILO 1977, Table 2B).

There are other untestable explanations for why the survey and census data might differ as much as they do. Besides the sampling error associated with the surveys, there are methods effects due to: differences in the way the data were collected, differences in how the economically active population was defined, differences in how occupational information was coded into the ISCO major group classification, differences in the age ranges of the employed populations, and so forth. In addition, there are errors introduced by any substantive changes that occurred between the year of the survey and the year for which the census data were available (in a few of the countries, the difference between the survey and census date was as large as three years). The existence of these differences suggest that one should be cautious about interpreting sex and country differences in occupational behavior occurring in the analysis. At the minimum, differences of substantive importance should be large enough so that they could not be solely attributable to systematic sampling errors existing in the data.

METHODS

The question of the extent to which the survey data adequately represents the characteristics of the working population of a country is separate from the issue of the comparability of variables across the set of countries chosen for analysis, the task of the present section. In this study, I rely on cross-country comparisons of within-society relationships—comparisons of the occupational behavior of men and women, and of ever-married and never-married women, within a particular society. Thus, I determine the extent of cross-country variation in sex and marital differences in occupational behavior. Rather than abstracting traits to be compared crossculturally, this form of comparative analysis allows the comparison of relationships between variables within the societal context (Przeworski and Teune, 1970). Since I am not interested in comparing specific parameters of attainment models, I can concentrate on establishing logical or substantive equivalence rather than exact equivalence in measurement. In this section, I describe the efforts made to establish such equivalence. I restrict myself here to describing the coding of variables. Justifications for variable inclusion are presented in the individual chapters. There are five major variables: father's occupation (as a measure of social origins), age, marital status, educational achievement, and occupational position.

Description of Variable Measurement

Age of respondent. Establishing comparability among the data sets with regard to respondent's age was straightforward. In half of the data sets actual age in years was already available. In West Germany and Israel, the year of birth variable was transformed to age and in the four Scandinavian countries age was estimated by assigning the midpoint to categories representing five-year age groups. I use age in the analyses as a metric variable (in the regression analyses) and as a categorical variable (in comparing the age patterns of labor-force participation).

I also included age-squared in the regression analyses to take account of the potential curvilinear relationship between age and occupational attainment. Since age and age-squared are highly correlated, a constant (equal to the mean of age) was subtracted from age before squaring it to improve the stability of the coefficients.

Marital status. Like age, respondent's marital status was easily recoded. In each country, presently married, separated, divorced, and widowed women were assigned a code of "0," and women who never married a "1." The distinction was made between ever- and never-married women, rather than between currently and not currently married women, because women who have been married are more likely to have childcare and other home responsibilities left over from their marriage that affect their occupational choice and advancement. Sample-size limitations preclude separating a "previously married" or an "ever married with children" group, either of which would be preferable theoretically to what I used. Treiman and Terrell (1975b) found that educational, prestige, and earnings attainment patterns of formerly and currently married women are substantially similar in the United States, a finding that supports combining the two groups (although see Hudis 1976).

Educational achievement. I measured education by years of school completed. In five of the countries (Austria, the Netherlands, Great Britain, Israel, and the United States), education was already coded into years of school. In the remaining countries, I estimated years of schooling by using available education variable(s) and referring to area studies or special reference volumes on crosscultural educational attainment. In Northern Ireland, for example, I estimated educational attainment by subtracting "5" (the age at which children in Northern Ireland typically enter school) from the age at which the respondent left school. Similarly, in Japan, I subtracted "6" (the average school-entering age in Japan) from the respondent's school-leaving age. In addition, because of the excessive number of Japanese respondents with no value on the "age left school variable," I transformed a "level of education" variable to years of schooling by referring to other relevant source material (UNESCO 1966; Whitaker 1974; Mainichi Newspapers 1976). I then assigned this value to the Japanese respondents who had a missing value on school-leaving age (mostly older men and women who went to school in the very different educational system which existed prior to World War II). Similarly, the ten-category West German education variable and the eight-category Scandinavian variable were transformed to their years of schooling equivalent by reference to United Nations data on educational achievement (UNESCO 1966).

While years of schooling does not fully capture crosscultural variations in the quality of education in such countries as the Netherlands and Great Britain (see Treiman and Terrell 1975a for a more detailed discussion of the crosscultural measurement of education), I use this variable because it is straightforward and readily interpretable, and because the more detailed information required to take account of more complex educational systems was not available in the majority of the data sets. Since this study is specifically concerned with cross-country variation in within-society relationships, an exact equivalence is not required. Use of years of schooling in a gender comparison, however, may be less desirable than some alternative measure since men and women do not generally receive the same types of schooling (for example, men specialize in science and engineering and women in the humanities; see Finn et al. 1979, 1980 for crosscultural evidence in this regard). Since the appropriate variables are not available in these data, however, the effect of type of schooling on gender differences in occupational attainment crossculturally must await further analysis.

Occupational attainment. Given its role as the dependent variable, the decision about how to measure occupation is an important one. I use four separate measures, for both fathers and respondents, depending on the form of the analysis: a metric occupational prestige scale, a fourteen-category "type of work" variable, a seven-category major group classification, and a metric occupational wage-rate scale.

Given its wide use in crosscultural comparisons, I use the *Standard International Occupational Prestige Scale* (Treiman 1977). In preparing each data set for analysis, two coders assigned prestige scores to each country's detailed occupational classification, usually available at the three-digit level, and discrepancies of three points or more were discussed and reconciled. This coding was found to be highly reliable (Treiman 1977, Chapter 9). In those countries where additional distinctions were possible, the prestige coding was refined to take account of available information (for example, supervisory distinctions, self-employment, firm size, number of employees, size of farm; Treiman and Kelley 1978).

Because a metric prestige scale is not sufficient when investigating gender differences in occupational attainment patterns, I supplemented prestige with three other variables. These variables take into account the kinds of work men and women do, and thus reflect the gender differentiation of the labor market. First, the *Standard International Occupational Classification* was derived by dividing the seven ISCO (International Standard Classification of Occupations) major groups on the basis of prestige (Treiman 1977, 204). This classification, ordered according to average prestige, makes the usual type of work distinction between large occupational sectors (such as, professional, clerical, sales, production), but also differentiates between prestige groupings within each major group.[3] This latter feature makes the classification particularly useful for analyses of sex differences in occupation, since it distinguishes between the high-prestige classical professions (such as, doctor and lawyer) and the low-prestige technical and semiprofessions (such as, primary school teachers, nurses, and librarians). Such distinctions are made throughout the occupational hierarchy and correspond quite closely with the distribution of men and women in major groups. I use the fourteen-category classification as the variable of choice whenever a categorical variable is required.

Due to sample-size limitations, however, it is not possible to use the fourteen-category classification in all cases. In those analyses where a small sample size precludes using a more-detailed classification, I employ the seven-category *International Standard Classification of Occupations* (ISCO) (ILO 1969).[4] The seven-category classification thus provides a cruder estimate of gender and marital differences. I use this classification in two major analyses—comparing, via log-linear analysis, the occupational mobility of women and men (that is, mobility from father to respondent) and comparing the occupational distributions of ever- and never-married women. The seven categories of this classification are: (1) professional and technical, (2) administrative and managerial, (3) clerical and related, (4) sales, (5) service, (6) agricultural, and (7) production and related.

The fourteen- and seven-category classifications are useful for analyses where categorical variables are required, but they are not appropriate for regression analyses where respondent's occupation is the dependent variable. Although occupational prestige could be employed, I argue (in Chapter 5) that a more useful measure of occupational attainment would take into account differences in the kinds of work done by men and women. To have a summary measure of men's and women's occupational attainment for application in a multivariate framework, I thus create the *occupational wage-rate scale.* This scale was constructed to measure the extent to which women are concentrated in low-wage employment, relative to the occupations in which men are employed, and to study the determinants of such concentration. To create the scale I relied on the knowledge, derived from this and previous research, that a striking consistency exists across countries in the income hierarchy of occupations. Using data from eleven countries, Treiman (1977, Table 5.2) documented that a substantial degree of similarity exists in the relative wage rates of occupations. Similarly, Table 3.5 in the present analysis confirms the existence of a standard earnings hierarchy across industrial societies. The average intercountry correlation in occupational earnings levels for the ten countries with earnings data is .90 (calculated from Table 3.5).[5]

The raw data on which this scale is based are the average earnings of men within each of the fourteen categories of the Standard International Occupational Classification, in each of the ten countries with earnings data. For each country, I computed the average earnings of high-prestige professional men, male administrators and managers, low-prestige male clerical workers, and so forth. These average occupational earnings of men were then converted to a common metric, using the following formula (the United States was used as the standard):[6]

$$X'_{ij} = \frac{s_u}{s_j} (X_{ij} - \bar{X}_j) + \bar{X}_u$$

where, X'_{ij} = the transformed occupational earnings score for occupational category i as computed in country j;

s_u = the standard deviation of the United States scores;

s_j = the standard deviation of country j scores;

X_{ij} = original occupational earnings score for occupational category i as computed in country j;

$\bar{X}_j$ = mean occupational earnings of country j scores;

$\bar{X}_u$ = mean occupational earnings of the United States scores.

Once the transformed scores were obtained, I computed the weighted average (over the ten countries with earnings data) for each of the fourteen occupational categories. A weighted average was necessary since the countries varied in sample size and hence reliability of the earnings estimates. Occupational categories with large numbers of incumbents thus contributed proportionately more to estimating the average occupational wage rate. Finally, I transformed the resulting metric scale one more time to a 0- to 100-point scale for easier interpretability; "0" was assigned to the occupation with the lowest average male earnings across the ten countries (low-prestige agricultural occupations) and "100" to the groups with the highest male earnings (administrative and managerial occupations).[7]

In creating the occupational wage-rate scale, I used the average occupational earnings of men rather than the average earnings of all incumbents in the occupation. If one is to make valid gender comparisons, the same occupation scale should be used for both sexes. Adjusting the occupation scale to take account of the fact that women's occupations do not reap the same economic reward that men's do, which is what one does using total earnings, would obfuscate the important gender differences that do exist (for example, in economic returns to occupational attainment) (see Featherman and Hauser 1976, 465 for additional documentation of this point). The choice of male earnings is further justified by Treiman's and Terrell's (1975c, Table 7) finding that occupations that pay men poorly also pay women poorly (the correlation between male and female earnings computed over detailed occupational categories invariably exceeds .9). The occupational wage-rate scale thus represents a standard crosscultural earnings hierarchy of occupations. Using this metric scale as a dependent variable allows the researcher to determine the effects of hypothesized independent variables on the pay level of a particular occupation (for example, what effect does father's employment in high-paying jobs have on the likelihood that their sons or daughters will be employed in such jobs).

Gender Differences in Labor-Force Participation and Occupational Distribution

INTRODUCTION

To the extent that U.S. levels of occupational segregation also exist in other industrial societies, historical, cultural, and political traditions unique to this country cannot, in large measure, account for observed patterns of occupational concentration. Rather, similar patterns of occupational differentiation crossculturally suggest that fundamental features of the organization of work are more likely to be responsible for men's and women's different occupational locations. This chapter presents descriptive data on men's and women's labor-force participation, the nature of that participation, and the degree of occupational segregation, in order to examine the generality of the observation that men and women perform different work.[1] Additionally, I discuss the characteristics of sextyped employment. My goal is to lay the descriptive and empirical groundwork for subsequent occupational mobility and attainment analyses.

Recent analyses have documented that occupational segregation by sex in the United States is substantial and shows little sign of lessening (Gross 1968; Oppenheimer 1968, 1970; Treimen and Terrell 1975c; Blaxall and Reagan 1976; Treiman and Hartmann 1981). Between 1960 and 1970, the small changes that did occur mainly resulted from men's integration into traditionally female employment and not vice versa (Blau and Hendricks 1979). Since 1970, however, women have made some progress moving into selected male jobs, although the occupational structure as a whole remains highly sex segregated (for a review of the evidence, see Reskin and Hartmann 1985). Attempting to put numbers on the extent of this segregation, recent studies (Gross 1968; U.S. Commission on Civil Rights 1978) found that approximately two-thirds of women would have to change occupations to have their distribution correspond to that of men. Notably, gender segregation is substantially greater than occupational segregation by race (Gross 1968, 202). And, furthermore, not only do women and men work in different occupations, but the jobs in which women work are also poorly remunerated (Treiman and Hartmann 1981).

In contrast to the wealth of evidence regarding occupational sex segregation in the United States, evidence for other countries is more limited (although see Galenson 1973; Safilios-Rothschild 1975; Barrett 1976; Giele and Smock 1977; Standing 1978; OECD 1975, 1979; Volgyes and Volgyes 1977; Gaskin 1979; McAuley 1981). The most systematic of these analyses is Gaskin's, who investigated gender differences in occupational distribution in seven industrialized countries (Norway, Sweden, Canada, England, the United States, Germany, and Italy). She found (p. 96) uniformly high indexes of gender dissimilarity in six of the seven countries, ranging from a low of 58 in West Germany to a high of 73 in Norway.[2] Italy has a somewhat lower (but still quite large) index of 42 percent, which Gaskin (p. 141) attributed to the large numbers of women in agricultural work.

Gaskin also found uniformly high levels of occupational sextyping—the average intercountry correlation between the percent female in each category of Gaskin's occupational classification is .88 [when Italy is excluded, the correlation rises to .91 (calculated from Table 5–5 in Gaskin 1979)]. In the seven countries, women predominate in similar occupations—professional nurses; sewers, embroiderers, and such; housekeepers; maids and service workers, n.e.c.; nurses, n.e.c.; launderers; telephone operators; and waiters and bartenders. Women are also somewhat overrepresented as tobacco workers; stenographers, clericals, n.e.c.; packers and labelers; cooks; dressmakers, tailors, and so forth; salesworkers, shop assistants; teachers, except university; barbers and hairdressers; textile workers; and bookkeepers and cashiers (p. 117).

While sex-segregated occupational structures appear to be the rule, crosscultural variation does exist. Women in the Soviet Union, for example, are more highly integrated into the occupational structure than women in other highly industrialized countries (Dodge 1971; Galenson 1973; Blekher 1979). Despite women's integration into some jobs mainly held by men, the studies indicate that sex segregation in the Soviet occupational structure persists—women comprise 35 percent of all engineers, but 71 percent of all technicians, employed in production and design work; 46 percent of all engineers, but 71 percent of technicians, employed in technology; and 71 percent of the teachers in daytime schools (Blekher, p. 114). In addition, Dodge (p. 218) reported that although there are a large number of women doctors, they are less likely than men to be directors, deputy directors, and chief physicians; moreover wages for doctors were set at a level below those of highly skilled blue-collar workers (Cook 1979, 12).[3]

There is evidence of female integration into typically male employment in several Eastern European and some Western societies. Safilios-Rothschild (1975, 53) found that pharmacy and dentistry are feminine occupations in Finland, Poland, and Hungary. Gaskin (1979, Appendixes B and E) showed that in 1960, Norway, Sweden, England, and Germany had twice the percent female in the occupational category physicians, surgeons, and dentists than the comparable category in Canada, Italy, and the United States.

While these results are suggestive of substantial occupational sex segregation across industrial societies, previous analyses were limited in scope and (with the exception of Gaskin 1979) hampered by a lack of comparability in the measurement of occupation. As a consequence, it is impossible to know if observed country differences represent "true differences" or merely differences due to measurement error. The present study tackles this problem by presenting standardized data on the labor-force patterns of women and men.

LABOR-FORCE BEHAVIOR AND OCCUPATIONAL DISTRIBUTION

Gender Differences in Labor-Force Participation and Employment Status

This section sketches the extent and nature of female labor-force participation in twelve societies. Although the focus is on working women, it is important to bear in mind that the percentage of women engaged in wage employment varies quite substantially across countries (Galenson 1973; Durand 1975; Standing 1978).

Table 3.1 and Figure 3.1 present overviews of labor-force participation rates, by sex and age. In each country male's age pattern of labor-force participation can be described as an inverted U-shape curve: the percentage of men working increases with each successively older cohort, reaching a peak rate in the thirty to forty-four age period, and declining thereafter. In each country, at least 89 percent of the peak-age men are employed.

Table 3.1 Percent Employed, by Sex and Age for Twelve Industrialized Countries[a]

Age	Austria	Denmark	Finland	Germany (Fed. Rep.)	Great Britian	Israel	Japan	Netherlands	Northern Ireland	Norway	Sweden	United States
Male												
Less than 20[b]	41.9	51.0	61.5	[63.6]	60.6	16.3	21.1	34.8	—	60.0	61.4	51.9
20–24[c]	89.7	95.0	90.8	73.3	85.5	40.1	84.4	67.9	83.1	81.4	87.5	69.7
25–29	96.6	95.2	98.2	85.4	92.3	87.5	98.0	93.4	92.6	92.6	94.9	85.4
30–34	98.8	97.6	100.0	89.1	98.1	92.6	99.2	93.2	91.4	100.0	97.9	89.4
35–44	98.6	100.0	95.6	97.7	98.9	94.8	97.5	95.8	92.7	95.6	100.0	87.4
45–54	97.3	92.8	88.5	95.2	95.8	94.1	97.0	85.5	88.3	93.6	99.1	88.0
55–64	64.3	88.0	65.3	67.2	89.9	89.5	90.9	72.9	83.8	80.8	88.4	69.5
65+[d]	17.2	—	—	12.9	23.4	35.1	70.1	10.1	20.5	—	—	15.6
Total	80.0	89.9	85.3	76.2	78.8	67.4	85.1	70.4	79.5	87.5	92.2	69.6
Total (20–64)	92.4	94.6	90.6	89.1	93.9	85.6	95.4	85.8	88.7	91.1	95.4	82.5
Female												
Less than 20[b]	34.8	50.0	55.4	63.7	78.4	8.3	15.6	36.5	—	51.0	54.7	46.6
20–24[c]	62.0	80.0	85.2	67.3	55.1	41.2	65.4	79.3	63.1	42.9	82.9	52.0
25–29	45.1	68.3	80.4	49.3	53.2	46.2	35.5	44.3	43.5	38.1	66.7	50.4
30–34	44.9	60.0	85.2	41.3	48.7	37.5	39.7	42.0	35.9	44.6	65.5	51.0
35–44	57.5	60.7	86.0	36.7	51.4	32.6	50.5	28.9	39.7	44.0	72.6	50.3
45–54	49.5	64.1	72.3	36.5	65.9	35.4	50.8	22.4	36.2	48.6	75.7	49.9
55–64	27.1	31.2	50.0	25.6	44.3	22.2	43.9	17.3	28.7	32.9	41.0	41.8
65+[d]	5.5	—	—	3.2	4.8	6.1	27.1	3.0	10.1	—	—	8.1
Total	40.6	56.5	71.4	34.1	43.6	29.6	42.1	34.3	36.4	43.2	65.7	42.2
Total (20–64)	48.9	61.7	76.7	42.3	55.0	37.3	49.5	50.0	41.8	43.0	69.5	49.3

[a] Bracketed percentages based on less than 20 cases.
[b] Age less than 20 varies by country: Austria, Denmark, Finland, Great Britain, the Netherlands, Norway, Sweden (15–19); Germany (Fed. Rep.), United States (18–19); Israel (14–17); Japan (14–19). The Northern Ireland survey sample did not include persons younger than 21.
[c] Israel (18–24); Northern Ireland (21–24).
[d] The Scandinavian survey samples did not include persons older than 64.

While the male patterns are notable for their consistency, women's patterns are variable, reaffirming earlier findings of nonuniformity in women's age patterns of participation (Durand 1975; OECD 1975). Each country can be characterized by one of three basic types (see Figure 3.1):[4]

1. *Early peak*—substantial participation of women in the labor force prior to their marriage and childbearing years, followed by a sharp decrease;

2. *Double peak*—substantial female participation prior to marriage and childbearing, a drop off during childbearing years, an increase after childbearing has occurred (but before children are grown), and a final tailing off;

3. *Single peak*—like the male pattern, with an increase in participation until the thirties or forties and then a tailing off, but with lower rates than males of the same age.

The Federal Republic of Germany, Israel, the Netherlands, and Northern Ireland can best be described as early peak countries. In three of these countries, female labor-force participation is greatest in the twenty to twenty-four age cohort (the three-country average is 70 percent), the age by which most women will have finished their schooling but not yet married. The peak participation rate for females in Israel occurs in the twenty-five to twenty-nine age cohort, and is a much lower 46 percent, results that may reflect the three-year universal military service for Israeli men and women.[5] In the twenty-five to twenty-nine age cohort (or the thirty to thirty-four age cohort for Israel), there begins a typically uninterrupted decline in the percentage of working women. These are the ages when childbearing and rearing demands are heaviest. What particularly distinguishes the early peak countries, however, is that even women who have completed their childbearing have not returned to the labor force. Not surprisingly, the early peak countries have low average levels of female participation, ranging from 30 percent in Israel to 36 percent in Northern Ireland, or 37 (Israel) to 50 (Netherlands) percent of the twenty- to sixty-four-year old populations.

Six countries have double peak patterns. As with the early-peak countries, the first participation peak occurs in the early age groups— the twenty to twenty-four age cohort for Austria, Denmark, Japan, and Sweden, and the less than twenty age cohort for Great Britain and Norway. Following this early peak (which ranges from 51 percent in Norway to 83 percent in Sweden), women in their late twenties and early thirties are less likely to work (ranging from 36 percent in Japan to 66 percent in Sweden). By the time women have completed their childbearing, usually in their late thirties, they are likely to return to the labor force. The second participation peak generally occurs in the forty-five to fifty-four age cohort, and is always somewhat less than the first peak. The six double peak countries are characterized by middle levels of female labor-force participation, ranging from 41 percent in Austria to 66 percent in Sweden, or 43 percent (Norway) to 70 percent (Sweden) of the twenty- to sixty-four-year old populations.

Only Finland can be considered a single peak society. This country has the highest female participation rate of any of the included countries—an average of 71 percent of the Finnish women work, 77 percent of the twenty to sixty-four age group. With only a small decline between the twenty to twenty-four and twenty-five to twenty-nine age cohorts, the Finnish pattern is one of increasing percentages of women working until the thirty-five to forty-four age cohort; after this age, women's participation declines.

The United States appears to be in transition from the double peak pattern, which it exhibited in 1960 (Oppenheimer 1970, 9), to the barely single peak pattern suggested by the present data. Analyses of cohort trends in labor-force participation document that younger cohorts of United States women are remaining in the labor force even during their prime childbearing years (Kreps and Leaper 1976, Chart 1B). The average female participation rate of 42 percent (49 percent of the twenty- to sixty-four-year old group), however, is significantly lower than those of Denmark and Sweden, two of the double peak countries.[6]

Extrapolating from the historical experience of the United States (see Oppenheimer 1970, 9), these three types of female participation may be viewed as three points on a continuum, with countries first exhibiting an early peak pattern (with low levels of female participation). With the growth in demand for female workers [partly due to an increase in the number of jobs that typically employ women (such as, clerical and service)], countries shift to a double peak pattern (with medium levels of participation) and then to a single peak pattern (characterized by high participation levels). This transition is consistent with research noted earlier documenting the recent influx into the labor forces of the United States and other industrial societies of married women with small children, traditionally the group least likely to work (Sweet 1975; Finland Central Statistical Office 1975; OECD 1979, 25).

Table 3.2 presents information on employment status. In the societies for which a full-time/part-time distinction is available (all except Great Britain and Northern Ireland), men are much more likely to work full time than women. In each country except Israel

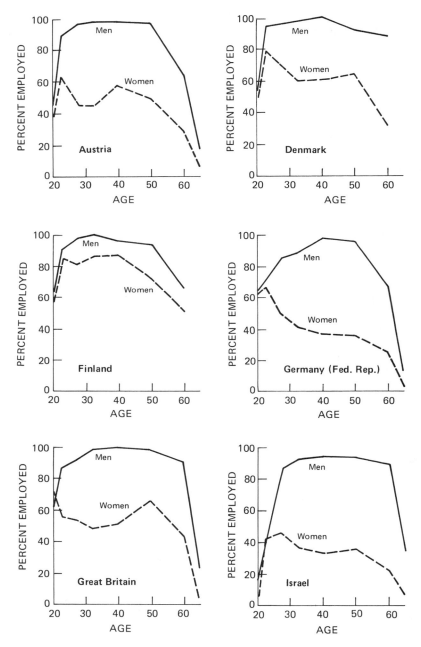

Figure 3.1   Percent Employed, by Sex and Age, for 12
Industrialized Countries

Figure 3.1   Percent Employed, by Sex and Age, for Twelve Industrialized Countries

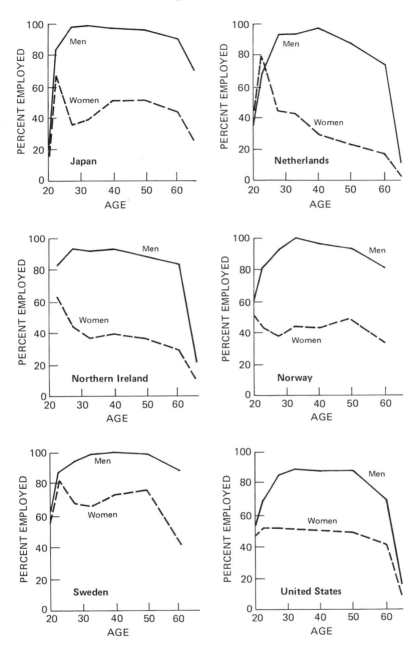

Figure 3.1 Percent Employed, by Sex and Age, for 12
Industrialized Countries (Cont.)

Figure 3.1 Percent Employed, by Sex and Age, for Twelve Industrialized Countries
(Cont.)

and the United States, well over two-thirds of the sampled men are employed full time. Notably, in Finland, Israel, Norway, and Sweden at least 10 percent of the men work part time. Relative to men, women are less likely to work full time and more likely to work part time. Perhaps the most salient characteristic of women's employment to be gleaned from Table 3.2 is that so few women work—in nine of the twelve countries well over half the sampled women are not employed.[7]

In sum, there is consistency across the twelve countries in the percentage of men who work, their age pattern of participation, and their propensity to work full time. These consistent patterns undoubtedly reflect, at least in part, men's historical role as family provider. The employment patterns of women, in contrast, vary substantially. The differences between men and women on these measures of employment are instructive, in the sense that they provide striking documentation of the extent to which women's labor-force behavior depends on their marriage and family life cycle. Women, on average, are less likely than men to participate in the labor force, especially during their prime childbearing and rearing years, and when they do work, they are more likely than men to be employed part time. Only in Finland do women come close to approximating men in their labor-force participation.

Lacking from the previous discussion is any explanation for why women's labor-force behavior varies so widely. To address this issue adequately would require a detailed analysis of the role of institutional arrangements, as well as historical, legislative, and cultural factors, that affect women's labor-force entry and extent of employment (see Semyonov 1980 and Ward and Pampel 1983 for investigations of structural determinants of women's labor-force participation cross-culturally).[8]

While such analyses are beyond the scope of the present study, I am able to speculate on the origin of these diverse patterns. It may be that the availability of part-time employment is significantly greater in countries exhibiting single or double peak patterns and high levels of female participation, thus increasing women's opportunities for work outside the home (see Jonung's 1977 work with respect to Sweden). Alternatively, some countries may provide greater support (for example, tax deductions or state-supported childcare) for families with children, increasing women's flexibility in choosing to work outside the home. Finally, the lower rates of female participation in the Federal Republic of Germany may be attributable to decisions by the government to import foreign labor (Kamerman 1979, 645; Shaffer 1981). Faced with similar labor shortages, the Swedish government reduced their dependence on foreign labor by actively re-

Table 3.2   Employment Status of Men and Women (All Ages) for Twelve Industrialized Countries (in percentages)

Country and sex of respondent	Full time	Part time	Not employed	Total	N
Austria					
Male	79.5	0.5	20.1	100.1	(683)
Female	31.5	9.1	59.5	100.1	(867)
Denmark					
Male	83.0	7.0	10.0	100.0	(458)
Female	34.1	22.3	43.6	100.0	(560)
Finland					
Male	70.9	14.5	14.7	100.1	(484)
Female	55.0	16.3	28.7	100.0	(509)
Germany (Fed. Rep.)					
Male	72.9	3.3	23.8	100.0	(889)
Female	18.7	15.4	65.9	100.0	(1,294)
Great Britain					
Male	73.9	4.9	21.1	99.9	(703)
Female	25.7	17.8	56.4	99.9	(721)
Israel					
Male	54.4	12.9	32.6	99.9	(13,220)
Female	16.0	13.6	70.4	100.0	(15,013)
Japan[b]					
Male	85.1		14.9	100.0	(896)
Female	42.1		57.9	100.0	(1,131)
Netherlands					
Male	68.5	1.8	29.7	100.0	(663)
Female	25.0	9.3	65.7	100.0	(471)
Northern Ireland[b]					
Male	79.5		20.5	100.0	(602)
Female	36.4		63.6	100.0	(607)
Norway					
Male	77.5	10.1	12.4	100.0	(516)
Female	21.4	21.9	56.7	100.0	(462)
Sweden					
Male	77.8	14.3	7.9	100.0	(468)
Female	28.0	37.7	34.3	100.0	(554)
United States					
Male	60.8	8.8	30.3	99.9	(2,837)
Female	30.3	11.9	57.8	100.0	(3,067)

Employment status[a]

[a] See Chapter 2 for definition of employment status variable.
[b] Full-time/part-time status not available.

cruiting married women (Cook 1979, 48). Similarly, the recruitment of married women to fill labor shortages caused by excessive emigration is probably one of the major explanations for Finland's high level of female participation (see Finland Central Statistical Office 1975 and Haavio-Mannila and Sokolowska 1978 for additional details). These explanations must be left for others to pursue.

The remainder of this study investigates similarities and differences in the occupational distributions and attainments of men and women. I thus focus exclusively on employed persons.[9]

Gender Differences in Occupational Composition

Table 3.3 presents data on sex differences in occupational location. I focus on the extent to which other industrial societies approximate the characteristic United States pattern. As suggested by previous research, men and women are concentrated in quite different kinds of occupations. Although crosscultural variability exists, the United States pattern is fairly typical—large numbers of women are employed in high-prestige clerical occupations, low-prestige professional and technical positions, and low-prestige service jobs. Only in Austria and Northern Ireland do women predominate in low-prestige clerical jobs as they do in the United States. Men, in contrast, are located mainly in high- and medium-prestige production work, and, in the United States, in high-prestige professional and administrative/managerial employment. Five countries (Austria, Denmark, Finland, Japan, and Norway) also have large numbers of agricultural workers.[10]

The summary statistic presented in the bottom panel of Table 3.3 estimates the extent of occupational segregation by gender for each country. The index of dissimilarity measures the percentage of one sex that would need to change occupations to make the two distributions identical. All the indexes are high, with most falling in the 40 to 50 percent range, indicating the existence of a substantial amount of occupational sex segregation.[11]

There are two major exceptions to the uniformity in indexes: Japan has a relatively low index (28 percent) and Sweden has a relatively high index (60 percent). The low index in Japan is partly a reflection of insufficient detail in the occupational classification: Japan's classification is a two-digit scheme while those of the remaining countries are three-digit. Another explanation is the large proportion of women employed in agriculture. At the time of the survey, 37 percent of Japanese women were employed in agriculture compared with 19 percent of Japanese men. Japanese women in 1967 (the survey date) were thus still in the process of moving out of the primary sector of the economy. Consistent with this hypothesis, the percentage of Japanese women employed as family workers decreased from 43 to 25 percent of all women workers from 1960 to 1978. Moreover, the percentage of female paid employees increased from 41 to 61 percent during the same period (Cook and Hayashi 1980). According to recent OECD (1979, 30) figures, by 1975 fully 97 percent of all stenographers and typists were women. In addition, the percentage of Japanese clerical workers who were female increased from 36 percent in 1960 to 50 percent in 1978 (Cook and Hayashi, p. 108). Thus, the same sort of concentration of women in clerical occupations characteristic of the United States has occurred in Japan, but more recently.[12]

In contrast to Japan, Sweden's index of dissimilarity is high relative to other countries. This finding is due primarily to two factors: a relatively large concentration of women in clerical occupations (the proportion of women in high-prestige clerical occupations is greater than the proportion of men by a ratio of 11 to 1) and a substantial underrepresentation of women in production work (the proportion of men employed in high- and medium-prestige production work outnumbers the proportion of women by factors of 8 to 1 and 7 to 1, respectively). This highly segregated occupational structure is probably due in part to the heavy concentration of Swedish women in part-time employment (see Table 3.2). Jonung (1977, 2), in fact, suggested that as much as 88 percent of the increase in the employment of Swedish women between 1965 and 1970 was the result of the expansion of part-time employment.

Ironically, Sweden is one of the few countries to actively reorient its social policy in an attempt to reduce occupational segregation and better integrate women into the occupational structure. The government's policy has been one of actively encouraging equal employment opportunities for, and equal acceptance of family responsibilities by, men and women. One of the best known of the Swedish initiatives was the 1974 conversion of maternity into parental insurance (OECD 1975, 96). Other policies increase women's opportunities in nontraditional employment by emphasizing training programs, increasing the availability of childcare, and providing subsidies to employers who offer on-the-job training for female workers in typically male employment (and male workers in typically female employment) (see Jonung 1977, 1978a). Unfortunately, it is impossible to determine, with the 1972 data used in this study, whether these reforms have resulted in any significant reduction in observed occupational segregation by gender. Certainly, in 1972, Sweden exhibited greater occupational segregation than other included countries.

Table 3.3 Occupational Distribution of Employed Persons (All Ages), by Sex, for Twelve Industrialized Countries (in percentages)

Occupational category[a]	Austria		Denmark		Finland		Germany (Fed. Rep.)		Great Britain		Israel	
	M	F	M	F	M	F	M	F	M	F	M	F
1. High-prestige professional and technical	5.1	1.4	5.4	3.2	3.5	3.1	7.5	3.5	4.8	2.3	6.7	7.9
2. Administrative and managerial	3.3	0.5	3.8	0.0	2.4	1.2	2.7	0.0	6.1	0.9	4.2	1.0
3. High-prestige clerical and related	3.7	12.7	3.8	24.1	0.8	14.8	18.4	31.7	5.5	29.4	8.2	25.7
4. High-prestige sales	8.4	4.3	4.7	2.4	3.3	3.1	5.8	4.3	4.9	3.5	6.7	2.1
5. Low-prestige professional and technical	4.5	6.0	6.6	14.5	7.1	10.2	6.0	11.0	7.2	12.6	7.5	21.4
6. High-prestige agricultural	15.0	19.2	22.1	17.3	22.8	24.7	4.6	1.9	2.5	0.0	3.6	2.0
7. High-prestige production and related	16.7	3.5	15.3	3.6	10.6	3.1	23.3	5.3	17.3	4.7	19.6	5.0
8. High-prestige service	3.9	4.6	1.4	4.4	1.9	4.3	5.0	5.8	5.5	7.3	2.9	6.4
9. Medium-prestige production and related	19.8	7.3	22.4	3.6	28.3	6.2	18.2	4.6	24.9	10.4	18.5	4.9
10. Low-prestige clerical and related	7.6	10.6	2.6	2.8	2.7	4.6	4.5	9.1	4.5	0.4	4.0	3.0
11. Low-prestige sales	0.8	7.6	1.9	6.4	0.5	6.5	1.2	12.1	2.2	8.3	2.5	6.3
12. Low-prestige												

	Japan		Netherlands		Northern Ireland		Norway		Sweden		United States	
	M	F	M	F	M	F	M	F	M	F	M	F
1. High-prestige professional and technical	5.4	4.8	7.3	6.3	6.6	12.3	8.3	5.8	8.5	6.2	11.1	6.7
2. Administrative and managerial	8.4	1.0	8.0	0.5	2.6	1.3	4.8	2.3	5.2	0.4	10.4	3.0
3. High-prestige clerical and related	15.5	15.2	11.7	27.3	0.4	6.4	6.0	18.1	2.4	26.3	2.4	22.9
4. High-prestige sales	6.2	6.3	10.0	3.9	7.4	1.7	5.0	1.2	4.7	1.1	4.4	1.5
5. Low-prestige professional and technical	3.3	2.5	9.0	18.0	3.1	4.7	12.1	13.5	10.7	17.2	6.5	15.6
6. High-prestige agricultural	16.8	30.4	4.6	0.5	13.1	0.8	14.9	16.4	7.6	1.1	3.4	0.1
7. High-prestige production and related	17.8	7.3	12.9	0.5	13.1	5.5	10.8	0.0	17.3	2.2	18.4	4.5
13. Low-prestige service	0.6	12.5	0.5	14.9	1.4	13.3	0.8	5.1	1.5	15.4	4.4	10.2
14. Low-prestige production and related	7.4	7.9	8.0	2.4	9.0	3.1	1.6	5.0	10.0	3.4	9.1	3.5
Total (%)	100.1	100.0	100.1	100.0	100.0	100.1	100.0	100.1	99.9	99.9	100.2	100.1
N	(541)	(342)	(393)	(281)	(373)	(319)	(642)	(386)	(545)	(314)	(8791)	(4407)
Index of dissimilarity	37.6		50.4		41.2		42.6		51.1		45.8	

[a] Standard International Occupational Classification (Treiman 1977, Chapter 9).

Table 3.3 Occupational Distribution of Employed Persons (All Ages), by Sex, for Twelve Industrialized Countries (in percentages) (*Cont.*)

	Japan		Netherlands		Northern Ireland		Norway		Sweden		United States	
	M	F	M	F	M	F	M	F	M	F	M	F
8. High-prestige service	2.0	2.8	4.4	3.4	2.8	16.9	3.5	2.9	3.8	5.5	5.0	8.8
9. Medium-prestige production and related	12.7	9.8	20.2	4.4	24.7	13.1	19.4	4.1	23.7	3.6	19.1	8.5
10. Low-prestige clerical and related	1.0	0.5	3.9	5.9	7.9	13.1	2.5	4.1	2.8	5.5	4.7	10.3
11. Low-prestige sales	2.0	4.9	1.5	11.2	2.6	6.8	1.5	12.9	2.1	10.6	5.1	5.3
12. Low-prestige agricultural	2.1	6.2	2.7	1.5	2.6	2.5	2.0	0.6	3.3	0.0	1.7	0.4
13. Low-prestige service	2.0	8.1	1.2	15.1	1.7	8.5	1.3	15.2	1.4	18.2	2.9	10.4
14. Low-prestige production and related	4.9	0.2	2.7	1.5	11.4	6.4	7.8	2.9	6.4	2.2	5.0	2.0
Total (%)	100.1	100.0	100.1	100.0	100.0	100.0	99.9	100.0	99.9	100.1	100.1	100.1
N	(719)	(454)	(456)	(160)	(472)	(222)	(413)	(155)	(397)	(299)	(1939)	(1298)
Index of dissimilarity	27.6		50.2		43.6		41.8		60.0		46.8	

[a] Standard International Occupational Classification (Treiman 1977, Chapter 9).

THE CHARACTERISTICS OF MALE AND FEMALE EMPLOYM

The Sextyping of Occupations

These uniformly high levels of occupational sex segregation document that men and women operate in very different labor markets, not only in the United States but also in other industrial societies. The present section delineates the nature of these labor markets by analyzing the characteristics of occupations mainly held by men and those mainly held by women. According to human-capital explanations, women's family responsibilities should have the consequence of concentrating women in jobs that require low levels of commitment to the labor force. In contrast, men, less encumbered by day-to-day family responsibilities, should work in jobs where continuous attachment is economically rewarded.

Table 3.4 presents the percent female in each of fourteen occupation groups, expressed as a deviation from the percent female in the country's total labor force. Using this latter figure as a standard against which the percent female in each occupation is compared provides a measure of the degree to which women are overrepresented (positive signs) or underrepresented (negative signs) in each occupation group, given their representation in the labor force as a whole. For example, women are equally underrepresented in high-prestige production work in Finland and Norway by approximately 26 percent. The percentage of women actually employed in such occupations in Norway and Finland, however, differs markedly because of the very different rate at which women are employed in the two countries— 20 (=46−26) percent of the high-prestige production workers in Finland are women, while the comparable figure for Norway is 0 (=27−27) percent.[13]

Inspecting Table 3.4 allows us to examine the nature of this substantial occupational sex segregation. Referring first to the twelve-country average (the final column in Table 3.4), it should be noted that women are slightly overrepresented in low-prestige professional, high-prestige service, and low-prestige clerical positions and substantially (greater than 20 percent) overrepresented in high-prestige clerical, low-prestige sales, and low-prestige service occupations. On the other hand, women are somewhat underrepresented in high-prestige professional, high-prestige sales, high- and low-prestige agricultural, and low-prestige production work and substantially underrepresented in administrative/managerial occupations and in high- and medium-prestige production work. The nature of occupational segregation in industrial society is clear: women are heavily concen-

Table 3.4 Percent Female in Each Occupation Group Expressed as a Deviation from Percent Female in the Total Labor Force, for Twelve Industrialized Countries[a]

Occupational category[b]	Austria	Denmark	Finland	Germany (Fed. Rep.)	Great Britain	Israel	Japan	Netherlands	Northern Ireland	Norway	Sweden	United States	Twelve-country average[c]
1. High-prestige professional and technical	-24	-12	-3	-16	-15	+4	-2	-3	+15	-6	-8	-11	-7
2. Administrative and managerial	-29	[-42]	[-16]	[-38]	-29	-23	-32	-24	[-13]	-12	-38	-24	-26
3. High-prestige clerical and related	+30	+40	+48	+13	+39	+28	-0	+19	[+55]	+26	+46	+46	+30
4. High-prestige sales	-14	-15	-1	-7	-7	-20	+0	-14	-22	-19	-28	-21	-14
5. Low-prestige professional and technical	+7	+19	+9	+15	+14	+26	-6	+15	+10	+2	+12	+22	+12
6. High-prestige agricultural	+6	-6	+2	-18	[-36]	-11	+15	-22	-29	+2	-33	-39	-12
7. High-prestige production and related	-27	-27	-26	-25	-23	-22	-18	-25	-15	-27	-34	-26	-25
8. High-prestige service	+4	[+27]	+20	+3	+7	+19	+9	-4	+42	[-4]	+9	+14	+12
9. Medium-prestige production and related	-20	-31	-30	-24	-17	-22	-6	-19	-12	-20	-32	-17	-21
10. Low-prestige clerical and related	+8	[+2]	+13	+17	-31	-6	—	+9	+12	[+11]	+16	+19	+6

11. Low-prestige sales	+47	+29	+45	+48	+32	+22	+23	+47	+23	+49	+36	+1	+34
12. Low-prestige agricultural	-12	—	-24	—	-16	-21	+26	[-10]	[-1]	—	[-43]	-28	-12
13. Low-prestige service	+54	+54	+43	+42	+49	+21	+34	+55	+38	+55	+48	+30	+44
14. Low-prestige production and related	+2	-24	-23	+28	-20	-17	-36	[-10]	-11	-15	-22	-19	-14
Total percent female	39	42	46	38	36	33	39	26	32	27	43	40	37

a Figures of sign opposite pattern for row are underlined. Percentages based on fewer than 10 cases not shown; percentages based on 10–19 cases are shown in brackets.
b Standard International Occupational Classification (Treiman 1977, Chapter 9).
c Bracketed percentages are not included in averages.

trated in three major occupational groups [on average 67 (=37+30) percent of high-prestige clerical workers, 71 (=37+34) percent of the low-prestige sales workers, and 81 (=37+44) percent of the low-prestige service workers are women]. Men predominate in three occupational groups [on average 89 [=100−(37−26)] percent of the administrators and managers, 88 [=100−(37−25)] percent of the high-prestige production workers, and 84 [=100−(37−21)] percent of the medium-prestige production workers are men]. I refer to these two sets of occupations as "occupations mainly held by women" and "occupations mainly held by men," respectively.[14]

There is extensive uniformity across the twelve countries in the pattern of occupational segregation by sex—the direction and magnitude of each country's over or underrepresentation of women in various occupational categories are similar. Departures from the modal pattern for the row (that is, where an individual country indicates an overrepresentation of women in a particular occupation group, while the major trend is one of underrepresentation, or vice versa) are underlined. Of 168 possible comparisons, only 16 (or 9.5 percent) indicate deviations from the modal sign for the row. The average deviation from expectation for those cells differing from the modal sign for the row is 9.8 percent; the average deviation from expectation for those cells conforming to the trend of the row is 23.8 percent.[15]

There are three major exceptions worth noting that are instructive in their own right. First, as previously discussed, the differing occupational pattern exhibited by Japanese women (five of the sixteen deviations are for Japan) can probably be traced to the heavy concentration of women in agricultural work at the time of the survey (as well as to the lack of detail in the occupational classification). The percentage of women in low-prestige agricultural work in Japan exceeds their percentage in the total labor force by 26 percent. In every other country, women are underrepresented in this category.

Second, women are substantially overrepresented in low-prestige production occupations in West Germany, a result that is partly an artifact of the way the German sample was selected. The *gastarbeiter* (guest worker) population, which comprised 11 percent of the total labor force in 1972 (German Federal Institute for Population Research 1974, 32), was excluded. This population has always been largely male and typically concentrated in the lowest status jobs. Thus it is probably true that, as elsewhere, low-prestige production work in Germany is mainly done by men, but by foreign men rather than by German nationals. This possibility is supported by Table 3.3, which shows that the percentage of the male labor force in low-prestige production work is smaller in Germany than in any other country.

Third, women are somewhat overrepresented in high-prestige professional occupations in Northern Ireland. A clue as to why this occurs may be found in the age pattern of participation of women in that country (see Figure 3.1). Northern Ireland is characterized by an early peak pattern of female labor-force participation, suggesting that women of marriage and childbearing age (and older) have permanently left the labor force. It may well be that in countries where such a pattern is common, women who hold high-paying (and hence high-prestige) occupations are particularly likely to remain in the labor force. This supposition is partially supported by Table 3.3, which shows that two of the four early peak countries (Israel and Northern Ireland) have the two largest percentages of their female labor force engaged in high-prestige professional work (relative to the remaining countries), and a third (the Netherlands) is among the largest. In addition, in Table 3.4 two of the early peak countries have a sign opposite the major trend in the high-prestige professional category (indicating female overrepresentation) and a third, though similar in sign, is smaller in magnitude than most of the other deviations in the row.[16]

Two other anomalous results are observed in Table 3.4 for which no immediate explanation is obvious: (1) women are underrepresented in low-prestige clerical work in Great Britain, and (2) contrary to the trend in other countries, women in the United States are less likely to be overrepresented in low-prestige sales occupations.

Detailed occupations and major groups. Given the high level of aggregation inherent in a major group occupational classification, it is instructive to examine what specific occupations fall into each of the fourteen major groups. I focus in this study on the six occupational categories characterized as either mainly held by men or mainly by women (see note 14). As previously mentioned, the occupations mainly held by women include high-prestige clerical and related employment, low-prestige sales work, and low-prestige service work. The kinds of detailed occupations falling into the high-prestige clerical category include such traditionally female occupations as clerical supervisors, secretaries, typists, bookkeepers, and keypunch operators. Similarly, the low-prestige sales group includes sales demonstrators, sales clerks, and street vendors, and the low-prestige service group includes waiters and waitresses, maids and related housekeeping workers, and launderers (see Treiman 1977, 206, Appendix A).[17]

The occupation groups mainly held by men include administrative and managerial jobs, high-prestige production employment, and medium-prestige production work. The administrative and managerial category includes such typically male occupations as government officials, heads of firms, bankers, business executives, and specialized and general managers. The high- and medium-prestige production major groups are also aggregates of typically male occupations (high-prestige production: foremen, steel-mill workers, chemical workers, cabinetmakers, and electricians; medium-prestige production: truck drivers, rolling-mill operators, and miners).[18]

Given the differences in the level of detail of the country-specific occupational classifications, it is important to ensure that occupations being coded into the same occupational categories are in fact comparable. Appendix A presents the interested reader a listing of the country-specific occupational titles that are coded into each of the fourteen categories of the Standard International Occupational Classification, separately by sex. For the sake of parsimony, countries with identical occupational classifications (that is, products of a single research project) are grouped and only those country-specific occupational titles containing at least 5 percent of the male (or female) labor force in the major group category are listed. The results are informative, for two reasons. First, they allow a check of the country-specific occupational titles coded into each major occupation group and, second, they permit a rough indication of the types of male and female jobs within each of the fourteen categories.

Reviewing the list of the occupational titles in Appendix A further documents the explanation offered for the low index of gender dissimilarity observed in Japan. The grossness of the Japanese occupational classification results in the combining of occupational titles that span major groups. The high-prestige professional and technical category, for example, includes quite heterogeneous titles such as "Teacher: Primary, Junior, and Senior High School, University, Special School, Kindergarten, etc." and "Specialist in Medicine and Health: Doctor, Pharmacist, Midwife, Public Health Nurse, Nurse, Masseur, Specialist in Moxacautery, Veterinarian, Other Related workers." Both titles fail to distinguish between typically female nursing and primary school teaching occupations and typically male doctors and university teaching jobs, thereby reducing the amount of sex differentiation observed in the occupational structure. Similar lack of specificity is visible throughout the Japanese occupational classification.

Although the Japanese classification is the most obvious example of how the level of occupational detail is insufficient, there are a few such examples in each classification. I have already noted that the Northern Ireland title "Teachers, n.e.c." fails to differentiate between high-prestige secondary teachers and low-prestige elementary school teachers. Overall, however, the coding appears to be adequate and the occupational titles falling into the major groups comparable.

The Characteristics of Sextyped Occupations

While it is clear from the evidence presented thus far that men and women work in different occupational groups, and very different occupations within those major groups, I have not yet discussed what is known about the characteristics of the jobs in which men and women work. I turn to this issue now, to begin to address the human-capital contention that men and women work in different jobs because of differing levels of family responsibilities. Fortunately, researchers in the United States have addressed this issue, and have focused recently on a comparison of the characteristics of jobs mainly held by men and those mainly held by women (Oppenheimer 1968; McLaughlin 1975; Treiman and Terrell 1975c; Wolf and Rosenfeld 1978).

Oppenheimer (1968) was one of the earliest researchers to describe the characteristics of male and female occupations. She claimed that jobs mainly held by women are likely to: (1) depend on cheap but well-educated labor, (2) not require extensive schooling or on-the-job training (instead requiring skills that exist prior to employment and that do not depreciate with labor-force interruptions), (3) not require career continuity or long-range commitment, (4) seldom require extensive sacrifices of time and energy either in preparation for employment or on the job, and (5) seldom require women supervising men. Oppenheimer argued that these characteristics (or some subset of them) are observable in typically female jobs, such as the female professions, white-collar clerical employment, sales work, and service work. While the classifications are not identical, the jobs Oppenheimer described as female are similar to those described in this study.

In contrast, Oppenheimer described men's jobs as: (1) requiring a substantial investment of time and energy, both in the amount of schooling required and on the job, (2) requiring continuity of employment for advancement, and (3) requiring geographic mobility or extensive traveling for upward mobility. The occupational groups Oppenheimer described as male include those designated as predominantly male in Table 3.4.

What else is known about women's versus men's jobs? Oppenheimer (1968) and Treiman and Terrell (1975c) showed that incumbents in jobs mainly held by women are underpaid relative to their average educational achievement. More recently, Wolf and Rosenfeld (1978, 840) documented that predominantly female occupations are easier to reenter after labor-force interruptions and offer limited opportunity for upward mobility.

Using the third edition of the *Dictionary of Occupational Titles* (DOT) scores,[19] McLaughlin (1975, 116) found differences in the characteristics of male and female occupations: on average male jobs tend to exhibit a more complex relationship to "things," to require greater physical strength, to be performed in more hazardous locations, and to require more specific vocational preparation than female occupations, while female jobs generally require more clerical skills. Cain and Treiman (1981), however, found that the third edition of the DOT overstates differences between the attributes of jobs mainly held by women and those mainly held by men. They documented that the fourth edition scores show jobs mainly held by women (especially clerical jobs) as more complex in their relationship to things than men's jobs.[20]

The evidence presented in this section, albeit sketchy, is consistent with the human-capital argument that the characteristics of jobs mainly held by women should be relatively compatible with family responsibilities, while the characteristics of men's jobs interfere with those responsibilities. While the present crosscultural data on sex-segregated occupational structures conform to these expectations, they do not address the more important question of whether women's differential occupational concentration derives from their marital and childrearing responsibilities or from some other factors, a question examined in subsequent chapters.

Crosscultural Differences in Male and Female Jobs

The current data do not permit a detailed assessment of whether the characteristics of female and male employment differ crossculturally. With the data available, however, I can examine the average educational achievement and the economic remuneration of incumbents of fourteen major occupational groups. This exercise addresses the question of whether women in other industrial societies, like United States women, concentrate in employment where they are underpaid relative to their educational achievement—that is, whether they constitute a cheap source of educated labor.

Table 3.5 shows, for each country with earnings data, the mean education and earnings level of each major group, expressed as a percentage of the education and earnings, respectively, of high-prestige professional workers in the particular country. A comparison of these percentages within and between countries tests whether, as Oppenheimer (1968) and Treiman and Terrell (1975c) found for the United States, jobs mainly held by women are low paying relative to their educational achievement, compared with jobs mainly held by men. Expressing each variable as a percentage of the education and earnings of the high-prestige professional category allows for easier interpretability and comparability across the countries. I chose the high-prestige professional category as the standard because the occupations included in this category (for example, doctors, professors, and scientists) are traditionally well paid (although as Table 3.5 indicates, not the best paid), generally require the highest levels of educational investment, and are universally regarded as highly prestigious (Treiman 1977). Additionally, there are sufficient numbers of incumbents in this category in each of the included countries to ensure reliable base estimates.

Inspecting the ten-country average in the final column of Table 3.5 (no personal earnings data were available for Great Britain or Northern Ireland), it is evident that occupations mainly held by women (indicated by two asterisks) are on average not particularly different from occupations mainly held by men (indicated by a single asterisk) in the educational achievements of their incumbents. The predominantly male administrative and managerial category has an average education level 83 percent that of the professional group. The comparable figure for the predominantly female high-prestige clerical category is 74 percent. The remaining sextyped occupations are quite similar with regard to the educational achievement of their incumbents—the female low-prestige sales and service workers average 62 and 55 percent, respectively, as much education as the high-prestige professional category. The comparable figures for the male high- and medium-prestige production workers are 62 and 59 percent, respectively.

This approximate gender similarity, however, does not hold when the average earnings of the sextyped jobs are compared—each of the predominantly female categories has lower average earnings than any of the predominantly male categories. The clerical, sales, and service categories have average earnings that are 54, 38, and 31 percent, respectively, of the high-prestige professional category, while the comparable figures for the administrative/managerial, high-prestige production, and medium-prestige production categories are 123, 60, and 55 percent, respectively. Particularly notable is that, although they have substantially more schooling, high-prestige clerical workers earn on average about as much as medium-prestige, and 6 percent less than high-prestige, production workers.

This average pattern is duplicated in nearly every country. The high-prestige clerical category has a higher average educational achievement than either the high- or medium-prestige production group in each country. With three exceptions, the predominantly female clerical group also has substantially lower earnings than the high-prestige production group, and these exceptions only prove the

Table 3.5 Mean Education and Earnings for Each Occupation Group Expressed as a Percentage of the Mean Education and Earnings of High-Prestige Professional and Technical Workers, for Ten Industrialized Countries[a]

Occupational category[b]	Austria	Denmark	Finland	Germany (Fed. Rep.)	Israel	Japan	Netherlands	Norway	Sweden	United States	Ten-country average[c]
						Education					
1. High-prestige professional and technical	100*	100	100	100	100	100	100	100	100	100	100
2. Administrative and managerial	91*	[82]*	[96]	[96]*	77*	88*	72*	92	82*	81*	83*
3. High-prestige clerical and related	76**	68**	67**	71	71**	90	68	78**	69**	77**	74**
4. High-prestige sales	74	[61]	[63]	72	56*	80	62	[70]	[65]*	83*	71
5. Low-prestige professional and technical	84	74	73	78	79**	92	78	77	70	90**	80
6. High-prestige agricultural	61	55	53	63	48	65	53*	56	55*	65*	57
7. High-prestige production and related	70*	58*	56*	68*	56*	70	63*	59*	56*	67*	62*
8. High-prestige service	71	[56]**	62**	67	48	70	61	[68]	61	70	64
9. Medium-prestige production and related	67*	56*	54*	63*	48*	69	59	55*	54*	65	59*
10. Low-prestige clerical and related	73	[57]	[55]	69	63	—	66	[62]	62	73	68
11. Low-prestige	73**	57**	55**	6?***	51**	73**	63**	55**	56**	75	63**

12. Low-prestige agricultural	62	—	53*	—	36*	[54]	—	[50]*	55*	54
13. Low-prestige service	61**	54**	53**	55**	38**	55**	50**	52**	63**	55**
14. Low-prestige production and related	62	53*	54*	56**	41	[52]	52	50*	64	56

Earnings

1. High-prestige professional and technical	100*	100	100	100	100	100	100	100	100	100
2. Administrative and managerial	140*	[135]*	[103]	[126]*	130*	114*	102	108*	118*	123*
3. High-prestige clerical and related	58**	46**	37**	58	66**	51	59**	46**	44**	54**
4. High-prestige sales	87	[85]	[50]	95	98*	67	79	80*	99*	86
5. Low-prestige professional and technical	72	68	56	62	75**	54	75	66	65**	68
6. High-prestige agricultural	43	77	37	56	—	49*	51	47*	95*	56
7. High-prestige production and related	66*	57*	41*	59*	73	46*	63*	59*	74*	60*

a Personal earnings not available for Great Britain and Northern Ireland. Figures based on fewer than 10 cases not shown; those based on 10–19 cases are shown in brackets.

b Standard International Occupational Classification (Treiman 1977, Chapter 9).

c Bracketed percentages not included in averages.

* Occupations held mainly by men (those with 20 percent or more underrepresentation of females in Table 3.4).

** Occupations held mainly by women (those with 20 percent or more overrepresentation of females in Table 3.4).

Table 3.5 Mean Education and Earnings for Each Occupation Group Expressed as a Percentage of the Mean Education and Earnings of High-Prestige Professional and Technical Workers, for Ten Industrialized Countries[a] (Cont.)

Occupational category[b]	Austria	Denmark	Finland	Germany (Fed. Rep.)	Israel	Japan	Netherlands	Norway	Sweden	United States	Ten-country average[c]
					Earnings						
8. High-prestige service	59	[47]**	[29]**	57	51	59	[50]	[81]	48	42	53
9. Medium-prestige production and related	59*	53*	45*	56*	64*	51	44	59*	56*	59	55*
10. Low-prestige clerical and related	57	[45]	46	57	68	—	42	[57]	51	48	53
11. Low-prestige sales	45**	26**	28**	32**	44**	40**	42**	40**	33**	53	38**
12. Low-prestige agricultural	[39]	[39]	29*	—	48*	35**	[40]	—	[53]*	35*	37
13. Low-prestige service	34**	20**	22**	—	41**	47**	27**	32**	27**	27**	31**
14. Low-prestige production and related	50	42*	32*	36**	53	64*	[38]	56	50*	44	47

[a] Personal earnings not available for Great Britain and Northern Ireland. Figures based on fewer than 10 cases not shown; those based on 10–19 cases are shown in brackets.
[b] Standard International Occupational Classification (Treiman 1977, Chapter 9).
[c] Bracketed percentages not included in averages.
* Occupations held mainly by men (those with 20 percent or more underrepresentation of females in Table 3.4).
** Occupations held mainly by women (those with 20 percent or more overrepresentation of females in Table 3.4).

general rule. In Germany, the average earnings of high-prestige production workers are nearly identical to clerical workers and in Japan and the Netherlands clerical workers earn more than high-prestige production workers. Notably, these three countries are the only ones in which the high-prestige clerical occupation is not mainly held by women (see the definition in note 14). Similarly, despite uniformly higher average levels of education, the high-prestige clerical group also earns less than, or approximately the same as, the medium-prestige production group.

In every country except one, the predominantly female low-prestige sales and service workers have substantially lower average earnings than any predominantly male occupation group in that country. Notably, in the one country where low-prestige sales employment is not mainly held by women, the United States, this category also has the highest relative earnings among the ten countries.

One final observation regarding Table 3.5 should be noted. In all ten countries with earnings data, women are underrepresented in administrative and managerial occupations (see Table 3.4). Only in Finland, where the estimate is not reliable, does the percent female in administrative and managerial work exceed 20 percent, reaching 30 percent.[21] In seven of the ten countries, the percent female in this group is 10 percent or less. Evident from Table 3.5 is that incumbents of this major group earn substantially higher salaries than workers in any other occupation—the figures range from 2 percent more than the high-prestige professionals in Norway to 49 percent more in Japan.

This evidence documents the low pay of jobs mainly held by women, relative to those mainly held by men, for a selection of industrial societies. Thus, as in the United States, workers in predominantly female employment in other industrial societies are underpaid relative to their average educational achievement. To provide a summary measure of this relationship for the present data, I used Tables 3.4 and 3.5 to generate occupational averages (over the ten countries with earnings data) for earnings, education, and percent female, where each occupational category equalled one case. I then regressed occupational earnings on education and percent female. The results show that average education and percent female alone account for 84 percent of the variation in average earnings across occupational categories. Most interesting, percent female has a substantial negative effect on the average earnings of occupations net of education (the standardized coefficient is −.449).[22] In sum, these results suggest that workers in predominantly female employment in other countries, as in the United States, do indeed provide a cheap source of educated labor.

CONCLUSION

The purpose of the present chapter was to investigate the generality of the claim that men and women work in different labor markets. I also investigated what is known about the characteristics of the types of jobs men and women do and tested the generality of the claim that women provide a cheap source of educated labor.

The data reveal a strong consistency across industrial societies in the percentage of men who work, their age pattern of labor-force participation, and their propensity to work full time. In contrast, women's labor-force behavior is heavily dependent on their family life cycle—women are less likely to participate in the labor force, especially during the typical childbearing and rearing years, and are more likely to be employed part time when they do work.

The evidence clearly documents that men and women work in very different types of jobs, both at the major group and detailed levels. In addition to being highly segregated, the occupations in which men and women work are highly sextyped and the degree of sextyping is remarkably consistent across the included countries. Furthermore, the jobs mainly held by women are low paying in all the countries and, as in the United States, incumbents of predominantly female employment in other industrialized countries are underpaid relative to their average educational achievement.

While consistent with the human-capital perspective, the data provided thus far do not test its adequacy. The sex-segregated labor markets observed could also derive from institutionalized features of the organization of work that inhibit women's access to sex-atypical jobs. The remaining chapters will address more directly whether women's family responsibilities account for their employment in low-paying jobs.

CHAPTER FOUR

Gender Differences in Intergenerational Occupational Mobility

The data presented thus far document substantial similarities across industrial societies in gender differences in occupational distribution, the sextyping of jobs, and the concentration of women in relatively poorly paid employment. These results occur even though extensive crosscultural variability exists in the labor-force behavior of women. It is appropriate to turn now to a description of the processes that help to create these gender differences.

There are two major ways gender differences in occupational location can arise. First, such gender differentials may reflect differences in background characteristics (such as, social origins or education). For example, most women workers in the early industrializing economies of the nineteenth century came from working- or lower-class backgrounds (Smuts 1959). If, in modern industrial societies, women's decisions regarding work remain dependent on social origins, then the majority of women workers will continue to come from predominantly working- or lower-class backgrounds, a factor likely to negatively affect women's occupational options relative to those of men.[1]

Second, the sex-segregated occupational structure may be attributable not to differences in background or individual characteristics, but to gender differences in the effects of these background factors on occupational attainment (that is, the process of attainment). For example, there is evidence (Oppenheimer 1968; Treiman and Terrell 1975c), that incumbents in traditionally female jobs are underpaid relative to their achieved education. Such a finding suggests that women and men receive different income returns to their education.

As described in Chapter 1, human-capital theory posits that women's work and family responsibilities should affect both the total amount of human capital accumulated (background factors) and processes of occupational attainment (effects of background factors on attainment), in ways that negatively affect women's job options relative to those of men. Chapters 4 and 5 investigate these issues within two traditions of stratification research. In the current chapter, I examine sex differences in intergenerational occupational mobility within the mobility table tradition (Blau and Duncan 1967, Chapter 2). Work in this tradition investigates the pattern of mobility from social origins to first or current occupation, where both origin and destination are measured by a categorical occupational classification. Recent applications to sex differences in the intergenerational transmission of occupational roles rely for the most part on log-linear analysis (Hauser et al. 1977; Rosenfeld 1978b; Dunton and Featherman 1979; although see Erikson 1976, and Pöntinen 1980 for recent adaptations of the more traditional mobility analysis).

In Chapter 5, I use the structural-equation (or status-attainment) approach to examine sex differences in the process of occupational attainment.[2] Current occupational position in this tradition is viewed as a function of various ascriptive factors (such as, father's occupation and education, mother's occupation and education, race, and sex), and achieved factors (such as, education, on-the-job experience, and marital status). Occupation, in this tradition, is generally measured by an interval-level socioeconomic or prestige scale. Unlike traditional mobility table research, which merely maps social origins and destinations, structural-equation analyses also investigate determinants of occupational mobility other than social origins. This investigation of the process of occupational attainment at the individual level thus permits a determination of the relative importance of hypothesized variables on attainment (such as the net effect of women's family responsibilities on occupational opportunities).

Gender Differences and Mobility Analysis

The focus of mobility research, in the United States and elsewhere, has been on the extent to which status advantages, as measured by occupational roles, are transmitted from one generation to the next (Glass 1954; Carlsson 1958; Svalastoga 1959; Blau and Duncan 1967,

Chapter 2). Researchers use mobility ratios to analyze cross classifications of respondent's and father's occupation. Societies are viewed
as having relatively more rigid stratification systems to the extent
that they depart from perfect mobility (that is, mobility predicted on
the assumption that respondent's occupation is not dependent on
father's occupation). The rigidity of a society's stratification system
is indicated by a high degree of intergenerational inheritance of
occupations (that is, larger numbers on the diagonal of the mobility
matrix than in the remaining cells). Countries with relatively lower
levels of occupational inheritance are viewed as fluid, with permeable
occupational boundaries permitting greater upward (but also downward) mobility. Comparative mobility research in this tradition thus
takes the form of investigating crosscultural differences in the rigidity
or openness of stratification systems.

The transmission of status advantages from one generation to the
next is straight-forward enough as a theoretical construct. Stratification
researchers have long been interested in estimating the extent to
which parents are able to pass on accrued advantages (as represented
by occupational position) to their children, and in investigating whether
this process varies across population subgroups or cultures. However,
this research has, for the most part, been restricted to men (for
example, United States men vs. Swedish men or black men vs. white
men). Svalastoga (1959), and more recently Erikson (1976) and Pöntinen (1980), are notable exceptions, in that their work compared
men and women within countries.

Applying mobility analysis to women, and hence to investigating
gender differences in mobility, however, requires certain modifications
in interpretation. The problem in applying the mobility perspective
to an analysis of women's intergenerational mobility has to do with
the way the abstract concept of status is measured. Because intergenerational mobility is defined as movement between occupational
categories, and because social origins are usually measured by father's
occupation, "social origin-current occupation" comparisons mean different things for men and women: for sons one makes a same-sex
comparison, while for daughters one makes a cross-sex comparison.
Since men and women have had quite different occupational destinations, it is not surprising that one of the findings of gender
comparisons is that women have been more mobile than men, which
should be interpreted as indicating that they move into occupations
different from those of their fathers (but not necessarily different
from those of their mothers). Interestingly, Rosenfeld (1978b) found
that when mothers work outside the home, their daughters are more
likely to inherit their mother's rather than their father's occupation.

Even though the transmission of occupational roles across generations means different things for men and women, I use mobility analysis because it permits investigation of the intergenerational transmission of status advantages within the context of specific occupations and not merely within levels of prestige or socioeconomic status. Since data from the United States (for example, Treiman and Terrell 1975b; Featherman and Hauser 1976) suggest that men and women on average tend to work in occupations of similar prestige and status, even though they are employed in very different kinds of occupations, it is important that investigations of occupational achievement not be solely limited to those analyses where occupation is measured by prestige or status. Use of mobility analysis permits an exact description of men's and women's occupations, the overall mobility process by which occupational origins affect occupational destinations, and how this mobility process differs by sex. Moreover, investigating mobility processes crossculturally allows a determination of whether male-female differences in mobility are substantially similar across industrial society.

In one of the first studies using mobility table analysis, DeJong and his colleagues (1971) compared male and female mobility patterns. Contrary to their expectations, the authors found no gender differences in social mobility ratios and thus concluded that working women have patterns of mobility similar to those of their brothers: occupational inheritance is greater than expected assuming statistical independence; upward mobility is more frequent than downward mobility; short distance mobility is more common than long-distance mobility; white-collar workers come from a narrower range of occupational origins than blue-collar workers; and barriers to downward mobility exist from white-collor to other occupations and from blue-collar to farm occupations.

Subsequent researchers (Havens and Tully 1972; Tyree and Treas 1974; and Hauser et al. 1977) criticized the findings of DeJong and his coauthors for two major reasons. First, the use of mobility ratios to compare two populations requires that the groups have similar marginals. Because men and women have quite different occupational destinations, the use of mobility ratios is thus methodologically inappropriate. Second, DeJong's and his coauthors' microlevel theory of role conflict is not appropriately tested by macrolevel mobility data. Mobility analysis that investigates patterns of occupational transference from social origins to current occupational position merely describes the process of occupational attainment; it offers no explanation for why observed differences exist.

More recently, research on gender differences in mobility has shifted from an analysis of mobility ratios, or inflow and outflow patterns, to log-linear analysis (for example, Hauser et al. 1977; Rosenfeld 1978b; Rosenfeld and Sørensen 1979; Dunton and Featherman 1979). This contingency table technique investigates differentials in mobility processes while controlling for differences in marginals, thus avoiding the pitfalls of mobility ratio analysis. Hauser and his coauthors (p. 208) summarized the consensus of these analyses:

> once [women's lesser propensity to be employed and different occupational distribution] are taken into account, more than 90% of the association between the occupations of persons and their fathers may be explained by a mobility regime that does not differ at all between the sexes.

Several results from these analyses are pertinent to the present study. First, gender differences in occupational mobility are shown to be due in large measure to the lesser likelihood that women engage in paid work—when "not in the labor force" is included as a category, the index of dissimilarity between the current occupational position of married (spouse-present) men and women ages twenty to sixty-four is nearly 70, compared with 53.2 for married men and women in the experienced labor force (Hauser et al. 1977).

Second, father's occupation does not affect whether men or women participate in the labor force, providing justification for limiting mobility analyses to currently employed men and women (Hauser et al. 1977). Similarly, Dunton and Featherman (1979) found, for a 1957 cohort of Wisconsin high school graduates, no difference in the patterns of mobility between all women and employed women. These results suggest that differing patterns of labor-force inactivity between all and employed women cannot account to any significant extent for gender differences in mobility patterns, at least in the United States.

Third, in a log-linear analysis of currently employed men and women, sex differences in current occupation, but not in father's occupation, account for much of the total association in a cross classification of all three variables (Hauser et al. 1977). This finding corroborates the results of inflow and outflow analyses showing that men and women have similar inflow (or recruitment) patterns but very different outflow (or supply) patterns. Thus, men and women in each occupational category come from similar origins, but men and women with the same origins tend to move into very dissimilar occupational destinations (Dunton and Featherman 1979).

Fourth, women are less likely than men to inherit their father's occupation, which the authors interpret as meaning that women are more mobile than men (Hauser et al. 1977). This result confirms the finding of inflow-outflow analyses that show less occupational inheritance from father to daughter than from father to son (Dunton and Featherman 1979).

Rosenfeld's (1978b) investigation of the intergenerational mobility of women points to some of the limitations of mobility analysis for gender comparisons that were previously described. Speculating that part of the sex difference in mobility found in previous mobility studies might have been due to measuring social origins by "father's occupation," Rosenfeld found (p. 45) that mother's labor-force status, and mother's occupation (if she works), are significant determinants of daughter's occupational location.

Evidence from the Scandinavian countries indicates that these results for the United States are generalizable to other cultural contexts (Erikson 1976; Pöntinen 1980). Using a three-category social group variable, Erikson found that employed men and women in Sweden come from similar social origins. Yet men and women who come from similar social origins move to very dissimilar destinations. Pöntinen (1980, 32) found that men move into manual employment and women into nonmanual white-collar positions (overwhelmingly clerical jobs).

Mobility Effects of Sex Segregation

While recognizing the importance of gender differences in occupational distribution, mobility researchers have generally been concerned with isolating pure differences in mobility regimes (that is, gender differences net of marginals). Searching for net gender differences in mobility, while interesting, should not be the only focus of mobility analyses. Rather, the more interesting gender differentials are structural differences in the occupational locations of men and women. Gender differences in occupational outcomes arise as a consequence of a whole host of allocative mechanisms affecting individual behavior, including traditional attitudes about jobs thought appropriate for men or women that derive from early sex-role socialization, statistical discrimination by employers, individual expectations regarding future labor-force behavior, and so forth.

Regardless of why sex-specific labor markets exist, there is compelling evidence (reviewed in Chapters 1 and 3) that the sex-segregated occupational structure is widespread and shows no sign of lessening. Because of its unchanging character, the sex-segregated labor market represents the opportunity structure available to new entrants and helps to shape men's and women's perceptions regarding their occupational opportunities. The sex-segregated occupational structure thus operates to constrain men and women from entering jobs deemed inappropriate for their gender (for a similar argument and an overview of the evidence, see Reskin and Hartmann 1985). For all these reasons, I view the different occupational outcomes of men and women not as a structural factor to be controlled, but as an important part of the overall process of intergenerational mobility that requires further description. I investigate the role this factor plays in the occupational mobility process and examine whether its importance varies crossculturally.

GENDER DIFFERENCES IN SUPPLY AND RECRUITMENT

Table 4.1 presents an overview of gender differences in recruitment (inflow) and supply (outflow) patterns of employed men and women in seven of the countries.[3] The indexes in Table 4.1 were calculated from Appendixes B and C, which provide complete inflow and outflow distributions for men and women.[4] The data in this table estimate the degree to which employed men and women differ in their occupational origins (first column) and in their occupational destinations (second column). An overall index of dissimilarity is presented first, followed by occupation-specific indexes. The occupation-specific indexes in column one show the degree to which sex differences exist in the process whereby incumbents of specific occupational categories are *recruited* from different occupational origins. Similarly, indexes in the second column show the extent to which gender differences exist in the process whereby individuals from specific occupational origins are *supplied* to different occupational destinations.

While previous research documenting occupational sex segregation leads to an expectation of large overall indexes of supply, one would not expect men and women, in general, to differ with respect to their occupational origins. However, it might be the case that social origins affect women's decision to work outside the home (for example, historically, daughters of professional workers were less likely to be engaged in paid employment than daughters of blue-collar workers). If this were still the case today, one might expect gender differences in social origins among employed men and women. While Hauser and his coauthors (1977) and Dunton and Featherman (1979) reported only small gender differences in social origins for the United States, the crosscultural variation in the age pattern of women's labor force participation (Figure 3.1) suggests that such differences may exist in other countries.

The present data for the United States confirms that the social origins of employed men and women are similar—only 5 percent of the women would have to change categories to have occupational origins identical to those of men. In contrast, 43 percent of the employed women would have to change categories to have occu-

pational destinations identical to those of men. Within major occupation groups, the index of recruitment is never greater than 21.9
(respondents in service occupations) and is generally much lower.

Table 4.1   Indexes of Dissimilarity Between Men and Women in Occupational Supply
and Recruitment Distributions; Employed Men and Women (All Ages) in Seven
Industrialized Countries[a]

Country and occupational category[b]	Recruitment (inflow)	Supply (outflow)
Austria		
Total	5.0	27.7
Professional and technical	22.9	[61.6]
Administrative and managerial	—	—
Clerical and related	19.8	46.6
Sales	12.5	[31.0]
Service	28.5	[47.9]
Agricultural	2.6	20.8
Production and related	14.8	32.3
Germany (Fed. Rep.)		
Total	10.9	32.0
Professional and technical	7.8	30.3
Administrative and managerial	—	—
Clerical and related	6.8	25.7
Sales	34.3	[30.7]
Service	26.7	[42.0]
Agricultural	[35.1]	40.0
Production and related	16.7	37.2
Israel		
Total	8.0	40.7
Professional and technical	8.6	30.6
Administrative and managerial	38.8	39.6
Clerical and related	11.4	37.9
Sales	6.3	31.4
Service	10.4	45.1
Agricultural	23.6	50.0
Production and related	14.7	47.4
Japan		
Total	9.4	25.6
Professional and technical	28.4	[37.8]
Administrative and managerial	—	—
Clerical and related	15.8	28.0
Sales	17.3	24.4
Service	19.1	[25.4]
Agricultural	3.8	26.9
Production and related	13.8	38.0

Table 4.1 Indexes of Dissimilarity Between Men and Women in Occupational Supply and Recruitment Distributions; Employed Men and Women (All Ages) in Seven Industrialized Countries[a] *(Cont.)*

Country and occupational category[b]	Recruitment (inflow)	Supply (outflow)
Netherlands		
Total	12.2	43.6
Professional and technical	19.5	[28.7]
Administrative and managerial	—	[42.8]
Clerical and related	15.3	32.6
Sales	42.6	[48.4]
Service	20.6	[27.0]
Agricultural	—	[59.4]
Production and related	—	54.2
Northern Ireland		
Total	11.4	39.6
Professional and technical	20.6	[31.6]
Administrative and managerial	—	—
Clerical and related	24.4	[58.4]
Sales	[27.3]	30.0
Service	11.6	[45.0]
Agricultural	—	50.4
Production and related	6.3	35.9
United States		
Total	4.6	43.0
Professional and technical	12.5	40.8
Administrative and managerial	14.0	34.6
Clerical and related	5.0	40.1
Sales	7.8	31.5
Service	21.9	47.7
Agricultural	—	48.2
Production and related	10.4	46.2

[a] Estimates based on less than ten men or women are not reported; those based on ten to nineteen men or women are bracketed. Great Britain and the Scandinavian countries are not included because of limitations in the way father's occupation was measured in these countries.
[b] The occupational classification is the seven-category International Standard Classification of Occupations (ISCO) (ILO 1969).

The index of supply is never less than 31.5 (respondents from sales origins), and ranges as high as 48.2 (agricultural occupations). This latter finding reflects the continuing decline of the United States agricultural sector since industrialization.

There are two important substantive conclusions that can be drawn from these United States findings, which are similar to those of Hauser and his coauthors (1977) and Dunton and Featherman (1979).[5]

First, the sex-segregated occupational structure plays a major role in accounting for gross gender differences in occupational mobility. Second, men's and women's different employment cannot be attributed to different social origins. Although the overall index of recruitment is quite low in the United States, indicating that on average employed men and women come from similar social origins, several occupation-specific indexes are somewhat larger. In particular, 22 percent of female service workers would have to change their occupational origins to have a distribution identical to that of men. Appendix B reveals the origin of this gender difference—female service workers are more likely than their male counterparts to originate from agricultural and production origins, while male service workers derive from professional, administrative, clerical, sales, and service backgrounds.

The patterns for the remaining countries are similar to those in the United States, although the recruitment indexes are slightly higher and the supply indexes slightly lower. The overall index of dissimilarity between men's and women's social origins exceeds 10.0 in only three of the countries (West Germany, the Netherlands, and Northern Ireland), and the seven-country average is 8.8. In contrast, the overall index of dissimilarity between the occupational destinations of men and women is never less than 25.6, and in most countries is much higher (the seven-country average is 36). There is even greater country variation in the occupation-specific indexes. However, with one exception, the supply indexes are always greater than the recruitment indexes, and often substantially so. These data indicate that, as in the United States, observed gender differences in occupational destinations cannot, in large measure, be attributable to sex differences in social origins. Although sex differences in origins do exist within occupational categories, these differences tend to balance out in the aggregate, at least for the sample of employed men and women used in this study.

The nature of these differing recruitment and supply patterns can be described more fully by referring to Appendixes B and C. Since sex differences in occupational origins appear to be relatively small in most of the countries, the focus here is on outflow (or supply) patterns (Appendix C). Using the United States data as the basis for comparison, certain clear patterns emerge from the data. First, large numbers of United States women move into clerical occupations regardless of their origins, ranging from 23 percent of the daughters of farmers to 49 percent of clerical daughters. Only women from professional or farm origins are more likely to work in other than clerical occupations, with professional daughters remaining in their origin category and farm daughters moving into service jobs. In no origin category does the percentage of men in clerical occupations exceed 10.1 percent. Second, large percentages of women work in professional occupations (albeit low-prestige professional occupations, see Table 3.4). The likelihood of working in a professional occupation is greatest for professional- or managerial-origin women and lowest for farm- and production-origin women, suggesting greater short-distance, as opposed to long-distance, mobility, a pattern visible among men as well. Service-origin women are more likely to move into white-collar (especially clerical but also professional jobs) than into blue-collar employment. Third, men from white-collar origins are most likely to move into professional or other white-collar occupations while men from blue-collar origins tend to remain in blue-collar jobs (for example, production work and secondarily service work). Fourth, the only notable movement of women into production work occurs among farm-origin women, and secondarily among the daughters of production workers.

These findings suggest two primary aspects of men's and women's occupational allocation: (1) daughters move into female clerical, low-prestige professional, and service occupations, while men move into male professional and production occupations; and (2) men and women tend to remain in their class of origin. These generalizations apply equally well in other countries. Pöntinen (1980, Appendix C) found similar results for the four Scandinavian countries.[6] The extent of crosscultural similarity in sex differences in mobility is investigated more systematically in a subsequent section and hence will not be discussed further here. One difference of note, however, should be mentioned at the outset—in Israel, half of the daughters from three occupational origin categories (professional, managerial, and clerical) themselves work in (albeit low-prestige) professional jobs.

GENDER DIFFERENCES IN MOBILITY: A LOG-LINEAR ANALYSIS

Mobility Hypotheses and Model Building

The results of the recruitment and supply analyses in the previous section lead to four hypotheses regarding father to respondent mobility, which can be tested in a more formal way in the present and subsequent sections. First, men's and women's occupational outcomes depend on the occupational achievements of their fathers, a factor reflected in the tendency for sons and daughters to remain in their class of origin. Second, men and women tend to move into male and female sextyped employment, respectively, as suggested by the differential supply indexes for men and women. Third, as suggested by the similar recruitment indexes in Table 4.1, sex differences in social origins do not account for a substantial portion of the gender difference in occupational outcomes. Fourth, due to the sextyping of occupations, men more often *inherit* the occupational positions of their fathers, while women are likely to be more *mobile* than men, moving into female sextyped employment different from that of their fathers. Previous research has addressed these issues for the United States. The purpose here is to determine whether these findings are generalizable to other industrial societies.

Table 4.2 presents the results of a log-linear analysis of gender differences in the occupational mobility of employed men and women. The analysis was performed on the $7 \times 7 \times 2$ classification of father's occupation, respondent's occupation, and sex within each of the seven countries where appropriate data were available (see note 3). The results for all possible models (that is, all combinations of variables) are presented in Appendix D. To maximize comparability between this study and previous work, I follow procedures of model building and hypothesis testing similar to those used by Hauser and his coauthors (1977) and Dunton and Featherman (1979).

The results in Table 4.2 allow a determination of which of several hypothesized models best approximate the observed frequencies in the three-way cross classifications. Before describing the findings, some preliminary explanation of the structure and symbols used in Table 4.2 is necessary. I denote the three variables by letters: O_F refers to occupation of respondent's father, O_R to occupation of respondent, and S to sex of respondent. Brackets are used to indicate null hypotheses, that is, which marginals or joint distributions are fitted for the specified model. Thus, $[O_F]$ indicates that the marginal values of father's occupation are fitted; $[O_F O_R]$ indicates that the joint distribution of father's and respondent's occupation is fitted. The purpose of such analysis is to specify the model that describes, in the most parsimonious manner possible, observed associations in the mobility table—that is, to determine how few parameters are needed to reproduce the observed frequencies.

The evaluation of whether a particular model fits the data is made by referring to the chi-square (likelihood ratio) test statistic (X^2_{LR}) and the index of dissimilarity (Δ) associated with the estimated model. A comparison of the likelihood ratio test statistic with its associated degrees of freedom formally tests whether the frequencies predicted on the basis of the model differ significantly from those observed. The index of dissimilarity between the expected and observed values for each model estimates the percentage of cases misclassified by the specified model. Hence, the smaller the index of dissimilarity (and the lower the chi-square value), the better the fit of the proposed model to the observed frequencies. Through hierarchical decompo-

Table 4.2 Log-Linear Analysis of Gender Differences in Occupational Mobility from Father's to Respondent's Current Occupation; Employed Men and Women (All Ages), in Seven Industrialized Countries[a]

Model (null hypothesis), by country	X^2_{LR}	df	ρ	Δ
Austria (N=773)				
A. Full mobility matrix (7×7×2)				
1. $[O_F]$ $[O_R]$ $[S]$	530.26	84	<.001	32.73
2. $[O_FO_R]$ $[S]$	107.18	48	<.001	13.82
3. $[O_FO_R]$ $[O_FS]$	104.42	42	<.001	13.93
4. $[O_FO_R]$ $[O_RS]$	27.60	42	>.5	5.76
5. $[O_FO_R]$ $[O_RS]$ $[O_FS]$	21.88	36	>.5	4.55
A2 vs. A1	423.08	36	<.001	18.91
A4 vs. A2	79.58	6	<.001	8.06
A5 vs. A4	5.72	6	>.05	1.21
B. Main diagonal blocked (movers)				
1. $[O_F]$ $[O_R]$ $[S]$	164.28	70	<.001	13.20
2. $[O_FO_R]$ $[S]$	89.11	41	<.001	9.51
3. $[O_FO_R]$ $[O_FS]$	68.15	35	<.001	8.29
4. $[O_FO_R]$ $[O_RS]$	21.78	35	>.5	3.92
5. $[O_FO_R]$ $[O_RS]$ $[O_FS]$	18.58	29	>.5	3.45
B2 vs. B1	75.17	29	<.001	3.69
B4 vs. B2	67.33	6	<.001	5.59
B5 vs. B4	3.20	6	>.05	.47
C. Hierarchical decomposition				
B5 vs. A5	3.30	7	>.05	1.10
Germany (Fed. Rep.) (N=967)				
A. Full mobility matrix (7×7×2)				
1. $[O_F]$ $[O_R]$ $[S]$	443.68	84	<.001	26.02
2. $[O_FO_R]$ $[S]$	157.02	48	<.001	15.87
3. $[O_FO_R]$ $[O_FS]$	140.71	42	<.001	15.26
4. $[O_FO_R]$ $[O_RS]$	50.88	42	<.250	6.59
5. $[O_FO_R]$ $[O_RS]$ $[O_FS]$	33.45	36	>.5	5.24
A2 vs. A1	286.66	36	<.001	10.15
A4 vs. A2	106.14	6	<.001	9.28
A5 vs. A4	17.43	6	<.01	1.35
B. Main diagonal blocked (movers)				
1. $[O_F]$ $[O_R]$ $[S]$	160.02	70	<.001	11.34
2. $[O_FO_R]$ $[S]$	107.35	41	<.001	9.48
3. $[O_FO_R]$ $[O_FS]$	77.15	35	<.001	7.88
4. $[O_FO_R]$ $[O_RS]$	31.54	35	>.5	4.40
5. $[O_FO_R]$ $[O_RS]$ $[O_FS]$	24.67	29	>.5	3.76
B2 vs. B1	52.67	29	<.005	1.86
B4 vs. B2	75.81	6	<.001	5.08
B5 vs. B4	6.87	6	>.05	.64
C. Hierarchical decomposition				
B5 vs. A5	8.78	7	>.05	1.48

Table 4.2 Log-Linear Analysis of Gender Differences in Occupational Mobility from Father's to Respondent's Current Occupation; Employed Men and Women (All Ages), in Seven Industrialized Countries[a] *(Cont.)*

Model (null hypothesis), by country	X^2_{LR}	df	p	Δ
Israel (N=9,058)				
A. Full mobility matrix (7×7×2)				
1. [O_F] [O_R] [S]	2897.65	84	<.001	22.95
2. [O_FO_R] [S]	1725.87	48	<.001	17.36
3. [O_FO_R] [O_FS]	1581.24	42	<.001	16.36
4. [O_FO_R] [O_RS]	168.06	42	<.001	4.02
5. [O_FO_R] [O_RS] [O_FS]	114.10	36	<.001	3.25
A2 vs. A1	1171.78	36	<.001	5.59
A4 vs. A2	1557.81	6	<.001	13.34
A5 vs. A4	53.96	6	<.001	.77
B. Main diagonal blocked (movers)				
1. [O_F] [O_R] [S]	1664.95	70	<.001	13.93
2. [O_FO_R] [S]	1221.90	41	<.001	12.44
3. [O_FO_R] [O_FS]	996.94	35	<.001	10.80
4. [O_FO_R] [O_RS]	146.42	35	<.001	3.49
5. [O_FO_R] [O_RS] [O_FS]	97.26	29	<.001	2.70
B2 vs. B1	443.05	29	<.001	1.49
B4 vs. B2	1075.48	6	<.001	8.95
B5 vs. B4	49.16	6	<.001	.79
C. Hierarchical decomposition				
B5 vs. A5	16.84	7	<.025	.55
Japan (N=938)				
A. Full mobility matrix (7×7×2)				
1. [O_F] [O_R] [S]	497.10	84	<.001	27.22
2. [O_FO_R] [S]	115.26	48	<.001	13.97
3. [O_FO_R] [O_FS]	105.77	42	<.001	13.52
4. [O_FO_R] [O_RS]	33.06	42	>.5	6.02
5. [O_FO_R] [O_RS] [O_FS]	29.61	36	>.5	5.83
A2 vs. A1	381.84	36	<.001	13.25
A4 vs. A2	82.20	6	<.001	7.95
A5 vs. A4	3.45	6	>.05	.19
B. Main diagonal blocked (movers)				
1. [O_F] [O_R] [S]	132.83	70	<.001	10.93
2. [O_FO_R] [S]	77.39	41	<.001	8.07
3. [O_FO_R] [O_FS]	68.73	35	<.001	7.37
4. [O_FO_R] [O_RS]	26.05	35	>.5	4.62
5. [O_FO_R] [O_RS] [O_FS]	20.50	29	>.5	3.76
B2 vs. B1	55.44	29	<.005	2.86
B4 vs. B2	51.34	6	<.001	3.45
B5 vs. B4	5.55	6	>.05	.86
C. Hierarchical decomposition				
B5 vs. A5	9.11	7	>.05	2.07

Table 4.2 Log-Linear Analysis of Gender Differences in Occupational Mobility from Father's to Respondent's Current Occupation; Employed Men and Women (All Ages), in Seven Industrialized Countries[a] *(Cont.)*

Model (null hypothesis), by country	X^2_{LR}	df	ρ	Δ
Netherlands (N=575)				
A. Full mobility matrix (7×7×2)				
1. $[O_F]\,[O_R]\,[S]$	315.93	84	<.001	28.20
2. $[O_FO_R]\,[S]$	137.67	48	<.001	17.79
3. $[O_FO_R]\,[O_FS]$	126.11	42	<.001	16.54
4. $[O_FO_R]\,[O_RS]$	46.75	42	<.500	8.49
5. $[O_FO_R]\,[O_RS]\,[O_FS]$	40.44	36	<.500	7.25
A2 vs. A1	178.26	36	<.001	10.41
A4 vs. A2	90.92	6	<.001	9.30
A5 vs. A4	6.31	6	>.05	1.24
B. Main diagonal blocked (movers)				
1. $[O_F]\,[O_R]\,[S]$	113.28	70	<.001	12.42
2. $[O_FO_R]\,[S]$	73.06	41	<.005	9.62
3. $[O_FO_R]\,[O_FS]$	71.51	35	<.001	9.16
4. $[O_FO_R]\,[O_RS]$	28.95	35	>.5	5.80
5. $[O_FO_R]\,[O_RS]\,[O_FS]$	27.10	29	>.5	5.26
B2 vs. B1	40.22	29	>.05	2.80
B4 vs. B2	44.11	6	<.001	3.82
B5 vs. B4	1.85	6	>.05	.54
C. Hierarchical decomposition				
B5 vs. A5	13.34	7	>.05	1.99
Northern Ireland (N=663)				
A. Full mobility matrix (7×7×2)				
1. $[O_F]\,[O_R]\,[S]$	387.50	84	<.001	29.68
2. $[O_FO_R]\,[S]$	148.88	48	<.001	18.57
3. $[O_FO_R]\,[O_FS]$	130.60	42	<.001	16.88
4. $[O_FO_R]\,[O_RS]$	37.01	42	>.5	6.62
5. $[O_FO_R]\,[O_RS]\,[O_FS]$	30.27	36	>.5	6.06
A2 vs. A1	238.62	36	<.001	11.11
A4 vs. A2	111.87	6	<.001	11.95
A5 vs. A4	6.74	6	>.05	.56
B. Main diagonal blocked (movers)				
1. $[O_F]\,[O_R]\,[S]$	127.90	70	<.001	13.29
2. $[O_FO_R]\,[S]$	84.91	41	<.001	10.53
3. $[O_FO_R]\,[O_FS]$	74.97	35	<.001	10.00
4. $[O_FO_R]\,[O_RS]$	30.56	35	>.5	5.27
5. $[O_FO_R]\,[O_RS]\,[O_FS]$	22.93	29	>.5	4.14
B2 vs. B1	42.99	29	<.050	2.76
B4 vs. B2	54.35	6	<.001	5.26
B5 vs. B4	7.63	6	>.05	1.13
C. Hierarchical decomposition				
B5 vs. A5	7.34	7	>.05	1.92

Table 4.2 Log-Linear Analysis of Gender Differences in Occupational Mobility from Father's to Respondent's Current Occupation; Employed Men and Women (All Ages), in Seven Industrialized Countries[a] *(Cont.)*

Model (null hypothesis), by country	X^2_{LR}	df	p	Δ
United States (N= 2,809)				
A. Full mobility matrix (7×7×2)				
1. $[O_F]$ $[O_R]$ $[S]$	1121.91	84	<.001	26.67
2. $[O_F O_R]$ $[S]$	715.46	48	<.001	20.89
3. $[O_F O_R]$ $[O_F S]$	706.54	42	<.001	20.52
4. $[O_F O_R]$ $[O_R S]$	64.66	42	<.025	4.62
5. $[O_F O_R]$ $[O_R S]$ $[O_F S]$	55.18	36	<.025	3.76
A2 vs. A1	406.45	36	<.001	5.78
A4 vs. A2	650.80	6	<.001	16.27
A5 vs. A4	9.48	6	>.05	.86
B. Main diagonal blocked (movers)				
1. $[O_F]$ $[O_R]$ $[S]$	610.38	70	<.001	16.46
2. $[O_F O_R]$ $[S]$	455.05	41	<.001	14.52
3. $[O_F O_R]$ $[O_F S]$	434.18	35	<.001	14.09
4. $[O_F O_R]$ $[O_R S]$	39.78	35	<.500	3.03
5. $[O_F O_R]$ $[O_R S]$ $[O_F S]$	31.54	29	<.500	2.48
B2 vs. B1	155.33	29	<.001	1.94
B4 vs. B2	415.27	6	<.001	11.49
B5 vs. B4	8.24	6	>.05	.55
C. Hierarchical decomposition				
B5 vs. A5	23.64	7	<.005	1.28

[a] O_F = occupation of father; O_R = occupation of respondent; S = sex of respondent. See Appendix D for the complete log-linear analysis from which this table is derived. Great Britain and the Scandinavian countries are not included because of limitations in the way father's occupation was measured in these countries.

sition, hypothesized models can be compared to determine whether specifying a particular interaction (for example, $[O_R S]$) significantly improves the fit of the model. To determine whether a specific interaction is significant, one need only subtract the chi-square value of the model including all possible lower-order interactions from the chi-square of the model including the specified interaction. If the difference in the chi-square values is significant ($p \le .05$), relative to its degrees of freedom (calculated by subtracting the degrees of freedom of the lower-order from those of the higher-order model), the specified interaction is considered to have significantly improved the fit between the expected and observed frequencies. As shall be seen, the significance of an interaction also depends on the model specified—an interaction may be significant when it is added prior to other interactions, although not net of them.

In Table 4.2 five specific models are tested for each country, first for the entire employed population (Panel A), and second only for those individuals who are in a major occupation group different from that of their fathers (Panel B). The Panel B tests investigate whether sex differences in occupational inheritance exist, and were accomplished by eliminating from the sample those men and women who inherited their father's major occupation group (persons on the main diagonal). Included as a base comparison, Model 1 hypothesizes that there is no association among father's occupation, respondent's occupation, and sex.

Model 2 fits the joint distribution of father's and respondent's occupation [O_FO_R] and the marginal values of sex [S], thus hypothesizing that father's occupation affects one's current occupation, but that no sex differences in origins or occupational destination exist. Given the large supply indexes reported in Table 4.1, I do not expect this model to fit the data.

Models 3 and 4 hypothesize, respectively, that, net of the mobility interaction [O_FO_R], there are sex differences in social origins or sex differences in current occupation. The results in Table 4.1 suggest (at most) a minor effect of social origins and a much larger effect of the "current occupation-sex" interaction.

Finally Model 5 serves a dual purpose: (1) it describes the degree of fit of the model specifying all possible two-way interactions (father's occupation affects current occupation, social origins differ by sex, and current occupational position varies by sex); and (2) it provides a global test of the three-way interaction [O_FO_RS]. The chi-square value for the fully saturated model [O_FO_RS] is necessarily zero. Thus, if Model 5 has a significant chi-square value, the three-way interaction is judged necessary to account for the cell frequencies. Substantively, this model tests for net gender differences in mobility, and is thus equivalent to what previous authors (for example, Hauser et al. 1977; Rosenfeld and Sørensen 1979) have termed "pure" mobility.

The comparisons of models in Panels A and B are structured to test the four hypotheses outlined above. First, the A2 vs. A1 comparison in each country tests the significance of the "occupation of father-current occupation of respondent" (or what I call the mobility) interaction—that is, whether the respondent's occupational position depends on his or her social origins. The B2 vs. B1 comparison performs the same test for the mobile population. Comparing the results of Model 2 with those of Model 1 permits a determination of whether the dependence of respondent's occupation on father's occupation is large enough to significantly improve the fit of the model ($p \leq .05$). On the basis of previous work, the expectation is that it will.

Second, the A4 vs. A2 comparison tests for the significance of the "current occupation-sex" interaction, that is, whether men's and women's occupational outcomes differ. Again, the B4 vs. B2 comparison makes the same test for the mobile population. Previous evidence suggests that this interaction will significantly improve the fit of the model.

Third, the A5 vs. A4 and the B5 vs. B4 comparisons test whether the social origins of men and women differ, net of the mobility and "current occupation-sex" interactions. Based on the inflow/outflow analyses, the expectation is that this will not be the case.

Fourth, in Panel C, I compare A5 (Model 5 estimated for the full sample of respondents) with B5 (Model 5 estimated for the mobile population). This comparison tests whether fitting separate diagonals for men and women results in a better fit to the observed frequencies (that is, whether sex differences in occupational inheritance exist). Since in analyses of intergenerational mobility one makes a cross-sex comparison for women but a same-sex comparison for men, and because men and women are traditionally employed in quite different jobs, the expectation is that sex differences in occupational inheritance will exist. Men will be more likely to inherit the occupational position of their fathers, while women will be more likely to move outside their occupational origin group to female sextyped employment.

Discussion of Findings

United States Results. In discussing my findings I begin with the results from the United States (presented in Table 4.2), to determine the comparability with previous analyses. I then turn to a discussion of the findings from the remaining six countries. As expected, the model hypothesizing no association among the three variables (the independence, or A1 model) can be rejected. The mobility interaction accounts for a significant 36 (=406.45/1121.91) percent of the total association in the table (the A2 vs. A1 comparison), while the "current occupation-sex" interaction explains 58 (=650.80/1121.91) percent (the A4 vs. A2 comparison). While adding sex differences in current occupation significantly improves the model's fit, the model including both interactions is not sufficient to fit the observed frequencies, and hence describe the gross mobility process. Model A4, however, does account for all but 5.8 (=64.66/1121.91) percent of the association in the table, substantially reducing the misclassification of cases. The A4 specification misclassifies only 4.6 percent of the cases, compared with 20.9 percent when the "current occupation-sex" interaction is not included. As expected, incorporating gender differences in social origins (the A5 vs. A4 comparison) does not significantly improve the fit of the model, accounting for only .8 (=9.48/1121.91) percent of the association. Recall that the results of Model 5 serve a dual purpose: describing the degree of fit of the model specifying all two-way interactions and providing a global test of whether sex differences in the mobility process, or pure mobility, exist. The unsaturated model (A5) does not fit the data; the three-way interaction [O_FO_RS] accounts for an additional 4.9 (=55.18/1121.91) percent of the association. Hence, there are small, but significant, sex differences in the relationship between father's occupation and respondent's occupation, net of the different distributions of social origins and destinations of men and women (that is, pure mobility).

The results for movers permit a determination of whether the gender differences observed for all employed persons can be solely attributed to sex differences in occupational inheritance. The overall mobility of movers is in some ways similar to that of all employed persons: the mobility interaction and sex differences in occupational composition both significantly improve the fit of the model, while sex differences in social origins do not. When restricting the analysis to movers, however, I find no sex difference in the process of intergenerational mobility net of the marginals (as indicated by a significance value for model B5 of greater than .05). This finding indicates that the global gender difference in pure mobility observed in Model A5 is due entirely to sex differences in occupational inheritance—fitting separate diagonals for men and women permits a better fit of the model. This result is confirmed by the significant result of the B5 vs. A5 comparison in Panel C, which shows that men and women do, indeed, have different net rates of occupational inheritance.

The log-linear results for the United States thus support the hypotheses I outlined. First, men's and women's occupational outcomes are heavily dependent on the occupational achievements of their fathers: the mobility interaction accounts for 36 percent of the association in the model. Second, the sex segregation of the occupational structure is an important factor affecting men's and women's gross mobility patterns, accounting for fully 58 percent of the total association in the three-way cross classification. Third, no significant gender differences in social origins exist. Fourth, sex differences in occupational inheritance result in a small, but significant, sex difference in the process of mobility net of differences in marginals.[7]

Crosscultural results. Comparing the United States findings with those from the remaining countries reveals interesting country differences in the gross patterns of father to respondent mobility. Israel's results come closest to duplicating the American pattern. As in the

United States, the mobility and "current occupation-sex" interactions significantly improve the goodness of fit of the expected to observed frequencies. Additionally, the global test in Model A5 suggests sex differences in pure mobility. However, Israel differs from the United States in two respects: there are small, but significant, sex differences in the social origins of employed men and women, and global gender differences in the mobility process that are attributable both to sex differences in the mobility of movers and to gender differences in inheritance.

These differences from the United States pattern are attributable to the large sample size of the Israeli data set (N=9,058), relative to the United States (N=2,809). Since the chi-square statistic is sensitive to sample size, the large number of cases in the Israeli sample may make even the smallest differences statistically significant. To circumvent this problem, I refer to the indexes of dissimilarity associated with specified models to put significant differences into perspective. In the United States-Israel comparison, the indexes for the A5 vs. A4 models in both countries suggest that the *nonsignificant* "father's occupation-sex" interaction in the United States reduces the misspecification of cases slightly more than the *significant* Israeli interaction (.86 to .77). Hence, although significant, the Israeli finding has less substantive significance in a comparison with the United States result, insofar as the latter is not purely an artifact of sampling error. A similar argument could be made for the other difference found between the two countries.[8]

The results for the remaining countries are similar in kind, although not in degree, to the United States and Israeli findings. First, in each country, an individual's occupational position is heavily dependent on his or her father's occupation—the mobility interaction significantly improves the model's fit to the observed frequencies.

Second, in each country, the sex-segregated occupational structure has important effects on an individual's occupational outcome. Except for the United States and Israel, however the effect of father's occupation is more important in the mobility process than the sex-segregated occupational structure. In Israel and the United States, the "current occupation-sex" effect (the A4 vs. A2 comparison) accounts for 54 and 58 percent, respectively, of the total association in the three-way table. The comparable figures for Austria, Germany, Japan, the Netherlands, and Northern Ireland are a much smaller 15, 24, 17, 29, and 29 percent, respectively. These findings reflect the fact that Israel and the United States have two of the highest indexes of gender dissimilarity in current occupational distributions (see Table 4.1). The Netherlands, however, also has a high index and the "current occupation-sex" interaction in that country accounts for 29 percent of the association. In these five countries, father's occupation is particularly important in determining one's occupational position, accounting for 80 percent of the association in Austria, 65 percent in Germany, 77 percent in Japan, 57 percent in the Netherlands, and 62 percent in Northern Ireland.

There are two possibile explanations for the greater effect of mobility in these five countries. In Austria and Japan, where the percentage explained by the mobility interaction is greatest, the labor force has a large agricultural component, a factor that undoubtedly accounts for the relatively greater intergenerational inheritance of occupational position. A possible explanation for the lesser importance of the mobility interaction in the United States and Israel, relative to the remaining countries, may be the historical role of these two countries as a refuge for immigrant populations. Certainly, the United States has historically been a nation of immigrants, as has Israel since its incorporation as a Jewish state in 1948. Large first generation immigrant populations in these countries might well account for the lesser role of the social origin-occupational destination connection [see Matras and Weintraub (1976) and Hartman and Hartman (1981) for investigations of the immigration factor in Israel].

Third, with two exceptions (Germany and Israel), there are no sex differences in social origins, net of the mobility and "current occupation-sex" interactions. Nearly 4 percent of the association in the German cross classification is due to this factor, the largest net contribution of social origins in any of the countries.[9] Along with Northern Ireland, both Germany and Israel are early peak countries. They have the lowest female participation rates of the twenty- to sixty-four-year old population of all twelve countries, and the lowest percentages working full time (see Tables 3.1 and 3.2). Recall that an early peak pattern indicates that women tend to leave the labor force permanently upon marriage or childbearing. In countries with such a pattern, women who work outside the home are more the exception than the rule. In such societies, those women who work might be those who have to work (for example, working- or lower-class women). If this supposition were true, a larger percentage of female than male workers would originate from working- or lower-class backgrounds, a factor that would lead to sex differences in social origins.

Alternatively, it may be that those women who work in such societies are those who would lose the most by not working (that is, the highly educated or those in high-paying or high-prestige employment). If this supposition were true, a larger percentage of female than male workers might originate from professional and other high-status backgrounds. In either case, the finding of gender differences in social origins suggests that selecting only the employed population introduces a selectivity bias. Chapter 5 will return to this issue, and investigate which of these alternative explanations for social origin differences is supported by the data.

Fourth, the gender differences in occupational inheritance found in the United States and Israel are not duplicated in the remaining countries. Both the Israel and United States results show sex differences in pure mobility, attributable in the United States to sex differences in occupational inheritance and in Israel to sex differences in inheritance and sex differences in mobility among movers. Thus, the more general finding among the included countries is that no sex differences exist in occupational inheritance. This finding does not suggest that the sex-segregated occupational structure is not important in affecting occupational outcomes but that, net of the differing marginal distributions of men and women, specifying separate diagonals for men and women does not significantly improve the fit of the model.

As previously suggested, the significance of some of these results may be an artifact of the larger sample sizes available for Israel and the United States, relative to the remaining data sets, a proposition supported by the indexes for Model A5 in each of the countries. In the United States and Israel, the indexes are 3.8 and 3.2, respectively, suggesting that excluding the three-way interaction $[O_FO_RS]$ misclassifies 3.8 and 3.2 percent of the cases. Contrary to what might be concluded on the basis of the tests of significance for the three-way interaction, the indexes for the remaining countries are somewhat larger than those for Israel and the United States (for example, they range from 4.6 in Austria to 7.2 in the Netherlands). Thus, in these five countries, pure sex differences in mobility are actually more important in reducing the misclassification of cases than is true in Israel and the United States (at least to the extent that the former are not due to sampling error).

COUNTRY DIFFERENCES IN THE MOBILITY PROCESS

To determine whether the small country differences observed in the previous section were due to chance, I introduce country as a variable. I test for country differences by conducting a log-linear analysis of the four-way classification of father's occupation, respondent's occupation, sex, and country (referred to in the models as "C"). Although the small number of countries and the ad hoc nature of their selection precludes a search for systematic country patterns, Table 4.3 does permit an investigation of whether differences in mobility exist among the included countries.

In the specified models, the interest is not in finding the best fit to the observed frequencies, but rather, in examining differences across countries in three bivariate relationships—father to respondent mobility, gender differences in social origins, and gender differences in current occupation. In order to test the significance of these three-way interactions, all lower-order interactions must also be specified. Following the independence model (Model 1), the base model (Model 2) controls for all possible two-way interactions (the joint distribution of sex with each variable, the joint distribution of country with each variable, and so forth). I thus assume a common set of interactions, relative to which I test for country differences (Models 3 through 5). Panel A presents the results for the employed population (all ages), Panel B for the mobile population. Panel C tests for country variation in gender differences in occupational inheritance, by comparing Models B6 and A6.

The results of Model A2 suggest that specifying all two-way interactions accounts for all but 11.8 (=1184.22/10035.20) percent of the total association in the table, reducing the misclassification of cases from 31 to 9 percent. Models A3 through A5 reveal that each hypothesized country difference makes a small but significant improvement in the fit of the model, although in no case does adding a three-way interaction result in a model that adequately fits the data. As suggested in the previous section, country differences are greatest with respect to the mobility interaction (the A3 vs. A2 comparison), which accounts for 4.3 (=431.60/10035.20) percent of the total association in the table and reduces the misclassification of cases by 2 percent. Sex differences in current occupation (A5 vs. A2) and in social origins (A4 vs. A2) also vary by country, accounting for 3.5 (=347.34/10035.20) and 1.0 (=98.04/10035.20) percent of the association, respectively. Similar country differences are evident among movers.

The data presented in Panel C suggest that no country differences exist in the occupational inheritance of men and women, net of country differences in the relationship between father and respondent's occupation, country differences in the social origins of men and women, country differences in the occupational destinations of men and women, and sex differences in the process of mobility across countries (Models A6 and B6). Thus the country differences that do emerge are not attributable to societal differences in the extent to which men and women inherit the occcupational categories of their fathers.

These findings suggest that small but significant societal differences do exist, although not in gender differences in occupational inheritance. The existence of such differences, however, must be viewed

Table 4.3 Log-Linear Analysis of Country Differences in Occupational Mobility, in Sex Differences in Social Origins, and in Gender Differences in Current Occupation; Employed Men and Women (All Ages)[a]

Model (null hypothesis)	X^2_{LR}	df	p	Δ
All seven countries (N=15,783)				
A. Full mobility matrix (7×7×2×7)				
1. [O_F] [O_R] [S] [C]	10035.20	666	<.001	30.85
2. [$O_F O_R$] [O_FS] [O_FC] [O_RS] [O_RC] [SC][b]	1184.22	540	<.001	8.80
3. [$O_F O_R$C]	752.62	324	<.001	6.80
4. [O_FSC]	1086.18	504	<.001	8.24
5. [O_RSC]	836.88	504	<.001	7.18
6. [$O_F O_R$C] [O_FSC] [O_RSC] [$O_F O_R$S]	223.41	216	<.350	2.97
A3 vs. A2	431.60	216	<.001	2.00
A4 vs. A2	98.04	36	<.001	.56
A5 vs. A2	347.34	36	<.001	1.62
A6 vs. A2	960.81	324	<.001	5.83
B. Main diagonal blocked (movers)				
1. [O_F] [O_R] [S] [C]	5319.30	568	<.001	27.26
2. [$O_F O_R$] [O_FS] [O_FC] [O_RS] [O_RC] [SC][b]	779.01	449	<.001	8.69
3. [$O_F O_R$C]	526.84	275	<.001	7.10
4. [O_FSC]	694.99	413	<.001	7.87
5. [O_RSC]	552.27	413	<.001	6.71
6. [$O_F O_R$C] [O_FSC] [O_RSC] [$O_F O_R$S]	170.76	174	>.5	2.17
B3 vs. B2	252.17	174	<.001	1.59
B4 vs. B2	84.02	36	<.001	.82
B5 vs. B2	226.74	36	<.001	1.98
B6 vs. B2	608.25	275	<.001	6.52
C. Hierarchical decomposition				
B6 vs. A6	52.65	42	>.05	.80

[a] Data from seven countries were included in the analysis: Austria, Germany (Fed. Rep.), Israel, Japan, the Netherlands, Northern Ireland, and the United States. O_F = occupation of father; O_R = occupation of respondent; S = sex of respondent; C = country.
[b] All second order interactions are also included in Models 3 through 5.

in the context of the much larger within-country differences in these relationships—nearly 90 percent of the total association in the four-way classification is due to within-country differences.

CONCLUSION

This chapter began by examining the processes that create gender differences in occupational location by mapping occupational outcomes to social origins. I use mobility analysis to compare the gross patterns of intergenerational mobility of employed men and women.

The large indexes of supply indicate that employed men move into quite different occupational destinations than employed women. The small indexes of recruitment suggest that although gender differences in social origins exist in several countries, they cannot be a major explanation for sex differences in occupational outcomes. A review of the pattern of movement between the generations reveals two factors affecting occupational allocation: men and women tend to move into sex-typical occupations, and to remain in their class of origin.

The log-linear results for the United States demonstrate the key role that occupational sextyping plays in the mobility processes of employed men and women, and the lack of any effect of gender differences in social origins. I also find gender differences in the mobility regime (or what previous authors have called "pure" mobility) in the United States, which are attributable entirely to gender differences in occupational inheritance.

In the remaining countries, occupational position depends to a significant extent on father's occupation. Moreover, occupational sextyping plays a major role in each country in determining men's and women's occupational destinations. In Germany and Israel, gender differences in social origins are a small but significant component of the mobility process, while sex differences in pure mobility exist only in the United States and Israel.

What do these mobility analyses tell us about the process of intergenerational occupational mobility of employed men and women? First, an analysis of this sort lays out the overall process of occupational transference to be explained, and does so with respect to specific occupational categories rather than to metric occupational scales. The results are extremely informative, describing, in a more precise manner than is possible with status attainment analyses, the nature of the substantial sex differences in intergenerational occupational mobility that exist. Second, the findings suggest that a crucial factor affecting the occupational outcomes of men and women is the sextyping of occupations (the opportunity structure) and not gender differences in pure mobility. Third, although the results suggest that country differences exist, these are relatively small compared with the gender and mobility differences found within countries. The existence of country differences, however small, do suggest that one must be cautious in generalizing from the United States results.

CHAPTER FIVE

Gender Differences in Intergenerational Occupational Attainment

INTRODUCTION

The mobility analyses in Chapter 4 mapped the overall process of occupational transference from father to respondent and investigated to what extent this process varied by gender and country. While useful in laying out global patterns of mobility, such analyses are ultimately limited because they do not control for variables other than social origins that have been proposed as explanations for observed sex differences in occupational destinations. The present chapter uses structural-equation analyses to more directly address determinants of occupational attainment at the individual level and to continue the task, begun in Chapter 4, of describing the processes of attainment that produce the striking patterns of occupational sex segregation that exist in the United States and other industrial societies.

The analyses in this chapter also allow us to address more directly the extent to which observed gender differences in occupational destinations reflect gender differences in composition (that is, background variables) and to what extent they reflect sex differences in the process of attainment (that is, the effects of background factors on occupational position). In so doing, it will be possible to test the human-capital contention that family responsibilities are *the* important explanation for gender differences in occupational location.

A final task of the present chapter is to investigate whether the occupational attainment processes of men and women in other countries are similar to those observed in the United States, and to speculate on why observed country differences exist. Because occupational attainment models have not previously been estimated for most of the countries, I view the descriptive part of my task as particularly important and therefore provide the basic data of the analysis more fully than might otherwise be necessary.

Gender Differences and Attainment Analysis

Like mobility analysts, status-attainment researchers have been interested in whether and how status advantages are transferred across generations and whether these processes vary across population subgroups. Structural-equation analyses, however, also permit a test of hypotheses regarding the determinants of occupational attainment, including the traditional human-capital variables (personal characteristics, or investments such as education and job experience). Occupation in these analyses is measured by a metric-status or prestige scale.

The first United States status-attainment analyses (Blau and Duncan 1967; Duncan et al. 1972) were restricted to men, as were the early comparative studies of status attainment (Cummings and Naoi 1972; Müller 1973; Iutaka and Bock 1973; Pöntinen 1974). These studies showed that the process of social mobility experienced by men in other societies was very similar to what Blau and Duncan reported for United States men: (1) respondent's education (and, secondarily, first job) is the most important factor determining son's occupational position, and (2) social origins affect occupational attainment mainly through education.

Applying this approach to gender differences, United States researchers have found results inconsistent with the aggregate differences observed in mobility analyses: despite an occupational structure that is highly differentiated by sex, men and women are employed in equally prestigious jobs and experienced similar processes of occupational attainment (Treiman and Terrell 1975b) [using different data and different sample specifications, McClendon (1976) and Featherman and Hauser (1976) found similar results]. Treiman and Terrell (p. 182) interpreted these findings as evidence that women, like men, essentially depended on their own achievements rather than on social origins for job allocation, and, furthermore, that women did not need to present higher educational qualifications to compete for equivalent (that is, prestigious) jobs.

Sewell and his coauthors (1980) provided the first evidence that the extent of gender similarity in patterns of attainment may be overstated. Using panel data for a 1957 cohort of Wisconsin high school seniors and incorporating first job, the authors found sharp distinctions between men's and women's status-attainment processes: (1) women are employed in jobs of higher status than men at labor-force entry, whereas men have the advantage in occupational status at mid-life; (2) although the total effect of education on current occupation is the same for the two sexes, the direct effect of schooling on *first* job is stronger for men and the direct effect of education on *current* job is greater for women; and (3) status of first job has a larger effect on current job for men than for women. These findings indicate that while men may be initially disadvantaged with respect to status of first job, they build on their prior achievements while women have to continue to rely on formal education for later job placement.

There are conflicting findings regarding marital status differences in attainment. While both Treiman and Terrell (1975b) and Mc-Clendon (1976) reported no marital status differences in the process of prestige attainment, their findings regarding the average prestige of married and nonmarried women differed: Treiman and Terrell (p. 185) found that never-married women had a prestige advantage, while McClendon (p. 62) found that married women worked in jobs of higher prestige. This difference is probably due to the different ways the authors operationalized marital status. While Treiman and Terrell distinguished between never- and ever-married women, McClendon compared married women living with their spouse with unmarried women (a group that included those who were single, divorced, widowed, or separated).

Sewell and his coauthors (1980, Tables 5 and 10), on the other hand, found that women's average status and occupational attainment patterns varied by marital status and number of children. Because their findings are consistent with the human-capital contention that family responsibilities negatively affect women's employment and occupational options, I review them in some detail. The authors found that: (1) never-married women hold the highest status jobs; childless married women, women with one or two children, and women with three or more children work in progressively lower status jobs; (2) when status of first job is included in models of occupational attainment, the direct effect of schooling on current occupational status is lowest for never-married women and increases steadily with marriage and childcare responsibilities; and (3) the occupational return to status of first job is greatest for never-married women and decreases steadily with marital and childcare responsibilities. These findings indicate that marriage and childrearing responsibilities do have negative effects on women's occupational outcomes and that never-married women are more like men than ever-married women in their process of occupational attainment.

While Sewell's and his coauthors' results certainly differ from those of previous analyses, they are not inconsistent. As the authors themselves noted, because previous analyses were based on cross-sectional data and did not include first job as an intervening factor between social origins and status of current occupation, marital and gender differences in patterns of occupational attainment, as well as in average status, were effectively masked.

An Alternative Explanation

In the present analysis I offer an alternative explanation to that of Sewell and his coauthors (1980) for the discrepancy between the results of macrolevel mobility analyses and those of microlevel status-attainment research. The clue as to why the results of these two research traditions differ can be found in the way occupation is measured: the aggregate mobility analyses use occupational categories (thus allowing a distinction for *kind of employment*, while status-attainment analyses abstract a metric-status or prestige dimension. The former analyses routinely find substantial gender differences in occupational distribution and mobility. The latter, in contrast, find that men and women are, on average, employed in equally prestigious jobs and are allocated to these occupations in similar ways (unless one controls for age and includes status of first job, as in Sewell et al. 1980).

Because men and women are employed in jobs of comparable prestige and status (at least in the United States), neither of these variables (as measures of occupational position) are useful in explaining existing male-female differences in earnings (for example), since they do not reflect existing differences in the *kinds* of work men and women do (England 1979; Boyd and McRoberts 1982; Jacobs 1981, 1982; Nam and Powers 1983).[1] In an earlier paper (Roos 1981) I documented that neither status nor prestige contributes to explaining the gender gap in earnings precisely because as measures of occupational attainment they do not reflect differences in the kinds of work done by men and women. In like manner, the present analysis tests whether gender similarity in the process of occupational attainment derives in part from the way occupation is traditionally measured in status-attainment research.

In Roos (1981), I proposed income-relevant measures of the characteristics of men's and women's employment and found that an important component of the gender gap in earnings is women's concentration in jobs that are low paying and heavily female. Relying on the knowledge that women's jobs are paid less than men's, for the present study I created a summary scale based on the occupation's wage rate rather than its prestige (see Chapter 2). Inclusion of the occupational wage-rate scale in a model of occupational attainment permits the addressing of a different, and possibly more interesting, set of questions than that addressed by traditional status-attainment analyses. For example, are there gender differences in wage-rate returns to education, even though no such differences are found in prestige returns?

In much of the early earnings-attainment literature, the fact that men and women work in such different jobs remained implicit in the lower female economic return accruing to occupational prestige and status. Moreover, in analyses of occupational attainment, the sex-segregated nature of the occupational structure was seldom explicitly addressed, much less incorporated into measurement procedures. The present study tests whether or not the failure to include a measure of occupation that more directly reflects differences in the kinds of work done by women and men masks existing gender and marital differences in occupational attainment. If this is the case, it may be that marital and childcare responsibilities affect the kinds of jobs women enter, even if differences in the average status of men and women do not readily indicate this. Thus, status (or prestige) is only one dimension of an occupation that can be investigated. The average remuneration is another.

Some evidence as to the importance of marital differences in explaining occupational differences among women is already available. Sewell and his coauthors (1980, Table 4) documented that never-married and childless married women differ from women with children in the kinds of occupations in which they work: never-married women are most likely to be employed in professional and technical work, and the percentage working in this major occupation group decreases consistently with increasing marital and childcare responsibilities. Women with children are more likely than never-married or childless women to be employed in clerical, retail sales, and service work. Table 3.5 indicates that these occupations are among the very lowest average earning occupations in each of the ten countries with personal earnings data. Finally, Doescher (1980) showed, for a sample of women aged thirty to forty-four in 1967, that women with larger families are more likely than those with small families to be in jobs with flexible hours (that is, jobs with high standard deviations in hours worked per week) and lower rates of skill depreciation during labor-force interruptions.

GENDER DIFFERENCES IN OCCUPATIONAL ATTAINMENT

Hypotheses and Analytic Strategy[2]

With the data available it is possible to identify four determinants of occupational attainment: father's occupation (a measure of social origins), age, marital status, and years of school completed. As previously described, each of these factors has been shown to affect occupational attainment, although there is some controversy as to whether the effects of these factors on occupation vary by gender.

Father's occupation. I include father's occupation as a measure of social origins.[3] Although there is no reason to suspect that all women and men differ in their social origins, it may be the case that *employed* women and men differ. This might occur if the samples of currently employed women are not representative of all women who have ever been employed. While Fligstein and Wolf (1978) found that this selectivity bias does not exist in the United States, the same may not hold true in other societies, especially in those countries where few women work outside the home.

The results in Chapter 4 suggest that small gender differences in social origins exist in West Germany and Israel, both early peak countries. In societies such as these where few women work, it may be that women who work outside the home are those who must work. If this is the case, then the larger proportion of employed women should originate from lower- and working-class backgrounds. Alternatively, it may be that women who work in societies where most women remain at home are those who stand to lose the most by not working. In this case, the larger proportion of employed women should originate from professional or other white-collar backgrounds. Whether the bulk of the female labor force comes from working-class or professional/white-collar origins should also affect the average rate of return women receive for their social origins, relative to those of men. Analyses using the wage-rate scale allow us to choose between these two explanations for social origin differences, and to determine whether father's occupation differentially affects men's and women's access to high-paying jobs, even if they do not produce differing levels of average prestige.

Age. I also identify age, measured in years, as a determinant of occupational status. Because of variability in the age cutoffs in the surveys, as well as variability in the age at which labor-force participation normally begins, the attainment analyses are restricted to the most economically active portion of the population, those aged twenty to sixty-four. Because women are more likely than men to have discontinuous labor-force participation, and given the lack of experience variables in the data sets, age is a particularly important variable to include in models of attainment. Previous research suggests that men's occupational status increases with age (presumably due to their increasing levels of experience), while the occupational status of employed women remains constant (presumably due to their discontinuous labor-force attachment) (Wolf 1976; Wolf and Rosenfeld 1978).

Rosenfeld (1980, 603), however, found that women employed continuously do experience some status gains with age, although these gains are smaller than those men receive. Notably, women's gains in status are not rewarded by a similar gain in earnings. Rosenfeld's findings suggest that the lack of a wage increase for women over their lifetime is not solely due to their intermittent labor-force attachment. Previous work thus suggests that occupational returns to age should be greater for men than for women, especially when occupation is measured by the wage-rate scale.

Because workers may move into relatively lower-paying employment as they near retirement, I also include an age-squared variable (I subtract the mean of age from age before squaring to avoid problems of multicollinearity).

Marital status. Human-capital theory predicts that women differ from men in their occupational achievement because family responsibilities affect the sexes differently. Hence, if human-capital theory is correct, women should be found disproportionately in jobs that are more compatible with childcare and home obligations, and underrepresented in jobs where family and work responsibilities are difficult to reconcile. I make the distinction between ever-married women (assigned a value of "0") and never-married women (assigned a value of "1") because of the greater likelihood that previously married women, like currently married women, have childcare and other home responsibilities left over from their marriage that may affect their occupational choice. If human-capital theory is correct, never-married women should be more like men in their occupational attainment than ever-married women, that is they should have an occupational advantage over women who do have marriage and childcare obligations.

For men, being married is likely to be an advantage since the responsibility for time-consuming home chores and childcare generally falls on the wife, regardless of whether or not she works outside the home (see Chapter 1). Men should thus be relatively more free to invest in lengthy training, both prior to employment and on the job, which in turn enhances their job prospects. Because of their traditional responsibility to ensure the financial security of their family, married men, in some sense, have no choice but to maximize their income-producing activities.

Education. Education is measured by years of school completed. It may be that the different occupational distributions of men and women are attributable to differences in achieved education, although previous work (Treiman and Terrell 1975b) showing that men and women complete nearly the same amount of schooling suggests that this is not the case, at least not in the United States. The work reviewed in this study also suggests that men and women receive similar prestige returns to their educational investments. While gender differences in prestige returns to education may not exist, educational investment permits men easier access to high-paying jobs than women (Oppenheimer 1968; Treiman and Terrell 1975c). I use the occupational wage-rate scale to determine, for the present set of countries, whether men do indeed receive a greater wage return for their educational investment.

Occupation. The dependent variable, occupation of respondent, is measured by prestige (to replicate previous United States work) and by the occupational wage-rate scale. If, as I hypothesize, gender differences in the process of occupational attainment exist, they are more likely to be observed when a variable such as the wage-rate scale is employed than if a status or prestige measure of occupational attainment is used, since the former reflects differences in the kinds of jobs in which women and men work.

Analytic strategy. In describing the results of the study, I pursue the following strategy: First, I present the distribution of variables by sex for each country. Second, I estimate two models of occupational attainment, separately for men and women within each country. One, to replicate past work, employs prestige to measure occupation, while the second uses the occupational wage-rate scale. I focus in the discussion on the wage-rate results to determine to what extent the findings from other countries approximate United States patterns. Third, I decompose the male-female gap in occupational attainment into its component parts.

Distribution of Variables by Sex

Table 5.1 presents the means and standard deviations for all included variables (the correlations for each country are presented in Appendix E).

Table 5.1 Means and Standard Deviations for Models of Occupational Attainment for Currently Employed Men and Women 20–64 in Twelve Industrialized Countries[a]

	Austria		Denmark		Finland		Germany (Fed. Rep.)		Great Britain		Israel	
	M	F	M	F	M	F	M	F	M	F	M	F
	Means											
Father's occupation-prestige	37.2	37.6	37.9	38.6	38.0	38.9	41.7	42.0	47.5	47.2	38.7 *	41.2
Father's occupation-wage-rate scale[b]	27.6	28.7	27.0	29.1	25.0 *	28.1	32.4 *	32.9	—	—	38.1 *	43.0
Age	40.6	41.1	41.7 *	39.2	38.1	39.6	40.5 *	38.9	42.5	42.1	39.8 *	35.2
(Age*)2	129	130	157	153	150	154	121	152	165	170	167	164
Marital status (Never married=1)	.174	.196	.131	.122	.264 *	.186	.140 *	.221	.141	.170	.151 *	.273
Years of schooling	9.95 *	9.20	8.23	8.18	7.94 *	8.42	11.2 *	10.4	10.4	10.3	9.57 *	10.8
Respondent's occupation-prestige	39.4 *	35.7	40.2	38.6	38.3	38.2	44.3 *	40.5	39.3	38.5	39.9 *	42.2
Respondent's occupation-wage rate scale	33.2 *	27.2	33.5	32.8	28.9	30.6	38.5 *	35.1	35.6	33.4	35.6 *	39.3

Standard deviations

Father's occupation-prestige	10.6	10.5	10.0	10.7	8.72	8.34	11.2	11.5	22.8	21.5	12.0	12.9
Father's occupation-wage-rate scale[b]	17.7	18.3	17.9	20.2	16.8	17.3	17.1	16.4	—	—	23.2	24.8
Age	11.4	11.4	12.6	12.4	12.3	12.3	11.0	12.2	12.9	12.8	12.9	12.7
$(Age^*)^2$	135	135	138	140	151	139	133	159	148	145	155	175
Marital status (Never married=1)	.379	.398	.338	.328	.442	.390	.348	.416	.348	.376	.358	.446
Years of schooling	2.11	1.61	2.26	1.86	2.21	2.77	2.35	2.05	2.23	1.93	4.18	4.05
Respondent's occupation-prestige	12.1	11.2	11.9	10.4	11.8	11.9	12.1	11.5	13.0	12.7	13.7	13.3
Respondent's occupation-wage rate scale	21.6	16.4	21.9	17.5	20.2	19.1	19.9	16.9	24.0	19.1	23.3	20.5
N[c]	445	293	363	253	353	286	610	365	473	271	5926	2653

a For details on scoring see text and Chapter 2. Note: Age* = Age − mean of age.
b The father's occupational wage rate scale could not be constructed for Great Britain, due to the way father's occupation was measured.
c Missing cases deleted pairwise, lowest number of cases reported.
* Difference in male and female mean is significant at .05 level, 2 tailed test.

Table 5.1 Means and Standard Deviations for Models of Occupational Attainment for Currently Employed Men and Women 20–64 in Twelve Industrialized Countries[a] (Cont.)

	Japan			Netherlands			Northern Ireland			Norway			Sweden			United States		
	M		F	M		F	M		F	M		F	M		F	M		F
						Means												
Father's occupation-prestige	36.1	*	34.6	39.6		40.9	38.1		37.9	38.7		40.2	37.4	*	39.4	39.6		40.2
Father's occupation-wage-rate scale[b]	23.3	*	18.6	35.3	*	37.0	24.2	*	28.2	29.6		32.2	27.2	*	33.1	35.8		36.8
Age	38.8		39.3	39.1		32.5	40.9		39.0	42.2		39.9	41.8	*	39.6	39.5		38.9
(Age*)²	136		147	156		147	152		154	158		145	156		138	153		155
Marital status (Never married=1)	.184		.202	.180	*	.412	.230	*	.358	.126		.133	.156		.115	.149		.142
Years of schooling	11.2	*	10.2	10.1		10.2	10.2	*	10.6	9.14		8.70	8.88		8.78	12.6		12.5
Respondent's occupation-prestige	42.1	*	36.5	43.7	*	40.4	39.3		37.4	42.7	*	39.2	41.0		39.8	41.9		41.8
Respondent's occupation-wage rate scale	39.5	*	30.3	42.9	*	37.1	31.5		32.4	37.6		33.3	37.0		35.0	41.6	*	38.2

Standard deviations

Father's occupation-prestige	8.59	7.77	12.7	13.4	13.6	13.5	9.82	10.2	10.0	10.8	10.9	11.7
Father's occupation-wage-rate scale[b]	27.1	24.7	25.5	25.7	16.7	22.0	20.4	22.2	19.0	22.4	26.6	27.5
Age	11.7	12.1	12.5	12.0	12.4	12.5	12.6	12.1	12.5	11.7	12.4	12.4
$(Age*)^2$	146	141	150	219	137	145	143	128	141	131	141	146
Marital status (Never married=1)	.388	.402	.384	.494	.421	.481	.332	.341	.363	.319	.356	.349
Years of schooling	3.20	2.37	2.97	2.42	1.88	2.01	2.91	2.61	2.91	2.66	3.23	2.64
Respondent's occupation-prestige	11.3	9.51	13.5	13.2	12.7	13.3	12.9	12.6	13.3	12.6	12.9	12.8
Respondent's occupation-wage rate scale	25.2	20.0	25.9	21.1	21.8	22.5	24.2	22.2	24.9	20.3	28.3	21.4
N[c]	521	366	404	132	442	201	382	147	383	289	1626	1046

[a] For details on scoring see text and Chapter 2. Note: Age* = Age – mean of age.
[b] The father's occupational wage rate scale could not be constructed for Great Britain, due to the way father's occupation was measured.
[c] Missing cases deleted pairwise, lowest number of cases reported.
* Difference in male and female mean is significant at .05 level, 2 tailed test.

The United States results. I begin my discussion by referring to the results for the United States. As in previous research, men and women come from essentially similar social origins, a result that holds for both measures of father's occupation. Furthermore, employed men and women are approximately the same age; are equally likely to have never married; and have, on average, the same education. The only significant difference in the United States data is that, relative to men, women work on average, in lower-paying, although equally prestigious, jobs (as evidenced by the 3.4 point male advantage on the wage-rate scale). Moreover, the occupations in which women work have, on average, a more restricted range of variation than the jobs in which men work. Since the sexes have similar aver; je values on these determinants of occupational attainment, the difference in the wage-rate scale must be attributable to *differences in return* to background factors and investments experienced by men and women, a topic that will be examined in a subsequent section.

Crosscultural results. The findings for the remaining countries indicate that the United States patterns are not representative. Gender differences in occupational determinants do exist and in some countries they are substantial. In highlighting these differentials, I refer only to those significant at the .05 level.

Although the differences tend to be small, men and women in three of the twelve countries (Israel, Japan, and Sweden) differ significantly in father's prestige. When the occupational wage-rate scale is employed, the gender differential widens and Finland and Northern Ireland also show gender differences in social origins. These findings increase the number of countries with significant gender differences in social origins from those noted in Chapter 4.[4] These results suggest that my earlier supposition that social origin differences might be attributable to the uniqueness of women workers in early peak countries is incorrect. Finland is a single peak country, and Sweden and Japan are double peak countries. Moreover, both Finland and Sweden have particularly high levels of female labor-force participation. It is clear that it is not only in early peak countries that employed women differ in their social origins from employed men.

The data used in this study permit a better delineation of the nature of sex differences in social origins. In Japan, men come from somewhat higher status social origins than women, while in the remaining countries the significant gender difference favors women. The Japanese result reflects the fact that employed Japanese women are more likely than Japanese men to originate from low-wage agricultural origins (56 percent of the employed Japanese women compared with 48 percent of the Japanese men; calculated from Appendix C).

The results for Finland, Israel, Northern Ireland, and Sweden represent the more general finding that employed women come from slightly higher status social origins than men, ranging from 3.1 points on the wage-rate scale in Finland to 5.9 points in Sweden. This finding suggests that women in a better competitive position in the labor market (in this case, those coming from higher status social origins) are more likely to be employed than women in a less competitive position. This result is in direct contrast to what was true in the industrializing societies of nineteenth century Europe and the United States, when the female labor force was composed almost entirely of daughters of lower- and working-class families.

Notably, in the four countries where social origin differences favor women, larger proportions of the male labor force originate from farm backgrounds. This finding does not hold true in those countries with no significant gender difference in social origins, nor is it true for Japan, where the gender difference favors men (see Appendix C).[5] It is possible to speculate from these results that perhaps women from farm origins (who tend to remain in agricultural occupations themselves—see Appendix C) are less likely to be enumerated as employed in these countries, probably because they are farm wives.

With respect to age, in five of the twelve countries (Denmark, Germany, Israel, the Netherlands, and Sweden), employed men are significantly older than employed women. Age differences are largest in Israel and the Netherlands, where men are, on average, 4.6 and 6.6 years older than their female counterparts, respectively. Recall that these two countries are early peak societies, suggesting that women work only until marriage or childbirth before retiring permanently from the labor force. Because most women in these two countries drop out of the labor force upon marriage or childbearing, it is not surprising that the female labor force is on average so much younger than the male.

With respect to marital status, in five countries (Finland, Germany, Israel, the Netherlands, and Northern Ireland), the proportion that are never married differs significantly by gender and, in each country except Finland, the prediction is in the expected direction—employed women are more likely than employed men to have never married. Each of these countries (except Finland) is an early peak country: 22, 27, 41, and 36 percent, of the female labor force in Germany, Israel, the Netherlands, and Northern Ireland, respectively, have never married. The comparable figure for the United States is a much lower 14 percent. In contrast, Finnish males are significantly more likely than their female coworkers to have never married, a finding that reflects, in part, the Finnish women's more continuous labor-force attachment. In single peak countries such as Finland, where a working wife is the norm rather than the exception, marriage and childcare responsibilities are not likely to be as much of a deterrent to labor-force participation.

While sex differences in percentage married exist in some countries, it is important to remember that in the majority (seven of twelve), there are no such differences. Thus, in most of the included countries, the human-capital expectation that a larger proportion of employed women would be married is not proven by the data.

The results for education are mixed. In half the countries (Denmark, Great Britain, the Netherlands, Norway, Sweden, and the United States), men and women complete similar amounts of schooling. In the remaining half of the countries (Austria, Finland, Germany, Israel, Japan, and Northern Ireland), males and females differ significantly in their achieved education, although the sex differences are not always in the same direction. In Austria, Germany, and Japan, men complete .8, .8, and 1 year more schooling than women, respectively, while in Finland, Israel, and Northern Ireland, women are significantly more educated than men, by .5, 1.2, and .4 year, respectively. The findings of higher female educational achievement may be partly due to the fact that in the three countries that exhibit this pattern, employed women also come from slightly higher social origins than employed men. In the three countries where males achieve the higher education, women come from social origins similar to those of men or, in the case of Japan, from significantly lower origins.

In half the countries (Denmark, Finland, Great Britain, Northern Ireland, Sweden, and the United States), there are no differences in the average prestige of men's and women's jobs. In the other half (Austria, Germany, Israel, Japan, the Netherlands, and Norway), men's and women's average prestige differs significantly, ranging from a gender difference of 2.3 prestige points in Israel to 5.6 points in Japan. In each country except Israel the prestige advantage favors the men. The results are similar with the wage-rate scale,[6] except that it generally widens the observed sex difference in occupational attainment. Only in Israel are women employed in significantly higher-paying (and higher-prestige) occupations than men. Note that this does not mean that women in Israel earn more than their male coworkers, but only that they are employed in higher-paying jobs than men on average. This advantage may be due either to their higher status social origins, to their significantly higher educational attainment, or to some combination of these factors. I examine these possibilities in a subsequent section.

Gender Differences in the Process of Attainment

United States results. Table 5.2 presents the coefficients for the prestige and wage-rate models, separately for United States men and women. As in previous work, the process of prestige attainment is nearly identical for men and women: educational investment is the most important determinant of occupational prestige for both sexes, and the prestige return to each year of schooling is also very similar. Father's occupation is also a significant, but less powerful, predictor of occupational attainment for both sexes, in the expected positive direction. Furthermore, the occupational return to father's prestige is the same for men and women.

Small gender differences in returns to other determinants of occupational attainment occur and all are in the predicted directions. Males return almost twice the prestige to age that women do, reflecting both sex differences in total amounts of time spent working and in returns to experience. The small, but significant, effect of age on the prestige of women is worth noting, however, in light of previous findings (Wolf 1976; Wolf and Rosenfeld 1978) that women's

Table 5.2 Coefficients for Two Models of Occupational Attainment, for Currently Employed Men and Women 20–64, United States (1974–1977)[a]

Independent Variables	Prestige model		Wage-rate model	
	Men	Women	Men	Women
	Metric coefficients			
Father's occupation	.104*	.109*	.151*	.068*
Age	.178*	.093*	.384*	.184*
(Age*)²	−.006*	−.002	−.018*	−.002
Marital status				
(Never married = 1)		1.43	−4.97*	.762
Years of schooling	2.36*	2.63*	4.34*	3.85*
Intercept	2.18	1.13	−30.2	−19.3
R²	.384	.331	.313	.247
	Standardized coefficients			
Father's occupation	.087*	.099*	.141*	.088*
Age	.171*	.090*	.168*	.107*
(Age*)²	−.061*	−.026	−.090*	−.013
Marital status				
(Never married = 1)	−.063*	.039	−.063*	.012
Years of schooling	.592*	.540*	.495*	.474*

[a] Age* = Age – mean of age. Means and standard deviations for all variables are provided in Table 5.1 and correlations in Appendix E. Occupational prestige is used to measure respondent's and father's occupations in the "Prestige model;" the wage-rate scale is employed in the "Wage-rate model."
* Metric coefficient is twice its standard error.

occupational status remains constant over time. Additionally, the significant coefficient for the age-squared variable for men suggests that as they near retirement age, their rate of occupational return to age begins to decrease. As expected, married men have a 2.3 point prestige advantage over never-married men. However, contrary to human-capital theory, married women are not disadvantaged relative to never-married women.

In comparing the wage-rate and prestige results for the United States, the overall picture is similar in kind although not in degree. While the broad patterns of occupational attainment remain the same with the wage-rate scale, several gender differences in rates of return emerge (or increase). First, United States men and women receive similar net prestige returns to social origins but quite different occupational wage-rate returns: men receive over twice the wage-rate return to social origins that women do. Thus, although United States men and women come from similar origins (as indicated by Table 5.1), men are better able than women to translate their origin advantages into higher-paying occupations. Second, women receive 52 percent of the occupation return to age that men do when prestige is employed, and a slightly lower 48 percent when the wage-rate scale is used. This result indicates that if increasing age does little for women's occupational prestige relative to men's, it does even less for their occupational wage. Third, gender differences in the effect of marital status widen. Married men have significantly higher-paying jobs than never-married men, but the expected difference between ever- and never-married women does not emerge. Fourth, the gender gap in the rate of return to education widens (the female return to education is 111 percent of the male return in the prestige model and 89 percent in the wage-rate model).

In sum, accounting for the fact that men and women work in jobs with different wage rates reveals differences in the process of occupational attainment of United States men and women that prestige models failed to detect. Although men and women in the United States attain prestige in similar ways, the process whereby they are allocated to positions in the male occupational wage hierarchy differs by gender, with men accruing greater returns than women to each occupational determinant.

Because the wage-rate scale makes distinctions on the basis of only fourteen major group categories (refer to Chapter 2), and since it is based on male earnings within these occupational groups, the results this exercise produces are a conservative estimate of gender differences in the process of occupational attainment. It is well known that in addition to gender segregation at the major group level, men and women work in different detailed occupations and, within occupations, in different jobs. Additionally, males and females are segregated within occupations by industries and firms.[7]

Crosscultural results. I turn now to a discussion of the results in the remaining countries, discussing only those from the occupational wage-rate models. Table 5.3 presents the coefficients, separately for currently employed men and women, in each of the twelve countries. The comparable prestige models are presented in Appendix F for the interested reader.

For men, social origins have a small, but significant, positive effect on occupational destination in each country except Sweden. Thus, sons with fathers in high-paying jobs are more likely than sons whose fathers worked in low-paying jobs to themselves work in high-paying occupations. For women, social origins have a significant

Table 5.3 Coefficients of a Model of Occupational Wage-Rate Attainment, for Currently Employed Men and Women 20–64, in Twelve Industrialized Countries[a]

		Father's occupation[b]	Age	(Age*)²	Marital status	Years of schooling	Intercept
				Metric coefficients			
Austria	Men	.301*	.124	−.003	−4.39	4.91*	−27.8
	Women	.123*	−.029	.006	−2.02	4.86*	−20.3
Denmark	Men	.109*	.106	−.006	−4.92	6.05*	−22.2
	Women	.010	−.049	.001	−.200	5.04*	−7.00
Finland	Men	.216*	.287*	−.005	−4.27	4.86*	−24.2
	Women	.084	.261*	−.007	−.125	4.93*	−22.4
Germany	Men	.254*	.068	−.001	−3.68	4.79*	−25.2
(Fed. Rep.)	Women	.033	−.016	−.011	−2.76	3.48*	.587
Great	Men	.103*	−.032	−.015*	−5.27	4.30*	−9.62
Britain	Women	−.037	.074	−.004	4.51	4.30*	−12.5
Israel	Men	.102*	.214*	−.010*	−1.39	3.09*	−4.44
	Women	.014	−.017	−.009*	−3.22*	3.25*	6.78
Japan	Men	.124*	.498*	−.008	−2.07	3.00*	−14.8
	Women	.158*	.073	−.013	7.57*	2.95*	−5.32
Netherlands	Men	.214*	.315*	−.014	−6.33	3.91*	−13.3
	Women	.037	.150	.009	3.60	4.37*	−16.4
Northern	Men	.251*	.056	−.001	−4.25	5.72*	−33.9
Ireland	Women	.067	.130	−.003	−2.72	7.36*	−51.0
Norway	Men	.153*	−.003	−.002	−6.81*	5.26*	−13.7
	Women	.027	.083	.006	5.05	5.98*	−24.4
Sweden	Men	.043	.189*	−.007	−11.2*	5.48*	−17.9
	Women	.025	.034	−.002	−4.53	4.65*	−7.26
United	Men	.151*	.384*	−.018*	−4.97*	4.34*	−30.2
States	Women	.068*	.184*	−.002	.762	3.85*	−19.3

[a]Age*= Age – mean of age. Means and standard deviations for all variables are provided in Table 5.1 and correlations in Appendix E.
[b]For Great Britain only, father's occupation = prestige of father's occupation; for all other countries, father's occupation = wage-rate scale.
*Metric coefficient is twice its standard error.

Table 5.3 Coefficients of a Model of Occupational Wage-Rate Attainment, for Currently Employed Men and Women 20–64, in Twelve Industrialized Countries[a] (Cont.)

		Father's occupation[b]	Age	$(Age^*)^2$	Marital status	Years of schooling	R^2
		Standardized coefficients					
Austria	Men	.246*	.065	−.020	−.077	.480*	.390
	Women	.137*	−.020	.052	−.049	.476*	.307
Denmark	Men	.089*	.061	−.035	−.076	.624*	.458
	Women	.012	−.035	.012	−.004	.537*	.303
Finland	Men	.179*	.174*	−.035	−.093	.530*	.393
	Women	.076	.168*	−.054	−.003	.715*	.534
German	Men	.218*	.038	−.009	−.064	.567*	.461
(Fed. Rep.)	Women	.032	−.011	−.106	−.068	.421*	.208
Great	Men	.098*	−.017	−.092*	−.076	.400*	.194
Britain	Women	−.042	.050	−.032	.089	.436*	.201
Israel	Men	.101*	.119*	−.068*	−.021	.555*	.347
	Women	.017	−.011	−.078*	−.070*	.639*	.438
Japan	Men	.133*	.231*	−.049	−.032	.381*	.223
	Women	.196*	.044	−.090	.152*	.350*	.238
Netherlands	Men	.210*	.152*	−.080	−.094	.448*	.323
	Women	.045	.085	.088	.084	.500*	.264
Northern	Men	.192*	.032	−.007	−.082	.491*	.338
Ireland	Women	.066	.072	−.017	−.058	.658*	.449
Norway	Men	.129*	−.002	−.012	−.094*	.634*	.488
	Women	.027	.045	.032	.077	.702*	.512
Sweden	Men	.033	.095*	−.038	−.164*	.640*	.453
	Women	.028	.020	−.011	−.071	.609*	.376
United	Men	.141*	.168*	−.090*	−.063*	.495*	.313
States	Women	.088*	.107*	−.013	.012	.474*	.247

[a] Age* = Age − mean of age. Means and standard deviations for all variables are provided in Table 5.1 and correlations in Appendix E.
[b] For Great Britain only, father's occupation = prestige of father's occupation; for all other countries, father's occupation = wage-rate scale.
*Metric coefficient is twice its standard error.

positive effect only in Austria, Japan, and the United States. In most countries, women's occupational attainment depends solely on their education, and even in Austria and the United States the female return is 41 and 45 percent of the male return, respectively. With the exception of Japan, where the male return is 78 percent of the female return, social origins benefit men more than women: either father's occupation has no significant effect on daughter's attainment or the benefit accruing to women is substantially less than that men receive.

Age is positively associated with the occupational attainment of men in ten of the twelve countries, significantly so in six (Finland, Israel, Japan, the Netherlands, Sweden, and the United States), while it has a significant effect for women in only two countries. Thus men are more likely than women to benefit occupationally from

increasing age. Interestingly, the only countries in which age has a significant effect for women are Finland, where the female age pattern of participation comes closest to approaching that of men, and the United States, which has historically been headed in the same direction (see Chapter 3 and Oppenheimer 1970, Chapter 1). In Finland, the female return is 90 percent the male return; in the United States women receive only 48 percent of the male occupational return for each yearly increment in age.

Married men in each country have an occupational advantage over never-married men, net of social origins, age, and education, although this advantage is significant only in Norway, Sweden, and the United States. The marital-status results for women are mixed: the coefficient is significant in only two countries (Japan and Israel) and, moreover, in seven of the twelve countries the sign is opposite what was expected. Only in Japan is a significant positive coefficient obtained, indicating that never-married women have the expected occupational advantage over ever-married women. In Israel, ever-married women have the advantage over never-married women, even net of differences in social origins, age, and education. Thus, contrary to human-capital theory, indications are that ever-married and never-married women do not differ significantly in most countries, at least with respect to the wage rate of the jobs in which they work.[8]

For both men and women, education is consistently the most important predictor of occupational attainment. In each country, and for each sex, the relationship between education and the occupational wage rate is always significant and positive: increasing education is thus always associated with incumbency in jobs of higher earnings. For men, however, education is generally only one of several determinants of occupational attainment; social origins, age, and occasionally marital status also enhance men's occupational outcomes in many of the countries. In contrast, in seven of the twelve countries, education is the only independent variable with significant effects on women's occupational attainment. These data thus suggest that while education might be the most important factor affecting men's occupational outcomes, for women it is very often the *only* factor, at least among those I have measured.

Interestingly, the occupational return to education is not always greater for men than for women. In half the countries (Austria, Denmark, Germany, Japan, Sweden, and the United States), the female return is somewhat less than the male return, averaging 88 percent that of men. Table 5.1 showed, in each of these countries, that men also complete slightly more years of schooling than women, although the difference is significant in only three (Austria, Germany, and Japan). In the remaining six countries (Finland, Great Britain,

Israel, the Netherlands, Northern Ireland, and Norway), the female return is either identical to or greater than the male return. These latter six countries are also the ones in which women have similar (nonsignificant differences) or greater achieved education than men. These results may indicate, as Sewell and his colleagues (1980) speculated, that women continue to rely on formal educational qualifications for occupational placement throughout their life (hence their receiving a greater occupational return to education than men in some countries), while men advance in their careers by building on their personal characteristics (for example, age and social origins) and previous occupational experience.[9]

The Male-Female Occupational Gap

To this point, I have compared the occupational attainment processes of men and women, identifying various factors as determinants of occupational position. Such analyses can be informative as to whether hypothesized variables are important in explaining variations in attainment among women or among men, but they give no estimate of the extent to which gender differences in achieved occupation reflect sex differences in distribution on these variables (that is, differences in composition). Since Table 5.1 highlighted several gender differences (in both determinants and achieved occupation) for some of the included countries, a decomposition of the male-female occupational wage-rate gap is necessary. Table 5.1 indicates that sufficiently large gender differences in occupational attainment exist in six countries, as indicated by a significant gender difference on the wage-rate variable. In Austria, Germany, Japan, the Netherlands, and the United States, men are employed in significantly higher-paying jobs than women. In Israel women work, on average, in higher-paying employment. This section investigates to what extent these gaps in occupational attainment can be attributed to social origins, age, marital status, and schooling.

To assess the extent to which the gender gap in achieved occupation reflects sex differences in composition I apply a regression standardization procedure (Duncan 1969, 100–102). In applying this technique, the generally higher male (or in the case of Israel, female) means on the factors included as occupational determinants were substituted into female (male) regression equations of occupation on a sequentially ordered set of independent variables.[10] The technique, when used with the wage-rate scale, provides an estimate of how much of women's relatively greater concentration in low-paying employment (that is, in jobs that pay even men poorly), can be attributed to compositional differences on identified occupational determinants, and how much can be attributed to gender differences in rates of return to compositional characteristics. It is thus possible to estimate how much of the gender gap in occupation could be accounted for if women (or in the case of Israel, men) had the same social origins, average age, marital status, and education as men (women), but continued to receive their own occupational returns to these background factors.

Table 5.4 presents the results of the decomposition. In Panel A, results are expressed as the "female occupational wage rate as a percentage of male's;" in Panel B, comparable findings are expressed as the "male occupational wage rate as a percentage of female's." In each case, the group with the greater wage rate is assumed to be 100 percent. Although primary interest is in explaining the gender difference in occupational attainment in those countries where significant differences existed (that is, Austria, Germany, Israel, Japan, the Netherlands, and the United States), also included is a decomposition of differences in the mean occupational wage rate for all twelve countries, since an observed nondifference might be masking offsetting effects.

The results in Panel A suggest that gender differences in educational attainment are an important explanation for women's lower average wage rate. If Austrian, German, and Japanese women had the higher education of their male coworkers, they would increase their relative wage rate by 12, 7, and 6 percent, respectively. In each of these countries, the observed difference is due both to the significantly higher male educational achievement and to the smaller return to education women receive. In the Netherlands, women's relative wage rate can be increased by 2 percent when educational differences are taken into account, a finding due more to the use of the female equation to decompose mean differences than to gender differences in composition on this variable. Finally, in the United States, the nonsignificant gender difference in education (.1 year) and the greater male return for education account for a modest 1.7 percent of the increase in the female wage rate. Of those countries with a significant gender difference in wage rate, only in Japan does any occupational determinant other than education account for an appreciable part of the gender gap. The fact that Japanese men come from significantly higher status social origins increases the relative female wage rate by 3 percent. Sex differences in social origins and education together account for 9 percent of the increase in the relative wage rate of Japanese women.[11]

By referring to column 8 of Panel A, it can be seen that women in Germany come closest to approximating men in their achieved occupational level when gender differences in background factors are

Table 5.4 Decomposition of Difference in Mean Occupational Wage, of Currently Employed Men and Women 20–64, in Twelve Industrialized Countries[a]

Panel A	Female mean as percent of male mean (1)	Percentage due to sex differences in: Father's occupation (2)	Age (3)	Marital status (4)	Years of schooling (5)	Total percentage difference due to composition (sum of 2–5) (6)	Adjusted female wage-rate percentage (sum of 1 and 6) (7)	Residual percentage (100%–7) (8)
1. Austria*	82.0	-1.0	.2	.0	11.5	10.7	92.7	7.3
2. Denmark	98.0	-1.1	-1.7	.3	2.8	.3	98.3	1.7
3. Germany* (Fed. Rep.)	91.1	-.3	.9	.1	7.0	7.7	98.8	1.2
4. Great Britain	94.0	.0	-.3	-.4	1.5	.8	94.8	5.2
5. Japan*	76.9	3.0	.3	-.2	6.0	9.1	86.0	14.0
6. Netherlands*	86.6	-.8	-1.0	-.6	2.0	-.4	86.2	13.8
7. Norway	88.5	-2.3	-.9	-.1	10.7	7.4	95.9	4.1
8. Sweden	94.4	-5.0	-1.5	-.3	7.1	.3	94.7	5.3
9. United States*	91.7	-.5	.1	.1	1.7	1.4	93.1	6.9

Panel B	Male mean as percent of female mean (1)	Percentage due to sex differences in: Father's occupation (2)	Age (3)	Marital status (4)	Years of schooling (5)	Total percentage difference due to composition (sum of 2–5) (6)	Adjusted male wage-rate percentage (sum of 1 and 6) (7)	Residual percentage (100%–7) (8)
1. Finland	94.2	4.3	1.2	1.1	6.6	13.2	107.4	-7.4
2. Israel*	90.7	3.0	.0	-.6	5.3	7.7	98.4	1.6
3. Northern Ireland	97.2	5.8	.6	-1.0	2.7	8.1	105.3	-5.3

[a] In Panel A countries, where the male occupational wage rates were greater than the female occupational wage rates, the male means were substituted into the female prediction equations. In Panel B countries, where the female occupational wage rates were greater than the male occupational wage rates, the female means were substituted into the male prediction equations. An asterisk (*) indicates that the gender difference in occupational attainment (wage-rate scale) is a significant one.

taken into account. With a residual of only 1.2 percent, the occupational difference between German men and women all but disappears. This finding is all the more remarkable when one considers that the German sample excludes the lowest-earning, and overwhelmingly male, guest worker population. This finding of near gender equality in Germany, however, must be viewed in the context of the relatively small number of employed German women. As indicated by their early peak age pattern of participation (Table 3.1), those who work tend to be younger women who then drop out of the labor force permanently upon marriage or childbirth. Additionally, as indicated in Table 3.2, approximately half of the German women who work do so only on a part-time basis. Thus, while women with background factors equivalent to men do relatively well, few women benefit since so few women work outside the home.

With the exception of Germany, in each country with a significant sex difference in occupation, a large portion of the gender gap can be attributed to differences in rates of return. In the United States case, compositional differences account for only a negligible part of the gender differential, leaving a 7 percent residual. Hence, nearly the entire male-female difference can be attributed to gender differences in rates of return (for example, women receive less of an occupational return than men for their social origins, age, and education). In the Netherlands and Japan, the portions attributable to differences in rates of return are especially large, with unexplained residuals of approximately 14 percent in each country.

Panel B presents a break down of the occupation gap between women and men in those countries where the average occupational wage rate of women is higher than that of men. The focus is on Israel, since only in that country is women's wage rate significantly higher than men's. The largest portion of the Israeli gender gap is attributable to differences in education—if men had women's higher education, they would increase their relative wage rate by 5.3 percent. An additional 3 percent is attributable to women's higher status social origins. When compositional differences between the sexes are taken into account, men's wage rate is 98.4 percent that of women, leaving only 1.6 percent to be attributed to differences in rates of return. The Israeli results suggest that if women have a slight occupational advantage over men, it is because they come from slightly higher status backgrounds and are somewhat better educated, and not because of large differences in rates of return that favor women over men (as is the case for men in several of the countries in Panel A).

Recent work by Kraus and Treiman (1980) and Hartman (1980) suggest a possible explanation for the seemingly anomalous Israeli findings—choosing only employed women for inclusion in the sample may have introduced a selectivity bias that affects the attainment results. Also, the immigrant nature of the population and the division of the Jewish population into the more Westernized and advantaged European- and American-origin Jews and the less advantaged Asian- and African-origin Jews makes the potential effect of such a selectivity bias particularly troublesome [see Matras and Weintraub (1976) and Hartman (1980) for additional information on the importance of ethnic origins on attainment patterns in Israel].

Recall that Table 3.1 indicated that few women in Israel work— only 30 percent of Israeli women 18 years and older (and 37 percent of the twenty to sixty-four-year old population) are employed. This figure is the lowest for any of the twelve countries. In addition, the results from Chapter 3 suggest that women in Israel tend to leave the labor force permanently upon marriage or childbearing. Kraus's and Treiman's (1980) and Hartman's (1980) results allow a more precise description of just who these Israeli women are. Using the same data this study does, Kraus and Treiman found that almost no Arab women work in the paid labor force [15 percent of the population of Israel is Arab (Israel Central Bureau of Statistics 1975)]. In addition, 64 percent of women aged twenty-five to sixty-four in the civilian labor force in 1974 originated from European or American back- grounds. Almost half of the women from European or American origins are employed, compared with 29 percent of the Asian/African women, a finding supported in principle by Hartman's results. There is no similar distinction among men: 92 percent of the European/ American and 90 percent of the Asian/African men are employed. In comparing male and female workers in Israel, therefore, one is comparing groups with different likelihoods of success based solely on their social origins. In sum, the overrepresentation of European- and American-origin Jews in the employed female population is apparently an important explanation for why women in Israel are, on average, employed in jobs that pay better than the jobs in which men work.[12]

CONCLUSION

This chapter offers an alternative explanation for why previous analyses failed to detect gender differences in occupational attainment. Building on the knowledge that the occupational wage hierarchy is essentially invariant across industrial societies, and the fact that women are concentrated in lower-paying jobs even within occupa- tional groups, I proposed a measure of occupation, for use in regres- sion analyses, which reflects differences in the wage rates of men's and women's jobs.

These analyses suggest that gender differences in the process of occupational allocation and average levels of attainment in the United States are masked when prestige is used as a measure of occupational achievement. The process whereby United States men and women are allocated to positions in the occupational wage hierarchy differs, with males accruing greater returns than females to each identified occupational determinant, even though the process of prestige attainment is nearly identical for men and women. Thus, taking into account the fact that men and women tend to work in jobs with different pay scales reveals differences in the process of occupational attainment of men and women in the United States that previous prestige models failed to detect.

While the general pattern is one of similarity across societies, several country differences in attainment patterns emerge. Overall, for each sex within each country, education is consistently the most important predictor of occupational attainment, documenting once again that in an industrial society one's occupational destination is likely to depend mainly on one's education. For men, however, education is generally only one of several significant factors affecting occupational position. Social origins, age, and marital status all have expected positive effects on men's attainment in many of the countries.

Like men, women are allocated to occupational positions mainly on the basis of their education. However, education is very often the only factor affecting female occupational attainment: in seven of the twelve countries, women's attainment is solely dependent on their education. Age is significant for women only in Finland and the United States and social origins contribute to women's occupational destination only in Austria, Japan, and the United States. Little support exists for the human-capital contention that never-married women have significant occupational advantages over ever-married women. Only in Japan is the result significant and in the expected direction. In addition to relying almost solely on educational qualifications for their occupational attainment, women more often than not receive lower occupational returns than men for their characteristics or investments.

The results of the decomposition of the occupational gender gap suggest that, in those countries where significant differences in achieved occupational attainment favor men, part of the explanation lies in women's generally lower level of education. Accounting for sex differences in education substantially increases women's relative wage rate in Austria, Germany, and Japan. Women's lower average social origins also account for an appreciable portion of the gender difference in Japan. However, with the exception of Germany, in each of the five countries with a significant male advantage in occupation, gender differences in rates of return are an important explanation for the wage-rate gap, signifying that women do not benefit as much as men from their background factors. On the other hand, in Israel, the only country where women's occupational wage rate is significantly greater than that of men, men's lower relative wage rate can be attributed almost entirely to gender differences in education and social origins.

Marital Status Differences Among Women in Labor-Force Behavior and Occupational Attainment

---

INTRODUCTION

Thus far I have shown that gender differences exist in labor-force behavior, occupational distribution, and the process of attainment, findings which are consistent with the human-capital explanation for occupational sex segregation. In these comparisons, I have assumed, for the sake of simplicity, that since most men and women are married, and most women and not their husbands have primary responsibility for home and childcare, the effect of differential family responsibilities on occupational attainment should be reflected in gender differences in the process of attainment. Strictly speaking, however, the negative effects of home and childcare responsibilities on occupational attainment (posited by human-capital theory) should not affect all women, but only those employed women who must contend with such responsibilities (that is, married women and women with children).

The present chapter compares the labor-force behavior, occupational distribution, and attainment patterns of ever- and never-married women to test the human-capital expectation that differing family responsibilities are the major explanation for observed gender differences in attainment patterns and occupational outcomes. If human-capital theory is an important explanation for observed gender differences in occupational distribution, the analyses in the present chapter should show differences in the distribution and attainment patterns of ever-married and never-married women. A finding that never-married women's occupational distribution and attainment closely approximate those of men would support human-capital theory, indicating that women's economic disadvantage, relative to men, depends in large measure on the responsibilities associated with marriage. If minimal or no differences exist in the attainment of ever- and never-married women, then human-capital theory would be called into question. This would suggest that other more fundamental features of the organization of work are responsible for the sex-segregated occupational structure.

An outline will summarize how the human-capital expectations regarding marriage and childrearing responsibilities are expected to operate negatively to affect the differences in occupational distribution and attainment of ever-married women, relative to those of never-married women: (1) by reducing their total amount of on-the-job experience, and hence their seniority, because of labor-force interruptions due to childbearing and rearing; (2) by reducing their incentive to invest in additional education or on-the-job training for purposes of occupational advancement; (3) by limiting the number of hours, time, and energy, they can commit to the work force because of familial constraints on their time; (4) by encouraging them to maximize job characteristics other than status or earnings (for example, better working hours, convenient job location); and (5) by limiting their geographic mobility (Hudis 1976). Since these factors do not operate for never-married women directly, and because their total amount of labor-force experience more closely approximates that of men (Treiman and Terrell 1975c), women who never marry should be more likely than ever-married women to pursue nontraditional work options and to optimize income-producing activities (that is, to be more like men in their occupational choice and attainment patterns).

Selecting a Committed Never-Married Group

The problem with making comparisons between ever-married and never-married women is that single women tend to be younger than married women, and hence likely to still be in school. This is a problem for two reasons. First, young workers are generally employed in different occupations from older workers. Second, among the younger women are an unknown number whose occupational decisions are affected by an anticipated assumption of the traditional responsibilities of marriage. To the extent that men and women are socialized to have different expectations regarding their adult roles, women may not have the same incentive as men to invest in education or on-the-job training to improve their occupational opportunities.[1] In order to make a more appropriate comparison of ever- and never-married women, a group of never-married women should be chosen whose current labor-force behavior and occupational choice are not affected by an anticipation that their stay in the workplace is a temporary one (that is, women who make employment decisions in much the same way as men do).

To select a more committed never-married group, I selected only those women older than the average age at which women in the particular country were likely to first marry.[2] Although conceptually, it would have been desirable to use a more stringent criterion (perhaps the age by which 75 percent of all women had married), the potential loss of cases made such a choice unacceptable. As it was, selecting a more committed never-married group resulted in a loss of a large number of cases (since the never married tend to be younger than the married), and hence a reduction in the reliability in the estimates of the percentage employed. The choice of mean age at first marriage as the cutoff point, however, appears to have been a satisfactory compromise. Although the reduction in cases was large for some countries, the cases eliminated were likely to be those still in school and those women in the labor force prior to an anticipated marriage. The resulting sample of older or committed never-married women is thus a best guess approximation of a group of women whose labor-force decisions are closest to those of men than that of all married or all single women.

Basic Assumptions

The basic assumption underlying the discussion thus far is that a woman's decision to work, and her occupational outcomes, are dependent on her marital and childrearing responsibilities, and not vice versa. I have thus ignored the likelihood that the causality runs in the other direction as well: that a decision regarding marriage and/ or children, especially how many children, depends on one's labor-force or occupational choices or expectations. Certainly, the historical relationship between women's labor-force participation and their fertility, and hence the amount and extent of their family responsibilities, has been a reciprocal one. Decreasing birth rates, completion of childbearing at an earlier age, and increasing life expectancy have all interacted to increase the proportion of all women engaged in paid employment outside the home (see Chapter 1). On the other hand, women's entry into the labor force in increasing numbers in recent years has further reduced fertility, and hence the level of

women's family responsibilities. Using data from the National Lon-
gitudinal Study of Young Women, Waite and Stolzenberg (1976)
found that this reciprocal relationship also operates at the individual
level.

The finding that labor-force plans affect fertility expectations suggests that the relationship between marital status and occupational
attainment is more complicated than the one being tested here. Labor-
force and fertility expectations presumably affect one's initial occupational choice, which usually occurs prior to marriage and childbearing; this initial job choice in turn affects whether and when one
marries, whether one has children, and how many children one has.
Initial job choice and subsequent marital and childrearing choices
both, in turn, affect one's occupational options later in life.

If appropriate data were available to test this more elaborate model,
one would expect to find that women who anticipated continuous
labor-force attachment would decrease their fertility expectations, and
make their initial job choice on the same basis as men do: expecting
a full life's work in the labor market, they would make investment
decisions (for example, regarding education and on-the-job training)
and job choices that optimize their opportunity for advancement and
economic and other nonmonetary returns. Unfortunately, it is possible
to test only a small piece of this more complicated process of
occupational attainment: the effect of current marital status on current
occupational position.[3]

Evidence of Marital Status Effects on Attainment

What evidence is there that marital responsibilities negatively affect
women's attainment? The present section documents what is known
about marital status differences in labor-force behavior, occupational
distribution, and patterns of attainment.

Labor-force behavior. It is possible to estimate the extent to which
marital and childcare responsibilities affect the employment options
of women by comparing the participation rates of never- and ever-
married women. Since never-married women do not have the same
home responsibilities as ever-married women, one would expect that
their levels of participation and age patterns of participation would
be closer to those of men than their ever-married counterparts. The
evidence for the United States suggests that this is the case. In 1982,
62 percent of all never-married women sixteen and older, and 51
percent of married (husband present) women, were in the labor force.
The comparable figures for never-married and married (wife present)
men were 70 and 80 percent, respectively (U.S. Bureau of the Census
1983, 57). These marital status differences for women are conservative

estimates since never-married women are likely to be younger on average than married women, and hence more likely to be in school. The Census Bureau (1982, 382) reports that 61 percent of married (spouse present) women age twenty-five to forty-four, and 82 percent of never-married women of the same age, were employed in 1981. Comparable figures for men were 97 and 88 percent, respectively.

Married women with children younger than eighteen are least likely to participate in the labor force: 67 percent of United States married (husband present) women sixteen to forty-four with children between the ages of six and seventeen, and 49 percent with children younger than six, were in the labor force in 1982 (U.S. Bureau of the Census 1983, 57). Data published by the Organisation for Economic Cooperation and Development (1975, Figure 2 and Table 6) document that the higher level of participation of single women, relative to married women and especially married women with children, holds true in other industrialized countries as well. Moreover, in each of the OECD countries for which data are available, the age pattern of participation of unmarried women is much closer in shape to the inverted U-shape male pattern than to the low level of participation characteristic of married women (OECD 1975, Figure 2).

Occupational distribution. Although few researchers have addressed marital status differences in occupational distribution on a comparative basis, Sewell and his colleagues (1980) documented that never- and ever-married women do differ in their occupational distributions. The authors found that never-married women are more likely than married women to be employed in professional or technical employment. Additionally, the likelihood that a woman is employed in a professional position decreases with the number of children she has. On the other hand, marriage and childbearing increase the likelihood that women work in clerical, retail sales, and service employment.[4]

The finding that married women, and especially married women with children, are more likely than single women to be employed in service-sector occupations (for example, clerical, retail, and service jobs) suggests that these occupations may be easier to reenter and/or perhaps more compatible with home and childcare responsibilities than other traditionally female or male employment. Similarly, the requirements of professional and managerial occupations, specifically continuous labor-force attachment, seem more likely to be compatible with the characteristics of (especially older) never-married women, the group most likely to have a well-established labor-force commitment. In line with this expectation, Grossman (1979, 47) recently documented that, among women, it is single women over twenty-five who were most likely to work in professional and managerial jobs.

Several researchers have also found marital status differences in the average prestige and status of women's jobs. Sewell and his coauthors (1980) found that the average SEI score for women's current occupation ranges from 40 for married women with three or more children to 54 for never-married women. Similarly, Treiman and Terrell (1975b) and Hudis (1976) found that never-married women, had a prestige advantage over their married counterparts (in the former study, the disadvantage due to marriage was 5.7 and 2.9 prestige points for white and black women, respectively).[5]

Presenting comparative data for seven industrial societies, Gaskin (1979, Table 6–4) found that although marital status differences in occupational distribution do exist, they are not as substantial as sex differences. Using a detailed occupational classification (see Chapter 3, note 2), Gaskin reported indexes of dissimilarity between men and single women ranging from 52 to 76, with a seven-country average of 66. The indexes for the comparison between all men and married women are similar, ranging from 44 to 70 (the seven-country average is 61). The index for married and single women exceeds 24 in only two of Gaskin's seven countries (in Germany, the index is 35 and in Italy it is 37). Gaskin's results suggest that although women's marriage and childrearing responsibilities might explain a small part of the sex difference in occupational distribution, a large residual gender effect remains.

Occupational attainment. While earlier studies found that single and married women work in jobs of slightly different status, they also reported that the process of attainment is substantially similar for these two marital groups (Treiman and Terrell 1975b; McClendon 1976). The lack of a marital status difference in Treiman's and Terrell's study is particularly noteworthy given the sample they used. Because it consisted of women aged thirty to forty-four, the likelihood of a large premarried group is minimized, and hence comes close to approximating a committed female labor force. Only Sewell and his coauthors (1980, Table 10) found marital status differences when they controlled for age and introduced first job into the attainment model: (1) the effect of first job on current job is greatest for never-married women and decreases with increasing marital and childcare responsibilities, and (2) the direct effect of schooling on current occupation is lowest for never-married women and increases somewhat with marriage and childcare responsibilities.

MARITAL STATUS DIFFERENCES IN LABOR-FORCE BEHAVIOR

The present section examines marital status differences in the labor-force behavior of ever- and never-married women in the twelve countries used in this study. Table 6.1 describes the modal woman worker in these countries as either currently or formerly married. The percentage of the twenty to sixty-four-year old female labor force who ever married ranges from a low of 58.8 percent in the Netherlands (an early peak country) to a high of 88.5 in Sweden, with a twelve-country average of 78.9 percent.[6] These data indicate that women workers are no longer in the labor force just until they marry, as has been the case historically (see Chapter 1). Instead, the majority of women workers are, or have been, married and, by implication, face dual responsibilities of work and family.

That marriage and childrearing responsibilities affect how much women work is evident in Table 6.2. With the exception of Finland,

Table 6.1 Composition of the Female Labor Force, Employed Women 20–64, for Twelve Industrialized Countries (Number of cases in parentheses)

Country	Percentage ever married[a]
Austria	80.4 (331)
Denmark	87.8 (287)
Finland	81.4 (323)
Germany (Fed. Rep.)	77.9 (418)
Great Britain	83.0 (287)
Israel	72.7 (4201)
Japan	79.8 (424)
Netherlands	58.8 (142)
Northern Ireland	64.2 (212)
Norway	86.7 (177)
Sweden	88.5 (332)
United States	85.8 (1221)

[a] Ever married includes those women who are currently married (and living with spouse), widowed, divorced, and separated.

Japan, and Sweden, where the two marital groups are about equally likely to be employed, never-married women are, as expected, more likely to work than ever-married women. In addition, except for Finland and Sweden, never-married women are substantially more likely than their married counterparts to work full time.

The anomalous result for Finland may, in part, be a consequence of the high participation rate for women in that country. Recall that 77 percent of Finnish women aged twenty to sixty-four were employed at some time during the year prior to the survey date (see Table 3.1). In addition, as Figure 3.1 showed, the age pattern of participation of Finnish women is similar to that of Finnish men (that is, an inverted U-shape pattern). If childbearing and rearing fails to reduce the proportion of all women who work, which is what the Finnish single peak pattern suggests, it cannot then be argued that family responsibilities significantly limit women's participation in the work force, although they may well affect the kinds of jobs in which women work. Sweden's small marital difference may be attributable to similar factors (the participation rate for Swedish women aged twenty to sixty-four is 70 percent, a rate second only to Finland among the twelve countries in this study). Thus, in societies where a high rate of female participation is the norm, marital responsibilities may not play an important role in explaining differences in participation, since most women work regardless of their marital status.

One of the problems with the data in Table 6.2 is that never-married women are, on average, younger than ever-married women, and hence likely to still be in school. Including these women thus reduces estimates of the overall percentage of women employed, and especially the percentage working full time. For this reason, comparing all never-married women with all ever-married women is not, strictly speaking, the best possible comparison.

In an attempt to correct for the younger average age of the never-married women in Table 6.2, Table 6.3 compares the percentage employed, and the percentage employed full time, of all never-married women (from Table 6.2) with comparable percentages for more committed never-married women (that is, never-married women older than the average age at which women in their country first marry). As previously described, the reason for restricting the analysis to older never-married women is to determine whether the lack of a marital difference in employment status in some of the countries (in Table 6.2) is due to an overrepresentation of younger (and hence school-age) women in the never-married group.

The results in Table 6.3 strongly support this expectation. Selecting committed never-married women substantially increases the per-

Table 6.2 Employment Status of Women (All Ages), by Marital Status, for Twelve Industrialized Countries (in percentages)[a]

| Country | Employment status | | | | N |
	Full time	Part time	Not at work	Total	
Austria					
Ever married	27.3	9.5	63.2	100.0	741
Never married	56.3	6.7	37.1	100.1	125
Denmark					
Ever married	32.0	22.9	45.1	100.0	463
Never married	43.4	20.2	36.4	100.0	99
Finland					
Ever married	58.7	12.6	28.7	100.0	373
Never married	45.5	26.1	28.4	100.0	134
Germany (Fed. Rep.)					
Ever married	13.2	16.2	70.6	100.0	1127
Never married	54.5	10.3	35.2	100.0	171
Great Britain					
Ever married	19.7	20.2	60.1	100.0	628
Never married	61.8	4.1	34.1	100.0	100
Israel					
Ever married	13.4	14.6	71.9	99.9	11283
Never married	23.8	10.4	65.8	100.0	3726
Japan[b]					
Ever married		42.1	57.9	100.0	865
Never married		41.9	58.1	100.0	253
Netherlands					
Ever married	13.2	10.8	76.0	100.0	353
Never married	60.3	4.6	35.2	100.1	118
Northern Ireland[b]					
Ever married		28.2	71.9	100.1	497
Never married		73.3	26.7	100.0	109
Norway					
Ever married	19.0	21.6	59.5	100.1	385
Never married	32.9	23.7	43.4	100.0	76
Sweden					
Ever married	27.7	37.4	34.9	100.0	455
Never married	28.6	39.8	31.6	100.0	98
United States					
Ever married	28.0	11.8	60.2	100.0	2755
Never married	49.4	11.5	39.0	99.9	327

[a] See Chapter 2 for definition of employment status variable.
[b] Full-time/part-time status not available.

centage employed, as well as the percentage employed full time, in each of the countries with anomalous results. When age is controlled, the percentage of employed never-married women in Finland, Japan, and Sweden increases substantially, from 72 to 89 percent in Finland, from 42 to 80 percent in Japan, and from 68 to 83 percent in Sweden. In contrast, the percentage of ever-married women employed does not change when age is controlled (figures not shown). In Finland and Sweden, where a full-time/part-time distinction is available, the

Table 6.3 Employment Status of Never-Married Women, by Age Group, for Twelve Industrialized Countries (in percentages)[a]

Country	Percentage employed		Percentage employed full time		Number of cases	
	All never married	Older never married[b]	All never married	Older never married[b]	All never married	Older never married[b]
Austria	63.0	70.1	56.3	63.6	125	71
Denmark	63.6	72.0	43.4	64.0	99	28
Finland	71.6	88.6	45.5	81.8	134	43
Germany (Fed. Rep.)	64.8	60.8	54.5	55.0	171	84
Great Britain	65.9	59.9	61.8	55.4	100	51
Israel	34.2	70.7	23.8	48.1	3726	526
Japan[c]	41.9	79.5	—	—	253	32
Netherlands	64.9	84.6	60.3	76.9	118	51
Northern Ireland[c]	73.3	69.5	—	—	109	89
Norway	56.6	77.8	32.9	74.1	76	24
Sweden	68.4	83.3	28.6	62.5	98	26
United States	60.9	65.1	49.4	55.6	327	228

[a] Chapter 2 for definition of employment status variables.
[b] "Older never-married women" includes only those older than the age at which the average woman in the particular country marries. See text for additional details.
[c] Full-time/part-time status not available.

percentage of never-married women working full time also increases markedly when age is controlled.

In addition to Sweden, the very low rates of full-time participation (in Table 6.2) of all never-married women in Israel and Norway are also unexpected. Restricting the analysis to older never-married women convincingly documents that these low rates of participation are also due to an overrepresentation of young, school-age women in the samples: the percentage working full time increases substantially when the age range is restricted (from 24 to 48 percent in Israel, from 33 to 74 percent in Norway, and from 29 to 62 percent in Sweden).[7]

Although the case base is small in some of the countries, the magnitude and consistency of the increases leave little doubt that the anomalous results observed in Table 6.2 are primarily attributable to the large number of young (and hence school-age) women in the samples. Overall, the more committed the never-married women, the more their labor-force behavior resembles that of men.

MARITAL STATUS DIFFERENCES IN OCCUPATIONAL DISTRIBUTION

The present section investigates the occupational distributions of ever- and never-married women. I first examine marital indexes of dissimilarity, comparing them with the gender indexes presented in Chapter 3. I then turn to a replication of previous United States research on marital differences in occupation and finally examine these differentials crossculturally.

Marital Indexes of Dissimilarity

Table 6.4 (column 1) presents indexes of dissimilarity based on the occupational distributions of never- and ever-married women (the occupational distributions themselves are presented in Table 6.6). I use the seven-category, rather than the fourteen-category, occupational classification (ILO 1969) because of the small number of never-married women in many of the countries. These indexes should thus be viewed as lower-bound estimates: if a more detailed occupational classification system were used, somewhat larger indexes would be expected. Even with the seven-category classification, however, the sample sizes of several countries (in particular, Denmark, Norway, and Sweden) are small. The data presented for these countries should thus be viewed as suggestive.

The indexes in column 1 suggest that small to moderate differences exist in the kinds of jobs at which ever- and never-married women work. The scores range from a very low 9.6 percent in West Germany

Table 6.4 Indexes of Dissimilarity Between Gender and Between Marital Groups[a]

Country	(1) Between ever- and never-married women (7-category)	(2) Between older ever- and older never-married women (7-category)	(3) Between men and women (14-category)	(4) Between men and women (7-category)	(5) Between men and ever-married women (7-category)	(6) Between men and never-married women (7-category)	(7) Between men and older never-married women (7-category)
Austria	15.5	20.7	37.6	27.7	30.2	31.8	29.8
Denmark	19.6	[20.8]	50.4	45.4	44.8	54.2	[51.8]
Finland	27.2	26.4	41.2	39.2	35.9	56.4	49.6
Germany (Fed. Rep.)	9.6	11.8	42.6	32.0	32.4	35.0	39.0
Great Britain	25.1	34.5	51.1	43.1	40.7	44.0	51.4
Israel	20.8	10.3	45.8	40.7	40.0	38.0	42.6
Japan	43.4	[43.0]	27.6	25.6	35.1	39.8	[34.6]
Netherlands	15.4	17.0	50.2	43.6	42.2	45.2	48.1
Northern Ireland	21.3	24.9	43.6	39.6	39.2	39.8	41.0
Norway	23.7	[31.8]	41.8	34.6	34.2	49.4	[47.6]
Sweden	22.4	[28.6]	60.0	54.3	53.6	64.9	[73.0]
United States	10.2	16.1	46.8	43.0	40.6	50.8	53.5

[a] Brackets indicate that one of the comparison groups used to calculate the index had less than thirty cases. In columns (2) and (7), the female samples were restricted to those older than the mean age at first marriage for women in that country.

to a high of 43.4 percent in Japan. Most of the countries fall within the 15 to 25 percent range, indicating small to moderate differences between ever- and never-married women. The twelve-country average is 21.2, meaning that 21 percent of the married women would have to change occupations to make their distribution equal to that of never-married women. Although not as large as gender differences in occupational distribution—the twelve-country average for the gender difference (based on the seven-category classification) is 39.1 (calculated from column 4)—the indexes are sufficiently large in most countries to merit serious consideration.

Japan is again the anomaly: marital differences in occupation in this country are substantially larger than gender differences (the gender and marital indexes are 26 and 43 percent, respectively). In Chapter 3 it was suggested that the relatively lower gender index in Japan is due to the large proportion of women working in agriculture. The relatively high Japanese marital index occurs for similar reasons. The large number of women employed in agriculture, noted in Table 3.3, is shown in Table 6.6 to be composed almost entirely of married women. Nearly half of the never-married Japanese women (but only 8 percent of the married women) work in clerical jobs. In contrast, 45 percent of married Japanese women, but only 4 percent of never-married women, are employed in agriculture. Most of these women are probably family farm workers: 77 percent of the women engaged in agriculture in Japan in 1972 were "family helpers" (OECD 1975, 23).

As mentioned in Chapter 1, the observed decrease in the labor-force participation of Japanese women (at least between 1965 and 1972) occurred only among married women, the traditional family farm workers (OECD 1975, 16), reflecting the very recent shift of the Japanese economy from a primary to a secondary (and tertiary) economy (Singelmann 1978). The results in Table 6.6 suggest that never-married Japanese women, with their lesser marital and child-rearing responsibilities, are evidently better able than their married coworkers to move into these newly emerging service occupations (for example, clerical, sales, and service jobs). Similar factors may be important in Finland, where nearly one-third of ever-married women still labor in agricultural employment (never-married Finnish women, like Japanese never-married women, are more likely to be concentrated in clerical and service occupations). Consistent with this interpretation, Finland has a relatively large index of marital dissimilarity (27 percent), second only to that of Japan.

Because single women are, on average, much younger than married women, it might be expected that the indexes presented in column 1 of Table 6.4 represent conservative estimates of the difference in the occupational distributions of ever- and never-married women. The lower marital indexes, relative to the gender indexes, might reflect the concentration of never-married women in particular occupations because they are young and hence inexperienced, or because they are in the labor force only temporarily prior to an anticipated marriage. To the extent that this is the case, occupational differences between ever- and never-married women might be partially masked. To address this, age is again controlled for and the occupational distributions are recalculated. The results of these calculations are presented in column 2 of Table 6.4 (Appendix G presents the accompanying occupational distributions).

The evidence in columns 1 and 2 supports, for the most part, the expectation that controlling for age increases the marital status differences in occupational distributions: in nine of the twelve countries, the marital index increases when the samples include only those older than the average age at first marriage (however, in only five of the countries is the increase as large as 5 percent). Comparing Table 6.6 with Appendix G describes why this increase occurs. The United States result is typical: excluding women younger than the average age at first marriage substantially increases the proportion of never-married women working in professional and technical employment. The occupational distribution of ever-married women remains approximately the same when age is controlled.

The Israeli result is an anomaly with the index of marital dissimilarity decreasing by 10 percent when age is controlled. As was true in the United States case, controlling for age substantially increases the percentage of never-married women engaged in professional employment (compare Table 6.6 with Appendix G). Unlike the United States, however, the increase in the percentage of professional workers among older never-married women in Israel brings these women to a parity with married women, rather than increasing the marital difference as is true in the remaining countries. Notably, the percentage of married women working in professional employment in Israel is the highest of any of the included countries, which probably reflects the overrepresentation of women from relatively high status social origins (see discussion in Chapter 5).

The remainder of Table 6.4 presents various gender indexes computed between men and different groups of women. Column 3 presents the indexes derived from comparing the occupations of all men and all women (repeating the information in Table 3.3 for the fourteen-category classification); column 4 presents the comparable indexes computed on the basis of the collapsed seven-category classification (repeating the information provided for some countries in Table 4.1). Comparing columns 3 and 4 thus allows an estimate of the loss of precision in each country due to collapsing the occupational classification. The largest decreases occur in Austria and Germany, where the indexes drop by 9.9 and 10.6 percent, respectively, due to the loss of prestige distinctions within each major group. These prestige distinctions are particularly important in distinguishing between which jobs are done by men and which by women. In Germany, for example, eliminating the prestige distinction in the professional category leads to the conclusion that men and women are equally likely to be employed in professional jobs. While this observation is technically correct, it is also misleading, since men have been shown to be more likely to work in high-prestige, and women in low-prestige, professions (see Table 3.3). This same loss of detail also occurs in the sales, service, and production categories. Gaskin's (1979, Chapter 5) larger gender indexes, based on even finer occupational distinctions, provide additional evidence that the level of aggregation used in this study underestimates the gender and marital differences in occupational distribution.

The indexes presented in columns 5 through 7 compare the amount of dissimilarity between the occupational distributions of all men and ever-married, never-married, and older never-married women, respectively. Regardless of the female sample used, the gender differences are, with the one exception again of Japan, notably larger than the marital differences reported in column 1. The comparisons most relevant to this study's task are those between columns 5 and 6 and 5 and 7. Recall that human-capital theory implies that the occupational distributions of never-married women should be more similar to those of men than those of ever-married women. The present data, however, contradict this expectation. The indexes computed between the occupational distributions of men and never-married women (column 6) are larger than those between men and ever-married women (column 5) in eleven of the twelve countries, although in only five of the countries is the difference as large as 5 percent. These results indicate that although the labor-force participation of never-married women is relatively closer to that of men than that of ever-married women, their occupational distribution is more dissimilar to men's than that of ever-married women.

When men's occupational distribution is compared with that of committed never-married women (column 7), the group expected to most closely approximate the male pattern, the indexes widen even further in seven countries, although in only two is the increase as large as 5 percentage points. The Israeli result is worth noting since the relative position of the never-married groups reverses when age is controlled: the gender index between never-married women and men is larger than that between ever-married women and men, but only when the younger Israeli women are excluded from the sample.

Replication of Previous United States Results

In order to understand why the occupational distribution of never-married women is more dissimilar, relative to men's, than that of ever-married women, a fuller investigation is needed of the nature of the marital status differences previously reviewed. Table 6.5 documents marital status differences in occupational distribution for the United States; the next section presents results for the remaining countries. Because of the larger sample from the United States than from most of the remaining countries, it is possible to use the more detailed fourteen-category classification for the United States only. Replicating Sewell's and his colleagues' (1980) results, the largest percentage of each marital group works in clerical employment (33 and 36 percent of the ever- and never-married women, respectively). Never-married women are shown to be slightly more likely to be employed in both high- and low-prestige professional employment than ever-married women, although not in administrative and managerial occupations.

Support for these generalizations is strengthened when age is controlled. Committed ever-married women do not differ from all ever-married women in the likelihood that they work in professional jobs. On the other hand, the likelihood that never-married women work in high- and low-prestige professional employment increases by 3.7 and 4.3 percent, respectively. Employment in service jobs also differs by marital status, but in a more complicated way: never-married women are somewhat more likely than married women to be employed in high-prestige, but slightly less likely to be employed in low-prestige, service occupations. Finally, ever-married women are more likely to work in (high- and medium-prestige) production employment than never-married women, a finding that remains when age is controlled.

These findings suggest that marital status affects the kinds of jobs in which women in the United States work. These effects, although small, are in the direction predicted by human-capital theory: marriage reduces the likelihood that women work in the more prestigious jobs. However, if human-capital theory is correct, then why is there greater dissimilarity in Table 6.4 between the occupational distributions of men and never-married women than between men and ever-married women? Comparing men's occupational distribution (repeated from Table 3.3) with each female sample permits one to address this question (see Table 6.5). There are three basic components of the larger gender index between men and never-married women (and especially older never-married women): (1) never-married women are substantially more likely than men (and slightly more likely than ever-married women) to be employed in high-prestige clerical occupations; (2) never-married women are more likely to work in low-prestige professional and high-prestige service employment than men or ever-married women; and (3) never-married women are substantially less likely than men (and somewhat less likely than ever-married women) to be employed in high- and medium-prestige production employment.

It might be argued that the kinds of jobs in which never-married women work require both a greater investment in training and stronger labor-force commitment than the jobs in which ever-married women are employed. Certainly the female professions (for example, nursing, librarianship, and school teaching) require extensive educational investment and on-the-job training. Intermittent labor-force attachment for workers in these occupations would inevitably lead to depreciation of skills and a loss of bargaining power for women who wanted to leave the labor force temporarily and reenter these occupations later in life. The jobs in which ever-married women work (primarily clerical, production, low-prestige sales, and low-prestige service employment) require less educational investment and in most cases are more easily reentered after a labor-force absence. These latter jobs remain primarily entry-level positions since they usually have short career ladders.

In sum, the data suggest that, as human-capital theory predicts, never-married women work in somewhat different occupations than those in which their married counterparts work. As an explanation for occupational sex segregation, however, human-capital theory is limited, since it fails to explain why women who are more like men in their labor-force behavior and occupational commitment (as never-married women are) are likely to work in the female professions (or other prestigious female employment), rather than in typically male (and higher-paying) employment.

Crosscultural Results

The data in Table 6.6 suggest that other industrial societies duplicate the United States pattern of marital status differences. With two exceptions (Israel and Sweden), never-married women are more likely than married women to work in professional and technical jobs (only in Denmark, Great Britain, the Netherlands, and the United States is the difference as large as 5 percentage points). When the sample is restricted to postmarriage age women (Appendix G), the percentage

Table 6.5 Occupational Distributions of Employed Men and Women, by Marital Status and Age, for the United States, 1974-1977 (in percentages)

Occupational category[a]	All men	All women		Older women[b]	
		Ever married	Never married	Ever married	Never married
1. High-prestige professional and technical	11.1	6.2	9.7	6.3	13.4
2. Administrative and managerial	10.4	3.4	0.9	3.5	1.3
3. High-prestige clerical and related	2.4	22.7	24.4	22.8	25.5
4. High-prestige sales	4.4	1.8	0.0	1.8	0.0
5. Low-prestige professional and technical	6.5	15.1	18.0	15.3	22.3
6. High-prestige agricultural	3.4	0.1	0.0	0.1	0.0
7. High-prestige production and related	18.4	4.9	2.3	4.9	1.9
8. High-prestige service	5.0	8.4	11.1	8.6	10.8
9. Medium-prestige production and related	19.1	9.4	4.1	9.3	5.7
10. Low-prestige clerical and related	4.7	10.0	11.5	9.7	8.9
11. Low-prestige sales	5.1	5.1	6.5	5.0	3.8
12. Low-prestige agricultural	1.7	0.4	0.0	0.4	0.0
13. Low-prestige service	2.9	10.7	8.8	10.7	5.1
14. Low-prestige production and related	5.0	1.8	2.8	1.8	1.3
Total	100.1	100.0	100.1	100.2	100.0
N	1939	1095	204	1065	148
Index of dissimilarity	—	14.6		19.1	

[a] Standard International Occupational Classification (Treiman 1977, Chapter 9).

of never-married women in professional positions increases in ten of the twelve countries (in seven of those by 5 or more percentage points). Only Swedish older married women are more likely than their never-married coworkers to work in professional jobs (and this result might well be due to sampling error, given the small case base).

With the exception of Japan, large portions of both ever- and never-married women in every country work in clerical occupations. Where an economy has a large agricultural component (for example, in Austria, Denmark, Finland, Japan, and Norway), ever-married women are much more likely than never-married women to be agricultural workers. The greater representation of married women in agricultural employment reflects the traditional mode of production, where work was based in the home and husband and wife each contributed to the productive effort. The concentration of ever-married women in clerical occupations is somewhat less in these five countries (at least when age is controlled).

Finally, in most (although not all) of the countries, ever-married women are more likely to be employed in sales and service work than never-married women, at least when young, single workers (who are more likely to work in such jobs) are eliminated from the sample.

Marital Status Differences in Occupational Attainment

In Chapter 5, I found little support for the human-capital expectation that ever- and never-married women differ significantly in their occupational wage rate, net of other relevant variables. Contrary to expectation, the marital status coefficient for women was significant in only two countries and, moreover, in seven of the twelve countries the sign was opposite that expected. Because no interaction terms were included, the only test could be for differences in the average occupational wage rate and not for marital status differences in the process of occupational attainment. The present section investigates this issue more thoroughly, describing how ever- and never-married women reach their somewhat different occupational destinations. The expectation of human-capital theory is evident—because never-married women do not contend with the same responsibilities as ever-married women, their pattern of attainment should be closer to that of men's.

Hypotheses and Analytic Strategy

In the gender comparisons, most of the hypotheses concerned differences in rates of occupational returns to various background

Table 6.6 Occupational Distribution of Employed Women (All Ages), by Marital Status, for Twelve Industrialized Countries (in percentages)

Occupational Category[a]	Austria		Denmark		Finland		Germany (Fed. Rep.)		Great Britain		Israel	
	Ever married	Never married	Ever married	Never married	Ever married	Never married	Ever married	Never married	Ever married	Never married	Ever married	Never married
1. Professional and technical	6.3	10.8	15.5	27.9	12.6	15.7	14.2	15.4	12.2	25.9	31.8	22.9
2. Administrative and managerial	0.7	0.0	0.0	0.0	1.2	1.4	0.0	0.0	1.1	0.0	1.2	0.6
3. Clerical and related	21.4	30.1	27.7	23.3	17.3	27.1	39.0	46.4	27.5	38.8	25.5	36.7
4. Sales	12.3	10.8	10.2	2.3	10.6	5.7	16.3	16.7	12.9	7.9	9.9	4.6
5. Service	17.9	14.5	18.4	23.3	14.6	28.6	12.5	5.5	25.9	9.4	17.8	13.6
6. Agricultural	23.2	13.3	18.9	11.6	30.7	11.4	3.2	0.6	1.3	1.4	3.2	1.4
7. Production and related	18.2	20.5	9.2	11.6	13.0	10.0	14.8	15.4	19.0	16.5	10.6	20.3
Total	100.0	100.0	99.9	100.0	100.0	99.9	100.0	100.0	99.9	99.9	100.0	100.1
N	264	77	232	49	250	69	292	93	249	64	3143	1264
Index of dissimilarity	15.5		19.6		27.2		9.6		25.1		20.8	

Occupational Category[a]	Japan		Netherlands		Northern Ireland		Norway		Sweden		United States	
	Ever married	Never married	Ever married	Never married	Ever married	Never married	Ever married	Never married	Ever married	Never married	Ever married	Never married
1. Professional and technical	6.7	9.9	21.1	28.1	16.8	17.6	18.7	21.9	24.8	13.9	21.3	27.6
2. Administrative and managerial	0.9	1.1	0.9	0.0	1.3	1.2	1.4	6.3	0.4	0.0	3.4	0.9
3. Clerical and related	7.6	45.8	31.2	35.4	13.4	30.6	21.6	25.0	29.0	50.0	32.7	35.9
4. Sales	11.0	12.4	20.2	9.4	8.1	9.4	14.4	12.5	12.6	5.6	6.9	6.5
5. Service	11.3	8.8	18.3	18.8	31.5	14.1	15.8	28.1	23.5	25.0	19.1	19.8
6. Agricultural	45.4	4.5	3.7	0.0	2.7	4.7	19.4	6.3	1.3	0.0	0.5	0.0
7. Production and related	17.1	17.5	4.6	8.3	26.2	22.4	8.6	0.0	8.4	5.6	16.1	9.2
Total	100.00	100.0	100.0	100.0	100.0	100.0	99.9	100.1	100.0	100.1	100.0	99.9
N	354	97	85	75	140	80	126	29	259	39	1095	204
Index of dissimilarity	43.4		15.4		21.3		23.7		22.4		10.2	

[a] International Standard Classification of Occupations (ISCO) major groups (International Labour Office 1969).

factors, rather than differences in composition. I focused on this type of difference because previous literature showed that men and women differed little, if at all, in their distributions on the independent variables used. The results of the Chapter 5 analyses confirmed that much of the gender differences in occupational attainment are due to differences in rates of return to background factors and investments and not to differences in composition, although this is not true for all the countries. In the present analysis, however, I have a different expectation: if human-capital theory is correct, never- and ever-married women should differ not only in the returns they receive for identified background factors but also in their distribution on these variables.

Social origins. The results in Chapter 5 showed that in the majority of the twelve countries, there were no gender differences in social origins. However, in four of the five countries with a significant gender difference, women are more likely to come from high status backgrounds, a finding contrary to what had been hypothesized. On the basis of these results I speculated that those women most likely to work are those who would stand to benefit the most by continuing to work (or, alternatively, to lose the most by not working). If there are origin differences in the probability of women working, and if higher-status women are more likely to work than lower-status women, one might expect that higher-status women would be less likely to marry than lower-status women. As a result, never-married women may come from higher status social origins than ever-married women.

Because the extent of participation and the occupational position of married women has historically depended on their family of procreation (for example, husband's earnings and number of children), I expect that their occupational attainment will be less dependent than that of never-married women on their social origins. Never-married women, with their lesser home responsibilities, should have an attainment pattern similar to that of men—the benefit they receive from social origins should be greater than that of married women.

Age. Not only are never-married women in general younger than married women, since many of the former are in the labor force in the interval between schooling and marriage, but the effect of age on occupational attainment should also differ by marital status. Age, in the present context, is a crude proxy for experience and it is well known that never-married women have substantially more labor-force experience than ever-married women, at least in the United States (Treiman and Terrell 1975b; U.S. Bureau of the Census 1984). Since married women are likely to spend a much larger proportion of their working lives out of the labor force, or to work intermittently or part time when they do work, one would expect their occupational return to age to be less than that of never-married women whose attachment is more continuous.

There is another, equally plausible, hypothesis for how age affects the occupational achievement of ever- and never-married women. Wolf (1976) and Wolf and Rosenfeld (1978) documented the non-responsiveness of women's occupational status to work experience. Although age is associated with incumbency in higher-status occupations for men, this is not the case for women (although see Rosenfeld 1980). Additionally, researchers have noted that women have a flatter age-earnings profile than men, even when they have the same achieved education (Barrett 1979, 37). While theoretically these findings might be attributable to the fact that most women are married and married women have less accumulated years of experience, Sawhill (1973) found that even single women have the same flat age-earnings profile characteristic of married women. Evidence such as this leads one to speculate that age may return very little in the way of occupational wage benefits to married or single women, and hence that ever- and never-married women will have similar occupational wage returns to age [a result that would be consistent with Rosenfeld (1980)].

As in Chapter 5, an age-squared term is added to allow for the possibility that the relationship between age and occupational attainment is curvilinear.

Education. One would expect that women with strong labor-force commitment would make a greater investment in education than women who anticipate leaving the labor force to raise a family. As previously described, this group of committed women was approximated by identifying never-married women who are older than the average age at first marriage in their country. It was assumed that these women would be more like men in taking advantage of opportunities for advancement. If these expectations are proven, never-married women, and especially older never-married women, should have completed more years of schooling than married women. For the same reasons, I expect the occupational return to education to be greater for never-married women. If women anticipate a lifetime of labor-force participation, and have no one else on whom they can depend for financial security, one would expect that they would pursue the same income-optimizing behavior that is traditionally followed by men. One manifestation of this type of behavior is enrolling in educational, vocational, or on-the-job training programs that have payoffs with respect to occupational position.

As with age, there is an alternative hypothesis to consider. It may be that educational investment has the result that never-married women work in different kinds of jobs than married women, but that these jobs do not really differ to any significant extent with respect to occupational prestige and/or average income. Women may be inhibited from moving out of traditionally female jobs, either because of socialization or because of access barriers to typically male jobs. If this were true, then the occupational return to educational investment would not vary by marital status, and ever- and never-married women would tend to be employed in jobs with comparable salaries. The analyses in this chapter should help to choose between these two competing hypotheses.

To test these hypotheses, I follow a strategy similar to that used for the gender comparisons. First, I describe the distribution of the marital groups on each of the variables included in the analysis. Second, I estimate occupation models separately for ever- and never-married women within each country, using as the measure of occupation the wage-rate variable described earlier. The basic strategy used is to present the United States results as an illustration of the general pattern, and then to determine whether, or to what extent, patterns found in other countries duplicate the United States findings. The results for older women are described in the text as appropriate but are not provided in tabular form. As in the gender comparisons, the samples are restricted to include only those currently employed, aged twenty to sixty-four.

Distribution of Variables by Marital Status

Table 6.7 presents the means and standard deviations for the occupation models. I discuss only those marital status differences with a significance at the .05 level. Referring first to the United States data, the results confirm previous research documenting marital differences, and differences are always in the expected direction (although not always significantly so). Never-married women in the United States are substantially younger, better educated, and employed in higher-prestige jobs than their ever-married counterparts in the work force. There is no marital difference, however, in social origins, when either the prestige or wage-rate scale is used. Selecting only older women workers (data not shown) affects the gap between the marital status groups in the expected way: the age gap narrows by a year, while the gaps between women's educational achievement, occupational prestige, and occupational wage rate increase somewhat, by .2 years, 1.0 prestige points, and 2 points, respectively. Each of these marital differences remains significant for the sample of committed United States women. Significant differences in the average earnings of the jobs in which ever- and never-married women work emerge only when age is controlled, a reflection no doubt of a number of premarried women in the never-married group who are working in low-paying jobs until they marry.

The results for the remaining countries are largely similar to, but also differ in several respects from, the findings reported for the United States. Like the United States, ever- and never-married women in most of the countries come from similar social origins. The social origins of ever- and never-married women differ significantly only in Denmark, Germany, and Japan (although the Japanese difference disappears when age is controlled), and never-married women have the advantage. This finding provides support for the alternative hypothesis that women from higher-status backgrounds are relatively less likely to marry.

Not surprisingly, the means for age show that never-married women are on average significantly younger than married women in each country except Norway, where the result is of doubtful reliability. Even when older ever- and never-married women are compared, the two marital groups still differ significantly in age in eight of the twelve countries. Never-married women also complete more years of education than married women in all twelve countries, significantly so in eight. Part of this differential is undoubtedly due to the younger average age of the single women, and the fact that educational attainment is negatively correlated with age. Even when women older than the average age at first marriage are selected, never-married women are significantly more educated than married women in seven of the countries (Denmark, Finland, Germany, Great Britain, Israel, Northern Ireland, and the United States).

Despite their age and educational advantages, however, never-married women are able to translate age and schooling into higher prestige or occupational wages in only a few of the countries. Although, generally, never-married women are in the more prestigious and higher-paying employment, only in Denmark, Great Britain, and Japan are those differences in prestige and wage rate significant. In the United States, never- and ever-married women work in jobs of significantly higher prestige, but not in average wage rate. Older ever- and never-married women work in jobs of significantly higher prestige in Denmark, Great Britain, Northern Ireland, and the United States. Only in Great Britain and the United States, however, do older never-married women work in jobs with significantly higher wages than married women.

Table 6.7 Means and Standard Deviations for Models of Occupational Attainment for Currently Employed Women 20–64, by Marital Status, for Twelve Industrialized Countries[a]

Means

	Austria		Denmark		Finland		Germany (Fed. Rep.)		Great Britain		Israel	
	Ever married	Never married	Ever married	Never married	Ever married	Never married	Ever married	Never married	Ever married	Never married	Ever married	Never married
Father's occupation-prestige	37.3	39.0	37.8 *	44.2	39.0	38.8	41.2 *	44.8	46.3	50.5	41.1	41.8
Father's occupation-wage-rate[b]	28.3 *	30.2	27.9 *	37.3	28.3	27.4	31.6 *	37.7	—	—	43.1 *	42.9
Age	42.6 *	34.7	40.2 *	32.5	40.7 *	34.6	41.8 *	28.8	44.1 *	31.7	39.3 *	24.4
(Age*)²	114 *	195	146 *	208	139 *	221	135 *	210	159 *	224	172 *	142
Years of schooling	9.13 *	9.53	7.98 *	9.43	8.20 *	9.33	10.2 *	11.2	10.1 *	11.5	10.6	11.1
Respondent's occupation-prestige	35.7	35.6	37.8 *	43.6	37.8	39.8	40.3	41.4	37.5 *	43.8	42.4	41.7
Respondent's occupation-wage-rate scale	27.1	28.0	31.8 *	39.6	30.1	33.4	35.1	35.1	32.0 *	40.9	39.5	38.6

											Standard deviations
Father's occupation-prestige	10.0	12.1	10.0	13.1	8.37	8.29	11.8	9.82	21.6	20.0	12.8	15.8
Father's occupation-wage-rate scale[b]	18.2	19.0	18.9	26.1	17.5	16.5	16.2	16.3	—	—	24.7	28.2
Age	10.6	12.5	12.1	12.9	11.8	13.3	10.7	11.9	11.7	12.9	12.0	6.95
(Age*)²	123	165	140	126	133	147	164	124	148	119	199	82.3
Years of schooling	1.57	1.74	1.64	2.62	2.67	3.01	1.96	2.19	1.82	2.14	4.33	3.15
Respondent's occupation-prestige	11.2	11.5	10.1	11.3	11.8	12.4	11.8	10.4	12.8	10.8	13.5	12.9
Respondent's occupation-wage-rate scale	16.6	16.1	16.9	20.2	18.8	20.5	17.4	15.2	19.5	14.7	21.1	18.8
N[c]	232	60	219	34	232	50	286	79	228	42	2571	82

a For details of scoring see text and Chapter 2. Note: Age* = Age – mean of age.

b The father's occupational wage-rate variable could not be constructed for Great Britain, due to the way father's occupation was measured.

c Missing cases deleted pairwise, lowest number of cases reported.

* Difference in ever married and never married mean is significant at .05 level, 2-tailed test.

Table 6.7 Means and Standard Deviations for Models of Occupational Attainment for Currently Employed Women 20–64, by Marital Status, for Twelve Industrialized Countries[a] (Cont.)

	Japan		Netherlands		Northern Ireland		Norway		Sweden		United States	
	Ever married	Never married	Ever married	Never married	Ever married	Never married	Ever married	Never married	Ever married	Never married	Ever married	Never married
						Means						
Father's occupation-prestige	34.2 *	36.5	40.9	41.0	36.9	39.8	39.8	42.5	39.1	41.7	40.0	41.5
Father's occupation-wage-rate scale[b]	16.5 *	27.3	36.6	37.5	26.3 *	31.9	31.3	37.6	32.6	37.4	36.3	40.0
Age	42.8 *	25.4	36.0 *	27.6	42.1 *	33.8	39.8	40.7	40.4 *	33.3	40.6 *	28.8
(Age*)²	118 *	259	173	110	139 *	181	143	163	129 *	205	146 *	207
Years of schooling	10.0 *	11.1	9.97	10.5	10.3 *	11.1	8.64	9.09	8.66 *	9.77	12.3 *	13.5
Respondent's occupation-prestige	35.8 *	39.3	39.3	41.9	36.4	39.4	38.6	42.9	39.8	39.2	41.3 *	44.7
Respondent's occupation-wage-rate scale	28.5 *	38.1	35.4	39.5	31.7	34.0	32.2	39.9	34.9	35.2	37.7	40.9

Standard deviations

Father's occupation-prestige	7.49	8.71	13.8	12.9	13.3	13.8	9.71	12.9	10.6	12.1	11.6	11.9
Father's occupation-wage-rate scale[b]	24.1	25.3	26.0	25.5	19.9	25.2	21.6	25.7	22.0	25.6	27.4	28.5
Age	10.3	8.22	12.0	10.1	11.4	12.5	12.0	13.0	11.3	13.3	11.9	10.5
$(\text{Age}^*)^2$	136	99.6	247	166	154	128	126	145	129	126	148	117
Years of schooling	2.47	1.72	2.48	2.33	2.00	1.94	2.61	2.62	2.60	2.94	2.62	2.51
Respondent's occupation-prestige	9.57	8.73	14.0	12.1	13.7	12.5	12.7	11.2	12.9	10.4	12.8	12.7
Respondent's occupation-wage-rate scale	20.0	18.2	21.9	19.9	23.1	21.6	21.5	25.6	20.6	17.9	21.5	20.5
N[c]	297	68	80	52	129	70	125	20	257	32	899	147

[a] For details of scoring see text and Chapter 2. *Note:* Age* = Age − mean of age.

[b] The father's occupational wage-rate variable could not be constructed for Great Britain, due to the way father's occupation was measured.

[c] Missing cases deleted pairwise, lowest number of cases reported.

* Difference in ever married and never married mean is significant at .05 level, 2-tailed test.

Marital Status Differences in Attainment

United States results. Table 6.8 presents the prestige and wage-rate results for the United States to allow for comparability with previous work. In addition, I include prestige and wage-rate models for the sample of women older than the average age at first marriage to eliminate the premarried women from the never-married group.

Referring first to the prestige results for all women, ever- and never-married women differ in their process of prestige attainment, but only minimally. Notably, the differences are generally in the direction opposite that predicted by human-capital theory. Education is, as in previous research, the most important determinant of occupational prestige, and the prestige return to this factor does not vary by marital status (or at most, benefits married women only slightly more than never-married women). This result holds even when age is controlled.

Although occupational attainment depends mainly on education, married women's attainment also depends in part on their social origins, which affects occupation in the expected positive way. The stronger effect of father's occupation on the attainment of married women is contrary to expectation: married women benefit more from their social origins than never-married women. This finding might reflect the fact that for some married women, work is more a matter of choice than it is for never-married women. Hence, married women may not work unless they find a position suitable to their social position. Finally, ever-married women's attainment also depends in part on age, an effect that loses significance when the smaller group of postmarriage age women are compared.

This overall picture of occupational attainment does not change much when the occupational wage-rate scale is employed: education is still the primary indicator of women's occupational attainment. The occupational wage attainment of married women also depends in part on their age and social origins, and that of never-married women depends partly on age (although the age effect for the latter group loses significance when postmarriage age women are compared). Although not much can be made of the difference, since the never-married coefficients are not significant, it is interesting to note that the metric coefficients for father's occupation are identical for the two marital groups in the wage-rate model, while the comparable coefficients for the prestige models favor married women. These results indicate that although married women's social origins return occupational prestige, they do not return occupational wages. Finally, the wage rate return to age is greater for never-married women than for ever-married women (although the age coefficient for older never-

Table 6.8   Coefficients of a Model of Occupational Attainment, for Currently Employed Women 20–64, by Age and Marital Status, United States (1974–1977)[a]

	Father's occupation[b]	Age	(Age*)²	Years of schooling	Intercept
		Metric coefficients			
Prestige model—all women					
Ever married	.120*	.077*	−.001	2.65*	.844
Never married	.042	.138	−.013	2.50*	7.82
Prestige model—older women[c]					
Ever married	.117*	.062	.001	2.64*	1.50
Never married	.083	.131	−.011	2.49*	6.21
Wage-rate model—all women					
Ever married	.068*	.155*	.001	3.91*	−19.2
Never married	.067	.317*	−.013	3.41*	−14.2
Wage-rate model—older women[c]					
Ever married	.071*	.134*	.002	3.89*	−18.4
Never married	.073	.249	−.004	3.32*	−12.2

	Father's occupation[b]	Age	(Age*)²	Years of schooling	R²
		Standardized coefficients			
Prestige model—all women					
Ever married	.109*	.072*	−.006	.542*	.336
Never married	.040	.114	−.117	.496*	.277
Prestige model—older women[c]					
Ever married	.107*	.056	.007	.546*	.340
Never married	.079	.110	−.095	.524*	.289
Wage-rate model—all women					
Ever married	.086*	.086*	.004	.476*	.249
Never married	.094	.162*	−.076	.418*	.230
Wage rate model—older women[c]					
Ever married	.090*	.072*	.014	.478*	.252
Never married	.103	.127	−.022	.422*	.212

[a] Age* = Age − mean of age. Means and standard deviations for "all women" equations provided in Table 6.7.
[b] For prestige models, father's and respondent's occupation = prestige; for wage-rate models, father's and respondent's occupation = wage rate scale.
[c] "Older women" includes those women older than the average age at which women in the particular country first marry.
* Metric coefficient is twice its standard error.

married women is not significant), reflecting the greater labor-force continuity, and hence accrued seniority, of never-married women.

In sum, these results generally replicate those of previous analyses (Treiman and Terrell 1975b; McClendon 1976) in suggesting that ever- and never-married women in the United States have similar processes of occupational attainment. Although small differences emerge when the occupational wage-rate variable is employed (for example, an equalizing of the ever and never married returns to social origins and a larger occupational return to age for never-married women), the overall pattern of results is largely similar to those found in previous work.

Crosscultural results. The results for the United States suggest that the patterns of occupational wage (or prestige) attainment of ever- and never-married women are largely similar, a finding contrary to human-capital theory. Before speculating as to why these findings occur, I turn to a discussion of whether the same pattern of occupational wage attainment exists in other industrial societies. Table 6.9 presents the coefficients for each country, separately for the two marital groups, and only for the occupational wage-rate models.[8]

The expectation was that never-married women, like men, would receive greater occupational rewards from their social origins than married women. Although I found in Chapter 5 that men accrue significant occupational advantages from their social origins in each country except Sweden, there is little evidence in the present data that never-married women receive similar benefits. The effect of social origins on occupational attainment is significant for never-married women only in Finland and Germany, and only in Finland in the expected positive direction.[9] Interestingly, Finland is the country where women's age pattern of participation most closely approximates the male pattern, and hence women, like men, have a chance to build on their social origins. On the other hand, social origins significantly benefit married women in Austria, Japan, and the United States. As suggested, this could reflect the greater flexibility that some married women have regarding labor-force entry.

As with social origins, there is little support for the human-capital expectation that age benefits the occupational outcomes of never-married women more than ever-married women. Only in the United States is age significantly associated with never-married women's occupational wage rate and even that association loses significance in the postmarriage age comparison. Moreover, in half of the countries the relationship is in the wrong direction. When older women are selected, the age coefficient for never-married women in Finland gains significance, probably reflecting the greater participation and attachment to the labor force of Finnish women. Finally, age is a significant predictor of the occupational position of married women in Finland, Israel, and the United States, although only in Finland and the United States are the coefficients in the expected positive direction.

Education is the primary determinant of the occupational wage rate for both ever- and never-married women, as the relatively large standardized coefficients for this variable attest. The only country in which education is not significant is in Norway, where a small case base for never-married women is probably the cause. Greater educational achievement is thus associated with incumbency in jobs of higher income, regardless of marital status. There is some support for the expectation that never-married women receive the larger return to education. In seven of the twelve countries (eight when post-marriage age women are compared), the return to education is slightly greater for never-married women, in one it is the same, and in four it is less than that of ever-married women. For those societies where

Table 6.9   Coefficients of a Model of Occupational Wage-Rate Attainment, for Currently Employed Ever- and Never-Married Women, 20–64, in Twelve Industrialized Countries[a]

		Father's occupation[b]	Age	$(Age^*)^2$	Years of schooling	Intercept
		Metric coefficients				
Austria	Ever married	.165*	−.026	.007	4.47*	−18.1
	Never married	−.055	−.075	.004	6.52*	−30.7
Denmark	Ever married	−.002	−.034	−.000	4.83*	−5.24
	Never married	.151	−.245	.009	4.72*	−4.46
Finland	Ever married	.058	.239*	−.002	4.90*	−21.2
	Never married	.224*	.227	−.028*	5.29*	−23.8
Germany	Ever married	.091	−.035	−.011	3.15*	2.83
(Fed. Rep.)	Never married	−.231*	−.040	−.012	4.41*	−1.85
Great Britain	Ever married	−.027	.162	−.008	4.70*	−20.2
	Never married	−.062	−.119	−.001	3.10*	12.5
Israel	Ever married	.022	−.080*	−.008*	3.09*	10.4
	Never married	−.002	.259	.011	3.86*	−12.2
Japan	Ever married	.218*	.162	−.021*	2.90*	−8.63
	Never married	−.054	.394	.031	3.29*	−15.1
Netherlands	Ever married	.062	.264	−.002	4.00*	−16.0
	Never married	.035	−.018	.029	4.45*	−11.2
Northern	Ever married	.009	.104	.005	7.35*	−49.3
Ireland	Never married	.126	.077	−.019	7.34*	−50.6
Norway	Ever married	−.014	−.017	.007	6.02*	−19.8
	Never married	.261	.385	.013	4.36	−27.3
Sweden	Ever married	.063	.085	−.002	4.61*	−10.2
	Never married	−.254	−.330	−.014	5.04*	9.39
United	Ever married	.068*	.155*	.001	3.91*	−19.2
States	Never married	.067	.317*	−.013	3.41*	−14.2

[a] Age* = Age – mean of age. Means and standard deviations for all variables are provided in Table 6.7.
[b] For Great Britain only, father's occupation = prestige of father's occupation; for all other countries, father's occupation = wage-rate scale.
* Metric coefficient is twice its standard error.

Table 6.9 Coefficients of a Model of Occupational Wage Rate Attainment, for Currently Employed Ever- and Never-Married Women, 20–64, in Twelve Industrialized Countries[a] *(Cont.)*

		Father's occupation[b]	Age	$(Age^*)^2$	Years of schooling	R^2
		Standardized coefficients				
Austria	Ever married	.181*	−.016	.051	.423*	.280
	Never married	−.065	−.058	.041	.707*	.477
Denmark	Ever married	−.002	−.024	−.004	.469*	.226
	Never married	.196	−.157	.056	.613*	.528
Finland	Ever married	.054	.150*	−.017	.697*	.500
	Never married	.181*	.147	−.201*	.775*	.714
Germany	Ever married	.084	−.022	−.101	.356*	.187
(Fed. Rep.)	Never married	−.248*	−.032	−.099	.635*	.395
Great Britain	Ever married	−.030	.098	−.058	.436*	.174
	Never married	−.085	−.104	−.009	.451*	.243
Israel	Ever married	.026	−.046*	−.078*	.633*	.454
	Never married	−.003	.096	.050	.645*	.416
Japan	Ever married	.262*	.083	−.142*	.357*	.260
	Never married	−.075	.178	.168	.312	.089
Netherlands	Ever married	.074	.144	−.017	.453*	.232
	Never married	.045	−.009	.241	.519*	.323
Northern	Ever married	.008	.052	.035	.639*	.410
Ireland	Never married	.147	.044	−.111	.661*	.543
Norway	Ever married	−.014	−.009	.043	.731*	.538
	Never married	.263	.196	.074	.447	.457
Sweden	Ever married	.067	.047	−.011	.582*	.369
	Never married	−.364	−.247	−.100	.831*	.619
United	Ever married	.086*	.086*	.004	.476*	.249
States	Never married	.094	.162*	−.076	.418*	.230

[a] Age* = Age − mean of age. Means and standard deviations for all variables are provided in Table 6.7.
[b] For Great Britain only, father's occupation = prestige of father's occupation; for all other countries, father's occupation = wage-rate scale.
* Metric coefficient is twice its standard error.

the results are in the expected direction, the ratio of the married to never married return ranges from a low of .69 in Austria to a high of .93 in Finland, with a seven-country average of .83 (when post-marriage age women are selected, the eight-country average is .82). In those countries where the return to education is greater for married women, the four-country average is .81.

CONCLUSION

The data presented in this chapter offer some support for the human-capital expectation that never-married women are more similar to men than ever-married women, but not in all respects related to their occupational behavior. Marital responsibilities substantially affect women's labor-force behavior: women who have never married have substantially higher rates of labor-force participation and are more likely to work full time than women who married.

These marital status differences in labor-force behavior translate into modest differences in the kinds of work done by ever-married and never-married women. While the largest percentage of each marital group works in clerical employment, never-married women are more likely than their married coworkers to work in professional jobs. Ever-married women, in contrast, are predominantly employed in sales and service work. One important factor contributing to crosscultural variation in marital differences in occupational distribution is the existence of a large agricultural work force. Where agriculture still plays a large role in a nation's economy, married women are relatively more likely than never-married women to work in this sector, while never-married women are employed in clerical occupations.

While small marital differences in occupational distribution exist, they should not be overinterpreted. Comparisons of indexes of dissimilarity reveal that the dissimilarity between marital status groups is substantially less than gender differences. Notably, when men's occupational distributions are compared with those of ever-married and never-married women, respectively, the indexes of dissimilarity are larger for the latter. This finding suggests that when women are more like men in their labor-force behavior and occupational commitment (as never-married women are), they are more likely to work in the female professions (or other prestigious female employment), rather than typically male occupations.

Attainment analyses reveal small marital differences in distribution and in rates of return to relevant background factors. While marital differences in social origins exist in only a few countries, never-married women are generally both younger and better educated than their married counterparts. Modest differences in the types of jobs done by ever- and never-married women do not always translate into differences in average prestige or wage rate. In only three countries are the prestige and wage rates of never-married women's jobs significantly higher than those of ever-married women, and in the United States never-married women work in jobs of significantly higher prestige, although not higher wage rate.

Contrary to human-capital theory, the attainment patterns in the United States of ever- and never-married women are largely similar. These United States results are not necessarily typical of other industrial societies. Although no support exists for the human-capital expectation that never-married women should gain greater benefits for their social origins and age, they are better able to capitalize on their education in seven countries.

What do these data tell us about the occupational positions and employment outcomes of women and the adequacy of human-capital theory to explain occupational segregation by sex? On the whole, they suggest that never-married women are more like men in their labor-force behavior, in the sense that they are more likely than married women to participate in the labor force, and to work full time when they are employed. At the same time, however, despite their greater labor-force commitment, never-married women are concentrated in very different jobs from those in which men are employed, working in clerical jobs and the female professions rather than in higher-paying male employment. As was learned in Chapter 3, the female professions do not differ very much in prestige or average pay, from the kinds of jobs in which married women are employed—clerical, sales, and service work. Thus, although marital responsibilities affect the kinds of jobs in which women work, these differences are not large and for the most part do not translate into differences in prestige or wage rate. The one benefit accruing to never-married women (in seven of the countries) is a relatively greater occupational return to education. Married women in these countries evidently catch up in other ways, however, since in six of these seven countries the occupational attainments of ever- and never-married women (measured by either prestige or wage rate) do not differ significantly. This is all the more surprising when one considers the higher achieved education of never-married women.

In sum, human-capital theory is useful in explaining certain differences in labor-force and occupational behavior of men and women. However, this perspective offers little insight into why never-married women, similar in many ways to men in their labor-force behavior and occupational commitment, are limited in their occupational outcomes and differ little from married women in their returns to background factors and personal characteristics. Women's economic disadvantage, relative to men, thus cannot be attributed solely to differential marital responsibilities. Never-married women, who have no immediate marital responsibilities, do not fare much better than married women in their occupational attainment.

CHAPTER SEVEN

Conclusions

A major purpose of the present study has been to test whether, and to what extent, observed gender differences in occupational distribution reflect women's need to reconcile market and domestic tasks. Because of its comparative approach, the analysis has also permitted an examination of whether sex differences in occupational distribution and attainment are attributable to historical or cultural circumstances unique to individual countries, or to more fundamental features of industrial society.

Before examining (in Chapters 4 through 6) the processes that help to produce occupational sex segregation, Chapter 3 investigated whether sex differences in occupational composition observed in the United States are also found in other industrial societies. Despite substantial variability in age patterns of labor-force participation, and in the extent to which women engage in paid employment, the evidence suggests substantial crosscultural occupational sex segregation. Moreover, the same occupations tend to be held mainly by women or mainly by men in all twelve countries. Whereas men predominate in administrative and managerial occupations, as well as in high- and medium-prestige production jobs, women predominate in high-prestige clerical, low-prestige sales, and low-prestige service occupations. Finally, occupations held mainly by women are low paying across industrial societies: incumbents in traditionally female occupations are underpaid relative to their average educational achievement.

Chapter 4 described the mobility patterns of men and women that help to produce these gender differences in occupational location. In each country, I found that, for both men and women, occupational position depends to a significant extent on father's occupation, as well as on the sex-segregated occupational structure. Sex differences in social origins play a small role in only a few countries. Country variation does exist in the process of occupational mobility, in sex differences in social origins, and in gender differences in occupational distribution, but these differences are very small relative to the gender and mobility differences existing within countries.

Chapter 5 described additional determinants of occupational achievement. Proposing a measure of occupation designed to reflect differences in the wage rates of men's and women's jobs, I viewed occupational attainment as a function not only of social origins, but also of age, marital status, and years of schooling. These crosscultural analyses revealed differences in the process of occupational attainment of men and women in the United States that previous prestige models failed to detect. For each sex within each country, education was consistently the most important predictor of occupational position. For men, however, education was generally one of several factors with significant effects on occupational position: men successfully capitalize on their social origins, age, and marital status in many of the countries. Although women, like men, are allocated to their occupational positions mainly on the basis of education, in most countries this is the only identifiable factor affecting women's occupational outcomes. In addition, the female occupational return to personal characteristics and investments is generally less than men's.

Decomposing significant gender differences in occupational attainment revealed that in several countries (although not in the United States) at least part of the occupational gap between men and women is attributable to gender differences in background factors (for example, the higher-status social origins of women or men's greater educational preparation). In most of the countries, however, sex differences in rates of return to background and individual characteristics are the major reason for women's inferior occupational achievement. Only in Israel is women's occupational attainment, as measured by the wage-rate scale, significantly greater than men's, and this difference can be entirely accounted for by differences in background factors (for example, women's higher-status social origins).

Chapter 6 addressed more fully the question of whether observed gender differences in the process of occupational attainment, as well as in occupational distribution, could be attributed in large measure to women's marital responsibilities, or whether other factors must also be taken into account. I examined this question by comparing the labor-force behavior, occupational composition, and attainment patterns of ever- and never-married women. Because many never-married women are in the labor force prior to an expected marriage, it was necessary to approximate a more committed group of career workers by restricting the never-married sample to those older than the average age of first marriage in the particular country. If human-capital theory is correct, then the labor-force behavior, occupational position, and attainment patterns of never-married women (and especially older never-married women) should be more similar to those of men than to the patterns of married women, since the former are less likely to have family and childrearing responsibilities.

The evidence offers some support for the hypothesis that never-married women are more similar to men than ever-married women, but not in all respects related to their occupational behavior. Like men, never-married women have substantially higher rates of labor-force participation and are more likely to work full time than married women in each of the twelve countries. Differing rates of labor-force continuity apparently translate into modest differences in the kinds of work done by ever-married and never-married women. Although both marital groups are most likely to work in clerical occupations, never-married women tend to work in professional employment while married women work in sales and service jobs. Comparing the occupational distributions of ever- and never-married women with that of men, however, reveals that men's and never-married women's distributions are more dissimilar than those of men's and married women's. This greater dissimilarity is apparently related to the fact that never-married women's greater labor-force continuity is more likely to result in incumbency in the female professions, than in male occupations.

There is some minimal support for the human-capital explanation that the occupational attainment processes of ever- and never-married women differ. Two types of marital differences emerge: differences in distributions and differences in rates of return, the former being the more important of the two. Never-married women tend to be younger and more educated than their married counterparts. Although in most cases, never-married women are in the more prestigious and higher-paid employment, these differences are significant in only a few countries. In the United States, for example, never-married women work in jobs of significantly higher prestige than married women, but not in jobs that are significantly better paid.

Although not true in the United States, never-married women do receive a larger occupational return to education than married women in seven countries. In these countries, the married return averages 83 percent of the never married return. There is little support, however, for the human-capital expectation that never-married women, like men, are better able than married women to capitalize on their age and social origins. These determinants of occupational position in general benefit neither married nor single women.

Taken as a whole, these results offer little support for the human-capital explanation for the gender gap in occupational location. Although never-married women are like men in their labor-force behavior, are somewhat more likely than their married counterparts to work in the professions, and are more educated than married women, they are not generally able to translate these advantages into higher-prestige or better-paid employment. Instead, the overall generalization one can derive from the results for the twelve countries is that married and never-married women hardly differ at all in their occupational attainment patterns. The small marital differences in occupational attainment found in a few of the countries are not sufficient to explain the observed gender gap in occupational achievement.

Human-capital theory is thus useful in explaining only a small part of the difference in the labor-force and occupational behavior of men and women. It is not particularly useful in explaining why never-married women, more similar to men in their labor-force behavior and occupational commitment, are still limited in their occupational opportunities and differ little from married women in their process of attainment. In sum, women's relative economic disadvantage cannot be attributed solely or even in substantial part to sex differences in marital responsibilities.

Although data limitations preclude testing the institutional explanation for gender differences in occupational concentration, the marital results described are certainly consistent with the expectation that women are limited in their access to high-paying employment because of their sex. Women may well have the option of entering only certain kinds of jobs, in secondary or peripheral sectors, because employers hesitate to hire them in occupations where continuity on the job is highly valued. Given the fact that women as a whole are more likely than men to be intermittently attached to the labor force, even women who individually have strong labor-force attachment might be less likely to be hired in jobs where continuous labor-force attachment is rewarded with access to promotional opportunities and economic rewards.

According to the institutional view, once women enter jobs in the peripheral sector, transferring to primary jobs is difficult, since most such job openings are at the entry level. If it is true that women are locked into certain types of jobs, which allow no opportunity for advancement nor offer any economic return to experience, then it is not surprising that never-married women's greater education, their more continuous labor-force attachment, and their somewhat greater concentration in the female professions do not translate into high-paid employment. Because of their sex, they may be initially allocated to employment where little advancement is possible, regardless of the extent of their labor-force continuity.

The consistency of the results across the countries suggests that occupational sex segregation observed in the United States is not due simply to the biases of employers, nor to the way that work is organized in the United States. Instead, the problem is more generally true across industrial society.

POLICY IMPLICATIONS: THE UNITED STATES PERSPECTIVE

Since over half of all United States women work (52 percent in 1981) and, moreover, since women currently constitute 43 percent of the employed population in this country (U.S. Bureau of the Census 1982, 378, 383), public policy deliberations must include consideration of the special problems facing women workers. The dramatic growth in the number of women entering the labor market is a recent phenomenon, and this increase has occurred most notably among young women with children, those most burdened by family responsibilities. Because employment projections indicate that the number of women who work outside the home is likely to increase even further in the near future (Smith 1979), now is the time for policymakers to begin to formulate appropriate policy strategies regarding women's employment.

This issue takes on even greater import when viewed in the context of decreasing fertility (perhaps below replacement level) in the United States (Westoff 1978; Ryder 1979) and elsewhere [see Rizza (1982) for a description of Finland's decreasing levels of fertility]. Barring repressive restrictions on contraceptive availability or women's employment options, more women will work a greater proportion of their adult years outside the home, thereby further reducing their fertility. In order to ensure continued fertility at the replacement level, policymakers and employers must respond with programs and policies designed to allow women to more easily accommodate work and family roles.

Not only has the traditional family structure undergone a transformation as a result of women's increased participation in the paid work force, but this transformation has wide-ranging implications for a whole host of public policy issues, including welfare programs, federal and state income tax schemes, childcare programs, social security and pension policies, housing and urban planning issues, and employment and training programs. It is only recently, however, that researchers and policymakers have begun to address these issues and to investigate possible policy approaches related to women's employment (Council of Economic Advisers 1973; Kreps 1976; Kanter 1977; Cook 1979; Kamerman 1979; Smith 1979; Ratner 1980; Treiman and Hartmann 1981). I do not propose to review past research on policy strategies, nor to present a comprehensive list of possible policy approaches. Instead, I limit myself to a brief description of how the results of the present study inform policy deliberations regarding women's employment. In particular, I describe the usefulness of crosscultural research in formulating and deciding among alternative policy strategies for ensuring equal employment opportunities for men and women.

As previously described, one focus of the present study has been to test the human-capital explanation for the different occupational locations of men and women. To the extent that the data support this theory, the appropriate policy strategy would be to reduce the effect of family demands that constrain women (but not men) from engaging in paid employment. Possible strategies include increasing the number and quality of childcare facilities, subsidizing employers to provide on-site childcare facilities (in factories, offices, and so forth), subsidizing parents to make their own childcare arrangements, increasing the availability of part-time and flexible working arrangements, and pursuing other policies designed to reduce the constraining aspects of one's family life on one's choice about whether and in what job to work.

Alternatively, to the extent that the data suggest that family responsibilities are not the only or even major explanation for the sex-segregated occupational structure, other policy approaches are required. Among the kinds of approaches suggested in the latter case would be affirmative action strategies designed to increase men's and women's representation in sex-atypical employment (for example, government subsidies to employers to train men and women for jobs mainly held by the opposite sex, special vocational education and apprenticeship programs).

The results of the present study imply that a two-pronged policy approach would be most useful. Since women's family responsibilities do affect labor-force behavior, United States policymakers should pursue strategies that lessen the constraining effect these responsibilities have on women's labor-force and occupational opportunities. Simultaneously, and perhaps more importantly, policymakers must investigate approaches that increase women's (and men's) access to nontraditional employment opportunities.

In pursuing the first of these strategies, policymakers need to recognize explicitly that family responsibilities are not just a woman's problem, but men's and society's responsibility as well. A crucial first step is the recognition that childcare is a parental and not just a maternal responsibility. Several researchers (Kanter 1977; Cook 1979) have offered suggestions to this end, in encouraging policy-makers to begin to consider the effects that the traditional pattern of employment has had, and will continue to have, on family life. Kanter (p. 3) speculated that organizations of the future will have to pay attention to the effects of their policies on the families of their employees and, in fact, allow the needs of families to influence their organizational decisions. Cook (p. 17) noted that strategies for achieving this goal are currently under discussion in the United States, including longer annual leaves, sabbatical leaves for industrial workers, and four-day work weeks. Such policies would serve to relax the rigid requirement that one's attachment to the labor force must be without interruption, a pattern more easily followed by men than by women, and encourage the recognition that one's work life should be responsive to one's family life (and not just vice versa). Such innovations would permit a greater sharing of family and childcare responsibilities.

The marital status results in Chapter 6, however, suggest that policies to reduce the effect of family responsibilities on women's employment options, whether by encouraging the sharing of family responsibilities or by increasing the availability of childcare, would not in themselves sufficiently alter women's disadvantaged occupational and economic position. The current findings imply that even when women have more continuous attachment patterns, their occupational patterns are still quite different from those of men. Gender differences in occupational location cannot be attributed solely to differential marital responsibilities, since even women without such responsibilities are in relatively low-paying female employment. Such a situation dictates that more aggressive affirmative action measures are required to reduce the structural barriers that tend to keep women in low-paid employment, since the source of occupational inequality lies partly in the structure of the labor market itself.

Crosscultural research is particularly useful in informing policy deliberations because it indicates the extent to which labor market inequalities observed in the United States are idiosyncratic to this country and to what extent they are more generally true of other countries. Different policy strategies are suggested depending on the outcome of such analyses. For example, if the occupational sex segregation observed in the United States had been unique to this country, then the policy approach would be the more simple one of adapting proven policies and workable programs from other countries to the United States context. Given that this phenomenon is more generally true across industrial societies, however, the implication is that these patterns are firmly entrenched and hence not easily changed.

The further finding that gender differences in occupational attainment cannot be solely attributed to differences in marital responsibilities, and that this is generally true across industrial societies, suggests that major changes in the organization of work are required to make any significant progress toward equal employment opportunity. Policymakers need to examine, for example, how the market compensates employment and how gender enters into the wage-setting process; how firms recruit and promote their employees and whether this process differs by sex; what barriers keep women out of higher-paying jobs and how these obstacles can be overcome; how the workplace might be restructured to accommodate women's child-bearing, and men's and women's childrearing, roles; and how government policies and programs such as social security, tax schemes, and veterans' benefits have inhibited women's full and equal participation in the United States labor force and what policies should be pursued to alleviate the impact of these factors (see Roos and Reskin 1984 for an overview of institutional barriers that inhibit men's and women's access to sex-atypical jobs).

A major implication of the present study is that solutions to occupational and economic inequality by sex observed in the United States labor market are not easily found, since the same inequality exists in other industrial societies. However, even though no other industrial society has found a workable set of programs to reduce the rigidly sex-segregated occupational structure does not mean that United States policymakers cannot learn from initiatives currently underway in other countries. To the contrary, several countries have developed a set of innovative policies designed to better women's position in the labor market. For example, as a direct result of its decision to discontinue importing foreign labor, the Swedish government instituted several policies to encourage the entry of married women into the labor force and to make work life more compatible with family responsibilities (Cook 1979, 48). Swedish initiatives include such programs as: recruiting workers into nontraditional employment by subsidizing employers who hire men and women in jobs where their sex is underrepresented; providing public daycare facilities; emphasizing educational and vocational training; instituting sex quotas for firms receiving regional development support; adopting a system of individual taxation; and instituting parental as opposed to maternity leave (see Jonung 1977, 1978a for additional details on these and other policies).

Any policy deliberations regarding women's employment issues and equal employment policy should thus include a close investigation of programs already underway in other countries, as well as in the United States. Crosscultural investigations of policy strategies regarding equal employment opportunity, most notably those by Cook (1979), Kamerman and Kahn (1978), Kamerman (1979), Ratner (1980), and Rizza (1982), are particularly useful in laying out policy alternatives potentially useful for the United States context. In addition to investigating initiatives currently underway in other countries, policymakers should continue to play an active role in international organizations. Most importantly, the Organisation for Economic Cooperation and Development (OECD) and the International Labour Office (ILO) have provided a useful international perspective on women's employment and equal opportunity issues for several years (OECD 1975, 1979; ILO 1950, 1975a, 1975b, 1976, 1979a, 1984). In sum, an international perspective not only allows the recognition that problems of labor market inequality are firmly entrenched, since they occur in other societies as well, but it also offers examples of policy strategies potentially useful for achieving the goal of equal employment opportunity in the United States.

Appendixes

Appendix A Country-Specific Occupational Titles, by Occupational Category, Country, and Sex[a]

Occupational category and country	Country-specific occupational titles	
	Male jobs	Female jobs
1. High-prestige professional and technical		
Austria, Great Britain, and the Netherlands	Chemists; Electrical and Electronics Engineers; Medical Doctors; Economists; Accountants; University and Higher Education Teachers; Secondary Education Teachers; Teachers, n.e.c.	University and Higher Education Teachers; Secondary Education Teachers; Special Education Teachers; Teachers, n.e.c.
Denmark, Finland, Norway, and Sweden	Civil Engineers; Mechanical Engineers; Medical Doctors; Teachers in Particular Subjects (esp. Secondary School)	Medical Doctors; Dentists; Head Nurses; Pharmacists, Owner-directors of Pharmacies; Physiotherapists, Occupational Therapists; Teachers in Particular Subjects (esp. Secondary School)
Germany (Fed. Rep.)	Chemists; Architects and Town Planners; Civil Engineers; Electrical and Electronics Engineers; Mechanical Engineers; Medical Doctors; University and Higher Education Teachers; Secondary Education Teachers	Mechanical Engineers; Pharmacists; Medical X-Ray Technicians; Accountants; Secondary Education Teachers; Special Education Teachers
Israel	Civil Engineer; Mechanical Engineer; Physician; Lawyer; Economist; Teacher; Secondary Education	Physician; Academic Worker in Humanities (e.g., Philosopher); Teacher, Secondary Education; Teacher, Special Education; Technician in Medical Science
Japan	Professional and Technical Workers and Self-Employed Workers in General; Teacher: Primary, Junior and Senior High School, University, Special School, Kindergarten, Etc.; Specialist in Medicine and Health: Doctor, Pharmacist, Midwife, Public Health Nurse, Nurse, Masseur, Specialist in Moxacautery, Veterinarian, Other Related Workers	Teacher: Primary, Junior and Senior High School, University, Special School, Kindergarten, Etc.; Specialist in Medicine and Health: Doctor, Pharmacist, Midwife, Public Health Nurse, Nurse, Masseur, Specialist in Moxacautery, Veterinarian, Other Related Workers

	Male	Female
Northern Ireland	Teachers, n.e.c.; Civil, Structural, Municipal Engineers; Mechanical Engineers; Accountants, Professionals, Company Secretaries and Registrars; Surveyors, Architects	Medical Practitioners (Qualified); Head Nurses; Teachers, n.e.c.; Professional Workers, n.e.c.
United States	Accountants; Electrical and Electronic Engineers; Lawyers; Clergymen; Secondary School Teachers	Accountants; Personnel and Labor Relations Workers; Clinical Laboratory Technologists and Technicians; Secondary School Teachers; Teachers, except College and University (n.e.c.); School Administrators (n.e.c.)

2. Administrative and managerial

	Male	Female
Austria, Great Britain, and the Netherlands	Members of Legislative Bodies; General Managers; Production Managers (Except Farm); Managers, n.e.c.	Members of Legislative Bodies; High Administrative Officials; General Managers; Managers, n.e.c.
Denmark, Finland, Norway, and Sweden	Officials in Leading and Higher Positions in Public Administration; Managers of Establishments (Managing Directors, etc.); Technical Managers; Commercial Managers; Other Occupations Related to Administration of Establishments and Organisations	Officials in Leading and Higher Positions in Public Administration; Managers of Establishments (Managing Directors, etc.); Technical Managers; Managers of Commercial and Ideal Organisations, Trade Union Managers; Other Occupations Related to Administration of Establishments and Organisations
Germany (Fed. Rep.)	High Level Officials, Judges, Those with Extensive Leadership Responsibility; Members of Legislative Bodies; General Managers; Production Managers (Except Farm); Managers, n.e.c.	None
Israel	Managers and Administrators Government Services, Municipal Services, and National Institutes; General Manager; Manager of Bank, Insurance Company; General Contractor; Other Managers (Nonpublic), n.e.c.	Managers and Administrators Government Services, Municipal Services, and National Institutes; General Manager; Manager of Bank, Insurance Company; Other Managers (Nonpublic), n.e.c.

a This table presents a listing, compiled separately for male and female jobs, of the detailed occupational categories included in each of the fourteen categories of the Standard International Classification of Occupations (Treiman 1977, Chapter 9) for each country (or set of countries). Countries with identical occupational classifications are grouped. Only those detailed occupations containing at least 5 percent of the male (or female) workers in the major occupation group are included.

Appendix A Country-Specific Occupational Titles, by Occupational Category, Country, and Sex[a] (Cont.)

Occupational category and country	Country-specific occupational titles	
	Male jobs	Female jobs
Japan	Other Executives and Managers: Manager of an Independent Enterprise, Chief of Personnel Office (Company), Branch Manager, Purchasing Section Chief (Department Store), Branch Manager of Bank, Chief of Loan Section (Bank), Inspector; President or Director of Company, Factory Manager, Consultant, Member of Board of Directors	Other Executives and Managers: Manager of an Independent Enterprise, Chief of Personnel Office (Company), Branch Manager, Purchasing Section Chief (Department Store), Branch Manager of Bank, Chief of Loan Section (Bank), Inspector; President or Director of Company, Factory Manager, Consultant, Member of Board of Directors
Northern Ireland	Ministers of the Crown, Members of Parliament (n.e.c.); Senior Government Officials; Local Authority Senior Officers; Managers in Building and Contracting; Managers in Mining and Production, n.e.c.; Company Directors; Managers, n.e.c.	Local Authority Senior Officers; Company Directors; Managers, n.e.c.
United States	Bank Officers and Financial Managers; Managers and Administrators (n.e.c.)	Bank Officers and Financial Managers; Managers and Administrators (n.e.c.)
3. High-prestige clerical and related		
Austria, Great Britain, and the Netherlands	Clerical Supervisors; Government Executive Officials; Bookkeepers and Cashiers; Correspondence and Reporting Clerks	Stenographers, Typists and Teletypists; Bookkeepers and Cashiers; Correspondence and Reporting Clerks
Denmark, Finland, Norway, and Sweden	Officials in Public Administration; Bookkeepers, Accountants; Office Clerks; Bank Clerks; Insurance Clerks	Bookkeepers, Accountants; Private Secretaries, Correspondents, Stenographers; Office Clerks; Bank Clerks
Germany (Fed. Rep.)	Civil Service Officials; Government Executive Officials; Bookkeepers and Cashiers	Government Executive Officials; Stenographers, Typists and Teletypists; Bookkeepers and Cashiers; Correspondence and Reporting Clerks

Israel	Clerical Supervisor in Government Service; Clerical Supervisor not in Government Service; Bookkeeper; Bank Teller, Post Office Clerk, Ticket Seller; General Clerical Office Workers	Bookkeeper; Bank Teller, Post Office Clerk, Ticket Seller; Typist, Secretary, Stenographer; General Clerical Office Workers
Japan	Other Clerical Workers; Office Workers in General (Including Company Employees); Public Servants in General; Employee of Government Organization; Accountant, Bookkeeper	Office Workers in General (Including Company Employees); Accountant, Bookkeeper; Radio Operator, Wireless Engineer, Telephone Operator
Northern Ireland	Civil Service Executive Officers	Typists, Shorthand Writers, Secretaries; Clerks, Cashiers (Supervisor)
United States	Inspectors, Except Construction, Public Administration; Office Managers (n.e.c.); Officials and Administrators; Public Administration; Bookkeepers; Clerical Supervisors; Computer and Peripheral Equipment Operators; Not Specified Clerical Workers	Bookkeepers; Secretaries (n.e.c.); Typists; Miscellaneous Clerical Workers; Not Specified Clerical Workers

4. High-prestige sales

Austria, Great Britain, and the Netherlands	Managers (Wholesale and Retail Trade); Working Proprietors (Wholesale and Retail Trade); Sales Supervisors; Buyers; Commercial Travelers and Manufacturers' Agents; Insurance, Real Estate and Securities Salesmen	Managers (Wholesale and Retail Trade); Working Proprietors (Wholesale and Retail Trade); Sales Supervisors
Denmark, Finland, Norway, and Sweden	Wholesalers; Retailers; Commercial Travelers; Buyers, Salesmen (Office)	Wholesalers; Retailers
Germany (Fed. Rep.)	Managers (Wholesale and Retail Trade); Working Proprietors (Wholesale and Retail Trade); Sales Supervisors; Buyers; Commercial Travelers and Manufacturers' Agents; Insurance, Real Estate and Securities Salesmen	Managers (Wholesale and Retail Trade); Working Proprietors (Wholesale and Retail Trade); Sales Supervisors; Technical Salesmen and Service Advisers; Commercial Travelers and Manufacturers' Agents

[a] This table presents a listing, compiled separately for male and female jobs, of the detailed occupational categories included in each of the fourteen categories of the Standard International Classification of Occupations (Treiman 1977, Chapter 9) for each country (or set of countries). Countries with identical occupational classifications are grouped. Only those detailed occupations containing at least 5 percent of the male (or female) workers in the major occupation group are included.

Appendix A Country-Specific Occupational Titles, by Occupational Category, Country, and Sex[a] (*Cont.*)

Occupational category and country	Country-specific occupational titles	
	Male jobs	Female jobs
Israel	Working Proprietors (Wholesale Trade); Store Owner; Buyers, Purchasing Agent; Traveling Salesman, Manufacturing Agent	Store Owner; Buyers, Purchasing Agent; Insurance Agent
Japan	Proprietor of Retail Store, Wholesale Store; Store Salesman, Salesgirl, Floorwalker (Supervisor); Salesman (Excluding Salesman at Insurance Company): Automobile, Newspaper, Bond Salesman	Sales Workers in General; Proprietor of Retail Store, Wholesale Store; Store Salesman, Salesgirl, Floorwalker (Supervisor); Insurance Agent and Salesman, Branch Chief (Life Insurance)
Northern Ireland	Proprietors and Managers, Nonfood Sales; Commercial Travelers, Manufacturers' Agents; Salesmen, Services, Valuers, Auctioneers; Sales Managers	Proprietors and Managers, Nonfood Sales
United States	Purchasing Agents and Buyers (n.e.c.); Sales Managers and Department Heads, Retail Trade; Sales Managers, Except Retail Trade; Insurance Agents, Brokers, and Underwriters; Real Estate Agents and Brokers	Credit Men; Sales Managers and Department Heads, Retail Trade; Insurance Agents, Brokers, and Underwriters; Real Estate Agents and Brokers; Insurance Adjusters, Examiners, and Investigators
5. Low-prestige professional and technical		
Austria, Great Britain, and the Netherlands	Physical Science Technicians; Draftsmen; Electrical and Electronics Engineering Technicians; Primary Education Teachers; Authors, Journalists, and Related Workers; Other Professional, Technical and Related Workers	Professional Nurses; Nursing Personnel, n.e.c.; Primary Education Teachers; Social Workers
Denmark, Finland, Norway, and Sweden	Engineers Working in Other Technical Branches; Civil Engineering Technicians; Technicians Performing Power-Electrical Work; Mechanical Technicians; Primary Education Teachers	Nurses; Auxiliary Nurses; Primary Education Teachers

Country		
Germany (Fed. Rep.)	Industrial Engineers; Draftsmen; Electrical and Electronics Engineering Technicians; Professional Nurses; Nursing Personnel, n.e.c.; Primary Education Teachers	Draftsmen; Medical Assistants; Professional Nurses; Nursing Personnel, n.e.c.; Primary Education Teachers; Pre-Primary Education Teachers; Social Workers
Israel	Teacher, Primary Education; Teacher, Other Education; Miscellaneous Engineering Technicians; Electrical, Electronic Engineering Technician; Mechanical Engineering Technician	Teacher, Primary education; Teacher, Pre-Primary Education; Professional Nurse; Uncertified Nurse, Midwife; Teacher's Aide
Japan	Other Professional or Technical Worker; Technician: Technician in Mining, Metallurgy, Machine, Electricity, Chemistry, Civil Engineering, Architecture, Etc.; Artist or Entertainer: Artist, Designer, Musician, Actor, Dancer, Photographer, Author, Reporter; Minister of Religion	Other Professional or Technical Worker; Technician: Technician in Mining, Metallurgy, Machine, Electricity, Chemistry, Civil Engineering, Architecture, Etc.; Artist or Entertainer: Artist, Designer, Musician, Actor, Dancer, Photographer, Author, Reporter; Social Worker
Northern Ireland	Builders (So Described): Clerks of Works; Nurses; Clergy, Ministers, Members of Religious Orders; Social Welfare and Related Workers; Draughtsmen; Laboratory Assistants, Technicians; Technical and Related Workers, n.e.c.	Nurses; Social Welfare and Related Workers
United States	Computer Programmers; Industrial Engineers; Elementary School Teachers; Draftsmen; Electrical and Electronic Engineering Technicians; Engineering and Science Technicians (n.e.c.); Painters and Sculptors	Registered Nurses; Elementary School Teachers; Teacher Aides, Except School Monitors; Practical Nurses

[a] This table presents a listing, compiled separately for male and female jobs, of the detailed occupational categories included in each of the fourteen categories of the Standard International Classification of Occupations (Treiman 1977, Chapter 9) for each country (or set of countries). Countries with identical occupational classifications are grouped. Only those detailed occupations containing at least 5 percent of the male (or female) workers in the

Appendix A Country-Specific Occupational Titles, by Occupational Category, Country, and Sex[a] *(Cont.)*

Occupational category and country	Country-specific occupational titles	
	Male jobs	Female jobs
6. High-prestige agricultural		
Austria, Great Britain, and the Netherlands	Farmers; General Farmers; Specialized Farmers	Farmers; General Farmers
Denmark, Finland, Norway, and Sweden	Farmers, Silviculturists, Horticulturists	Farmers, Silviculturists, Horticulturists
Germany (Fed. Rep.)	General Farmer	General Farmer; Specialized Farmer
Israel	Farmer-Vegetables; Farmer-Bananas, Citrus; Farmer-Chicken; Farmer-Diversified	Farmer-Chicken; Skilled Worker in Agriculture-Plants, Flowers (Unpaid Family Worker); Skilled Worker in Agriculture-Bananas, Citrus (Unpaid Family Worker); Skilled Worker in Agriculture-Chickens (Unpaid Family Worker); Skilled Worker in Agriculture-Diversified (Unpaid Family Worker)
Japan	Owner of Large, Medium, or Small Farm; Unpaid Family Worker	Unpaid Family Worker; Owner of Small Farm
Northern Ireland	Farmers, Farm Managers, Market Gardeners	Farmers, Farm Managers, Market Gardeners
United States	Farm Managers	Farm Laborers, Unpaid Family Workers
7. High-prestige production and related		
Austria, Great Britain, and the Netherlands	Production Supervisors and General Foremen; Machinery Fitters and Machine Assemblers; Motor Vehicle Mechanics; Electrical Wiremen; Other Production and Related Workers	Production Supervisors and General Foremen; Tailors and Dressmakers; Machine-Tool Operators; Electrical and Electronic Equipment Assemblers; Welders and Flame-Cutters; Other Production and Related Workers

Denmark, Finland, Norway, and Sweden	Precision-Instrument Makers; Turners, Tool-makers and Machine-Tool Setters; Fitter-Assemblers in Iron and Metal Ware Work; Machine and Motor Repairers in Iron and Metal Ware Work; Welders and Flame Cutters; Other Iron and Metal Ware Work Occupations; Electricians; Cabinetmakers; Typographers	Dressmakers; Metal Smelting Furnacemen; Other Smelting, Metallurgical and Foundry Work Occupations; Electric and Electronic Equipment Assemblers; Typographers; Printers
Germany (Fed. Rep.)	Industrial and Other Foremen (Salaried Employees): Foremen and Crew Leaders; Production Supervisors and General Foremen; Machine-Tool Setter-Operators; Machinery Fitters and Machine Assemblers; Motor Vehicle Mechanics; Electrical Wiremen	Industrial and Other Foremen (Salaried Employees): Foremen and Crew Leaders; Production Supervisors and General Foremen; Tailors and Dressmakers; Patternmakers and Cutters; Welders and Flame-Cutters; Printing Engravers (Except Photoengravers); Other Production and Related Workers
Israel	Locksmith, Buildings; Fitters, Assembler-Machine; Vehicle Repairman; Diamond Finishers; Furniture Maker	Fitter-Assembler-Electronic Equipment; Electrician, Electrical Equipment Operator; Diamond Finishers; Tailor, Custom Dressmaker; Cutter, Patternmaker
Japan	Other Technician, Production Worker, Common Laborer Occupations: Painting, Furnishing, Fine Gem Processing, Designing, Projectionist (Film) Packing, Wrapping, Delivery; Worker in Metallurgy: Steel Production, Pressing, Smelting, Worker in Machine Production, Assembly, Repair, Metal Pressing, Welding. Electrical Machinery Assembly and Repair, Wire Insulation Assembly and Repair of Transportation Machinery. Electric Power Generation, Transformer Worker, Wire Installation or Related Activity; Worker (Foreman) in Manufacture of Ceramic or	Other Technician, Production Worker, Common Laborer Occupations: Painting, Furnishing, Fine Gem Processing, Designing, Projectionist (Film) Packing, Wrapping, Delivery; Worker in Metallurgy: Steel Production, Pressing, Smelting, Worker in Machine Production, Assembly, Repair, Metal Pressing, Welding. Electrical Machinery Assembly and Repair of Transportation Machinery. Electric Power Generation, Transformer Worker, Wire Installation or Related Activity

[a] This table presents a listing, compiled separately for male and female jobs, of the detailed occupational categories included in each of the fourteen categories of the Standard International Classification of Occupations (Treiman 1977, Chapter 9) for each country (or set of countries). Countries with identical occupational classifications are grouped. Only those detailed occupations containing at least 5 percent of the male (or female) workers in the major occupation group are included.

Appendix A Country-Specific Occupational Titles, by Occupational Category, Country, and Sex[a] (*Cont.*)

Occupational category and country	Country-specific occupational titles	
	Male jobs	Female jobs
Northern Ireland	Earthen Products: Processing of Ceramic Material, Production of Glass Molds, Ceramic Making, Brick and Tile Production, Cement Manufacture. Construction Work: Laying Tiles, Laying Tatami, Carpentry, Plastering	
	Electricians; Motor Mechanics, Auto Engineers; Maintenance Fitters, Maintenance Engineers, Millwrights; Fitters, n.e.c.	Electricians; Electrical and Electronic Fitters; Assemblers (Electrical and Electronics); Machine Tool Setters, Setter Operators n.e.c.; Tailors, Dress, Light Clothing Makers; Hand and Machine Sewers and Embroiderers, Textile and Light Leather Products; Printing Workers, n.e.c.; Craftsmen, n.e.c.
United States	Electricians; Foremen, n.e.c.; Automobile Mechanics; Heavy Equipment Mechanics, Including Diesel; Welders and Flame-Cutters; Machine Operatives, Miscellaneous Specified	Checkers, Examiners, and Inspectors, Manufacturing; Dressmakers and Seamstresses, Except Factory; Machine Operatives, Miscellaneous Specified
8. High-prestige service		
Austria, Great Britain, and the Netherlands	Working Proprietors (Catering and Lodging Services); Cooks; Police and Detectives; Protective Service Workers, n.e.c.; Other Service Workers	Working Proprietors (Catering and Lodging Services); Cooks; Hairdressers, Barbers, Beauticians and Related Workers; Other Service Workers
Denmark, Finland, Norway, and Sweden	Fire-fighters; Policemen; Custom Guards; Other Guards (Civil Duties); Hairdressers and Barbers	Institution Nursemaids; Housekeeping Managers; Cooks, etc.; Other Housekeeping, Doorman Work Occupations; Hairdressers and Barbers
Germany (Fed. Rep.)	Working Proprietors (Catering and Lodging Services); Cooks; Hairdressers, Barbers, Beauticians and Related Workers; Firefighters; Police and Detectives; Protective Service Workers	Housekeeping and Related Service Supervisors; Cooks; Hairdressers, Barbers, Beauticians and Related Workers; Other Service Workers

Israel	Working Proprietors (Catering and Lodging Services), Food Service; Cook, Chef; Barber; Policeman, Detective; Doorkeeper	Cook, Chef; Housekeeper; Hairdresser; Beautician
Japan	Self-Defense Force Member; Policeman, Coast Guard, Railway Guards; Guard: Prison Guard, Night Watchman; Other Service-Related Workers; Barber, Beautician	Other Service-Related Workers; Service-Related Workers in General; Barber, Beautician
Northern Ireland	Police Officers and Men; Guards and Related Workers n.e.c.; Barmen, Barmaids (Supervisor); Cooks; Hairdressers, Manicurists, Beauticians; Hospital or Ward Orderlies, Ambulance Men; Service, Sport and Recreation Workers	Lodging House, Hotel Keepers, Stewards and Matrons; Cooks; Maids, Valets and Related Service Workers, n.e.c.; Hairdressers, Manicurists, Beauticians; Hospital or Ward Orderlies, Ambulance Men
United States	Managers and Superintendents, Building; Restaurant, Cafeteria, and Bar Managers; Cooks, Except Private Household; Nursing Aides, Orderlies, and Attendants; Firemen, Fire Protection; Guards and Watchmen; Policemen and Detectives	Restaurant, Cafeteria, and Bar Managers; Cooks, Except Private Household; Health Aides, Except Nursing; Nursing Aides, Orderlies, and Attendants; Child Care Workers, Except Private Household; Hairdressers and Cosmetologists

9. Medium-prestige production and related

Austria, Great Britain, and the Netherlands	Machinery Fitters, Machine Assemblers and Precision Instrument Makers (Except Electrical), n.e.c.; Bricklayers, Stonemasons and Tile Setters; Carpenters, Joiners and Parquetry Workers; Construction Workers, n.e.c.; Motor Vehicle Drivers	Spinners and Winders; Sewers and Embroiderers; Tailors, Dressmakers, Sewers, Upholsterers and Related Workers n.e.c.; Shoe Cutters, Lasters, Sewers and Related Workers
Denmark, Finland, Norway, and Sweden	Motor-vehicle and Tram Drivers; Plumbers; Construction Carpenters; Painters; Bricklayers, Plasterers and Tile Setters	Weavers, Sewers etc. (Also Leather Garments and Gloves); Other Cutting, Sewing and Upholstering Work, etc.; Bakers and Pastry Makers

a This table presents a listing, compiled separately for male and female jobs, of the detailed occupational categories included in each of the fourteen categories of the Standard International Classification of Occupations (Treiman 1977, Chapter 9) for each country (or set of countries). Countries with identical occupational classifications are grouped. Only those detailed occupations containing at least 5 percent of the male (or female) workers in the major occupation group are included.

Appendix A Country-Specific Occupational Titles, by Occupational Category, Country, and Sex[a] (*Cont.*)

Occupational category and country	Country-specific occupational titles	
	Male jobs	Female jobs
Germany (Fed. Rep.)	Semiskilled Workers; Metal Rolling-Mill Workers; Bricklayers, Stonemasons and Tile Setters; Motor Vehicle Drivers	Semiskilled Workers; Bakers, Pastrycooks and Confectionery Makers; Milliners and Hatmakers; Sewers and Embroiderers; Machinery Fitters, Machine Assemblers and Precision Instrument Makers (Except Electrical), n.e.c.; Painters, n.e.c.
Israel	Plumber; Scaffolding Erector; Bus Driver; Truck, Trailer-Truck Driver; Driver of Commercial Vehicle	Weaver; Knitter; Sewer; Leather Clothes
Japan	Miner, Coal Miner, or Stone Miner; Other Transportation and Communication Workers; Transportation and Communication Workers in General; Technician, Production Worker, Common Laborer in General; Worker in Thread Production or Weaving; Weaver, Bleacher, Dyer, Worker in Fabric Production, Tailor, Sewing Machine Operator, Worker in Production of Wool or Vegetable Products, Timber Processing, Wood Processing, Bamboo Processing, Furniture Making, Pulp and Paper Manufacture and Processing; Worker in Manufacture of Ceramic or Earthen Products: Processing of Ceramic Material, Production of Glass Molds, Ceramic Making, Brick and Tile Production, Cement Manufacture, Construction Work: Laying Tiles, Laying Tatami, Carpentry, Plastering; Worker in Food Processing: Processing of Chemical Products, Salt Production, Vegetable Oil Pro-	Technician, Production Worker, Common Laborer in General; Worker in Thread Production or Weaving; Weaver, Bleacher, Dyer; Worker in Fabric Production, Tailor, Sewing Machine Operator; Worker in Production of Wool or Vegetable Products: Timber Processing, Wood Processing, Bamboo Processing and Paper Manufacture and Processing; Worker in Food Processing; Processing of Chemical Products, Salt Production, Vegetable Oil Production, Animal Oil Processing

Northern Ireland	Carpenters and Joiners; Food Processers, n.e.c.; Bricklayers, Tile Setters; Construction Workers, n.e.c.; Drivers of Buses, Coaches; Drivers of Road Goods Vehicles	Spinners, Doublers, Twisters; Winders, Reelers; Textile Fabrics, etc. Production Process Workers, n.e.c.; Hand and Machine Sewers and Embroiderers, Textile and Light Leather Products; Clothing and Related Products Makers, n.e.c.; Food Processors, n.e.c.
United States	Carpenters; Painters, Construction and Maintenance; Assemblers; Truck Drivers; Construction Laborers, Except Carpenters' Helpers	Assemblers; Sewers and Stitchers; Miscellaneous Operatives; Bus Drivers
10. Low-prestige clerical and related		
Austria, Great Britain, and the Netherlands	Bookkeepers, Cashiers and Related Workers, n.e.c.; Transport and Communications Supervisors, n.e.c.; Mail Distribution Clerks; Stock Clerks; Clerks, n.e.c.	Bookkeepers, Cashiers and Related Workers, n.e.c.; Stock Clerks; Receptionists and Travel Agency Clerks; Clerks, n.e.c.
Denmark, Finland, Norway, and Sweden	Dispatching and Receiving Clerks, Shipping Agents; Building Caretakers, Storeroom Clerks; Other Clerical Occupations; Railway Traffic Supervisors; Postmen; Messengers, etc.	Doctor's and Dentist's Receptionist; Bank and Post Office Cashiers; Cashiers in Shops and Restaurants; Computing Assistants, Reproduction Machine Operators, etc.; Telephone Operators; Telephone Switchboard Operators
Germany (Fed. Rep.)	Bookkeepers, Cashiers and Related Workers, n.e.c.; Mail Distribution Clerks; Stock Clerks	Bookkeepers, Cashiers and Related Workers, n.e.c.; Mail Distribution Clerks; Stock Clerks; Receptionists and Travel Agency Clerks
Israel	Bookkeepers, Cashiers and Related Workers, n.e.c.; Stockroom Attendant; Mail Carrier and Post Office Worker; Messenger; Receptionist; Clerks, n.e.c.	Bookkeepers, Cashiers and Related Workers, n.e.c.; Stockroom Attendant; Stock Control Clerk; Receptionist; Clerks, n.e.c.

ᵃ This table presents a listing, compiled separately for male and female jobs, of the detailed occupational categories included in each of the fourteen categories of the Standard International Classification of Occupations (Treiman 1977, Chapter 9) for each country (or set of countries). Countries with identical occupational classifications are grouped. Only those detailed occupations containing at least 5 percent of the male (or female) workers in the major occupation group are included.

Appendix A Country-Specific Occupational Titles, by Occupational Category, Country, and Sex[a] (*Cont.*)

Occupational category and country

	Country-specific occupational titles	
	Male jobs	Female jobs
Japan	Clerk Concerned with Postal Service or Telegraph; Account Collector; Conductor; Train Dispatcher, Flagman, or Coupler; Postal Clerk, Mailman, Mail Sorter	Clerk Concerned with Postal Service or Telegraph; Conductor, Train Dispatcher, Flagman, or Coupler
Northern Ireland	Postmen, Mail Sorters; Warehousemen, Storekeepers and Assistants; Clerks, Cashiers	Clerks, Cashiers
United States	Cashiers; Estimators and Investigators, n.e.c.; Expediters and Production Controllers; Mail Carriers, Post Office; Postal Clerks; Shipping and Receiving Clerks; Stock Clerks and Storekeepers	Cashiers; Estimators and Investigators; Receptionists; Statistical Clerks; Stock Clerks and Storekeepers; Telephone Operators
11. Low-prestige sales		
Austria, Great Britain, and the Netherlands	Salesmen, Shop Assistants and Demonstrators; Street Vendors, Canvassers and Newsvendors; Sales Workers, n.e.c.	Salesmen, Shop Assistants and Related Workers; Salesmen, Shop Assistants and Demonstrators; Sales Workers, n.e.c.
Denmark, Finland, Norway, and Sweden	Shop Personnel; Service Station Attendants; Other Sales Work	Shop Personnel
Germany (Fed. Rep.)	Salesmen, Shop Assistants and Demonstrators	Salesmen, Shop Assistants and Demonstrators
Israel	Salesman; Proprietor of Food Kiosk	Salesman
Japan	Store Salesman, Salesgirl, Floorwalker; Peddler, Stallkeeper	Store Salesman, Salesgirl, Floorwalker; Peddler, Stallkeeper

Northern Ireland	Proprietors and Managers, Food Sales (Self-Employed with no Employees); Shop Salesmen and Assistants, Nonfood; Roundsmen (Bread, Milk, Laundry, Soft Drinks); Street Vendors, Hawkers	Proprietors and Managers, Food Sales (Self-Employed with no Employees); Shop Salesmen and Assistants, Food; Shop Salesmen and Assistants, Nonfood; Street Vendors, Hawkers
United States	Salesmen and Sales Clerks, n.e.c.; Deliverymen and Routemen	Demonstrators; Hucksters and Peddlers; Salesmen and Sales Clerks, n.e.c.; Sales Clerks, Retail Trade
12. Low-prestige agricultural		
Austria, Great Britain, and the Netherlands	General Farm Workers; Nursery Workers and Gardeners; Farm Machinery Operators; Loggers	General Farm Workers; Field Crop and Vegetable Farm Workers; Agricultural and Animal Husbandry Workers, n.e.c.
Denmark, Finland, Norway, and Sweden	Agricultural Workers; Garden Workers; Fishermen; Forestry and Floating Workers	Garden Workers; Livestock Workers; Fur-bearing Farm Animal Workers; Other Agricultural and Horticultural Work, Breeding of Animals Occupations
Germany (Fed. Rep.)	Field Crop and Vegetable Farm Workers; Livestock Workers; Nursery Workers and Gardeners	General Farm Workers; Nursery Workers and Gardeners
Israel	Skilled Worker-Plants, Flowers; Skilled Worker-Bananas, Citrus; Tractor Driver, Columbine Driver; Forester; Fruit Picker; Other Picker	Skilled Worker-Diversified; Other Picker
Japan	Farm Hand; Forestry in General, Wood Planter, and Wood Cutter; Fishing, Seaweed and Shellfish Gatherer; Tenant Farmer	Farm Hand; Fishery in General, Fishing, Seaweed and Shellfish Gatherer

[a] This table presents a listing, compiled separately for male and female jobs, of the detailed occupational categories included in each of the fourteen categories of the Standard International Classification of Occupations (Treiman 1977, Chapter 9) for each country (or set of countries). Countries with identical occupational classifications are grouped. Only those detailed occupations containing at least 5 percent of the male (or female) workers in the major occupation group are included.

Appendix A Country-Specific Occupational Titles, by Occupational Category, Country, and Sex[a] (Cont.)

Occupational category and country	Country-specific occupational titles	
	Male jobs	Female jobs
Northern Ireland	Fisherman; Agricultural Workers, n.e.c.; Agricultural Machinery Drivers; Gardeners and Groundsmen; Foresters and Woodmen	Agricultural Workers, n.e.c.; Gardeners
United States	Fishermen and Oystermen; Gardeners and Groundskeepers, Except Farm; Lumbermen, Raftmen, and Woodchoppers; Farm Laborers, Wage Workers	Animal Caretakers, Except Farm; Fishermen and Oystermen; Gardeners and Groundskeepers, Except Farm; Farm Laborers, Wage Workers
13. Low-prestige service		
Austria, Great Britain, and the Netherlands	Waiters, Bartenders and Related Workers; Maids and Related Housekeeping Service Workers, n.e.c.; Building Caretakers; Charworkers, Cleaners and Related Workers; Launderers, Dry Cleaners and Pressers	Waiters, Bartenders and Related Workers; Maids and Related Housekeeping Service Workers, n.e.c.; Charworkers, Cleaners and Related Workers; Launderers, Dry Cleaners and Pressers
Denmark, Finland, Norway, and Sweden	Head Waiters, Waiters; Caretakers (Building); Charworkers; Chimney Sweeps	Kitchen Hands; Housekeepers and Nursemaids (Private Service); Communal Home Sisters, etc.; Head Waiters, Waiters; Charworkers
Germany (Fed. Rep.)	Waiters, Bartenders and Related Workers; Building Caretakers; Charworkers, Cleaners and Related Workers	Maids and Related Housekeeping Service Workers, n.e.c.; Building Caretakers; Charworkers, Cleaners and Related Workers; Launderers, Dry Cleaners and Pressers
Israel	Waiter; Cafeteria Worker (Serving Food); Launderer; Guard, Watchman (in Factory Building or Store); Janitor	Cafeteria Worker (Serving Food); Nursemaid (No Credential); Launderer; Janitor; Kitchen Worker, Cook's Helper, Dishwasher
Japan	Cook, Bartender, Waitress, Waiter, Hostess, Chambermaid; Laundry Worker; Hat and	Workers in Domestic Service: Maid, House Servant; Cook, Bartender, Waitress, Waiter,

Northern Ireland	Barmen, Barmaids; Caretakers, Office Keepers; Charwomen, Office Cleaners, Window Cleaners; Launderers, Dry Cleaners, and Pressers	Barmen, Barmaids; Lodging House Hotel Keepers, Stewards and Matrons; Restaur- anteurs, Waiters, Counter Hands; Kitchen Hands; Caretakers, Office Keepers; Char- women, Office Cleaners, Window Cleaners; Launderers, Dry Cleaners, and Pressers
United States	Laundry and Dry Cleaning Operatives (n.e.c.); Cleaners and Charwomen; Janitors and Sex- tons; Bartenders; Busboys; Waiters	Chambermaids and Maids, Except Private Household; Cleaners and Charwomen; Food Counter and Fountain Workers; Waiters; Food Service Workers; Maids and Servants, Private Household

14. Low-prestige production and related

Austria, Great Britain, and the Netherlands	Butchers and Meat Preparers; Dockers and Freight Handlers; Transport Equipment Op- erators, n.e.c., Laborers, n.e.c.	Dockers and Freight Handlers; Laborers, n.e.c.
Denmark, Finland, Norway, and Sweden	Other Assistant Construction Workers; Butchers and Sausage Makers; Dockers; Warehouse Porters; Laborers	Textile Product Finishers; Dyers; Tanners, Fellmongers and Pelt Dressers; Packers and Labellers; Laborers
Germany (Fed. Rep.)	Unskilled Workers; Butchers and Meat Pre- parers; Dockers and Freight Handlers; Trans- port Equipment Operators, n.e.c.; Laborers, n.e.c.	Unskilled Workers; Dockers and Freight Handlers; Laborers, n.e.c.
Israel	Streetsweeper; Porter; Carrier; Unskilled Worker in Plastics Production; Unskilled Worker in Construction, Misc.; Unskilled Worker in Industry, Misc.	Packer and Sorter in Packing Plant; Un- skilled Worker in Food Production, Drinks, and Tobacco, n.e.c.; Packer in Industry (Ex- cept Agricultural Products); Labeller, Related Worker; Unskilled Worker: Paper Products Manufacturing; Unskilled Worker in Indus- try, Misc.

[a] This table presents a listing, compiled separately for male and female jobs, of the detailed occupational categories included in each of the fourteen categories of the Standard International Classification of Occupations (Treiman 1977, Chapter 9) for each country (or set of countries). Countries with identical occupational classifications are grouped. Only those detailed occupations containing at least 5 percent of the male (or female) workers in the major occupation group are included.

Appendix A Country-Specific Occupational Titles, by Occupational Category, Country, and Sex[a] (*Cont.*)

Occupational category and country	Country-specific occupational titles	
	Male jobs	Female jobs
Japan	Driver, Transportation and Communication	Driver, Transportation and Communication
Northern Ireland	Butchers and Meat Cutters; Bricklayers, Laborers, n.e.c.; Railway, Lengthmen Laborers and Unskilled Workers, n.e.c.; Textiles Laborers; Building and Contracting Laborers; Laborers, n.e.c.; Stevedores, Dock Laborers	Bleachers and Finishers of Textiles; Chemical and Allied Trades Laborers; Textiles Laborers; Laborers, n.e.c.; Packers, Labellers and Related Workers
United States	Garage Workers and Gas Station Attendants; Packers and Wrappers, Except Meat and Produce; Freight and Material Handlers; Garbage Collectors; Stock Handlers; Miscellaneous Laborers; Not Specified Laborers	Meat Cutters and Butchers, Manufacturing; Packers and Wrappers, Except Meat and Produce; Freight and Material Handlers; Stock Handlers

[a] This table presents a listing, compiled separately for male and female jobs, of the detailed occupational categories included in each of the fourteen categories of the Standard International Classification of Occupations (Treiman 1977, Chapter 9) for each country (or set of countries). Countries with identical occupational classifications are grouped. Only those detailed occupations containing at least 5 percent of the male (or female) workers in the major occupation group are included.

Appendix B Inflow (Recruitment) Distributions of Employed Men and Women (All Ages), in Seven Industrialized Countries (in percentages)

Occupation and sex of respondent[a]

Country and occupation of father[a]	Professional and technical		Administrative and managerial		Clerical and related		Sales		Service		Agricultural		Production	
	M	F	M	F	M	F	M	F	M	F	M	F	M	F
Austria														
1. Professional and technical	19.5	11.1	0.0	0.0	4.1	9.3	0.0	5.3	4.5	0.0	2.3	0.0	1.0	0.0
2. Administrative and managerial	4.9	7.4	23.1	50.0	6.1	5.3	0.0	2.6	4.5	3.8	0.0	0.0	0.5	0.0
3. Clerical and related	7.3	7.4	15.4	0.0	20.4	16.0	9.5	7.9	0.0	7.7	0.0	0.0	9.8	3.3
4. Sales	19.5	11.1	7.7	0.0	8.2	8.0	19.0	23.7	4.5	1.9	1.1	1.4	2.6	1.6
5. Service	2.4	7.4	7.7	0.0	4.1	6.7	7.1	5.3	22.7	9.6	0.0	1.4	6.2	1.6
6. Agricultural	9.8	3.7	0.0	0.0	22.4	8.0	9.5	5.3	36.4	28.8	92.0	92.9	25.8	24.6
7. Production and related	36.6	51.9	46.2	50.0	34.7	46.7	54.8	50.0	27.3	48.1	4.6	4.3	54.1	68.9
Total	100.0	100.0	100.1	100.0	100.0	100.0	99.9	100.1	99.9	99.9	100.0	100.0	100.0	100.0
N	(43)	(25)	(14)	(2)	(52)	(69)	(44)	(35)	(23)	(48)	(92)	(65)	(204)	(57)
Germany (Fed. Rep.)														
1. Professional and technical	25.9	23.0	20.0	0.0	4.1	5.9	6.8	9.6	7.2	3.7	0.0	0.0	1.7	0.0
2. Administrative and managerial	2.3	2.1	26.1	0.0	1.0	1.2	0.0	2.9	2.5	0.0	0.0	0.0	0.0	0.0
3. Clerical and related	25.1	23.4	19.5	0.0	27.2	26.6	23.8	20.6	12.4	30.3	4.1	0.0	9.6	11.3
4. Sales	3.3	5.0	0.0	0.0	7.9	4.5	21.0	4.2	0.0	0.0	0.0	0.0	2.4	0.0

aThe occupational classification is the major group International Standard Classification of Occupations (ISCO) (ILO 1969).

Appendix B Inflow (Recruitment) Distributions of Employed Men and Women (All Ages), in Seven Industrialized Countries (in percentages) (Cont.)

Country and occupation of father[a]	Professional and technical		Administrative and managerial		Clerical and related		Sales		Service		Agricultural		Production	
	M	F	M	F	M	F	M	F	M	F	M	F	M	F
5. Service	3.9	9.2	8.2	0.0	5.1	5.6	9.0	0.0	21.6	6.7	0.0	0.0	3.5	3.6
6. Agricultural	13.2	10.1	0.0	0.0	14.8	12.0	11.0	5.8	17.0	11.2	95.9	64.9	18.5	5.9
7. Production and related	26.4	27.2	26.1	0.0	39.9	44.2	28.3	57.0	39.3	48.1	0.0	35.1	64.3	79.2
Total	100.1	100.0	99.9	0.0	100.0	100.0	99.9	100.1	100.0	100.0	100.0	100.0	100.0	100.0
N	(82)	(51)	(17)	(0)	(140)	(143)	(43)	(60)	(37)	(38)	(31)	(10)	(259)	(56)
Israel														
1. Professional and technical	15.8	14.3	11.9	13.9	7.4	8.1	5.7	4.0	3.2	6.9	4.9	5.9	3.6	6.6
2. Administrative and managerial	6.8	9.7	13.9	2.8	5.6	7.9	2.1	5.8	1.9	2.6	2.2	0.0	2.3	4.6
3. Clerical and related	10.1	12.2	6.1	0.0	12.6	10.8	2.1	1.8	3.6	3.5	1.5	8.4	4.4	0.7
4. Sales	29.5	23.8	34.0	60.4	38.7	31.4	53.8	52.8	30.5	36.4	23.7	32.9	28.9	38.3
5. Service	3.2	3.6	7.8	16.7	3.2	4.9	4.3	3.6	8.6	7.8	4.3	7.4	5.2	3.6
6. Agricultural	9.4	8.0	4.7	6.1	6.4	4.1	8.6	6.0	14.0	6.4	41.5	20.1	14.7	5.5
7. Production and related	25.3	28.4	21.6	0.0	26.1	32.8	23.4	26.0	38.2	36.3	21.8	25.2	41.0	40.8
Total	100.1	100.0	100.0	99.9	100.0	100.0	100.0	100.0	100.0	99.9	99.9	99.9	100.1	100.1
N	(946)	(890)	(300)	(36)	(823)	(700)	(624)	(276)	(453)	(472)	(381)	(92)	(2802)	(263)
Japan														
1. Professional and technical	40.1	12.9	2.2	0.0	6.2	11.5	4.0	7.0	4.0	0.0	0.0	0.0	2.4	3.3
2. Administrative														

3. Clerical and related	15.6	17.4	15.9	25.0	30.5	29.2	8.0	7.0	24.2	15.8	0.0	0.0	11.2	4.9
4. Sales	7.0	10.5	22.1	75.0	17.2	10.4	17.1	16.4	16.1	9.4	0.9	2.5	7.0	9.8
5. Service	2.3	3.5	2.2	0.0	3.1	7.0	4.0	2.3	8.1	11.3	0.0	0.0	2.0	4.9
6. Agricultural	23.3	41.8	35.4	0.0	28.9	21.2	50.7	36.8	32.3	40.0	92.1	94.2	42.9	50.1
7. Production and related	11.7	10.5	17.7	0.0	10.3	15.5	16.1	30.4	15.3	23.5	5.3	2.5	30.6	27.1
Total	100.0	100.1	99.9	100.0	100.0	100.0	99.9	99.9	100.0	100.0	100.1	100.0	100.1	100.1
N	(41)	(31)	(43)	(4)	(92)	(62)	(47)	(46)	(24)	(46)	(108)	(130)	(194)	(67)

Netherlands

1. Professional and technical	23.3	14.6	0.0	0.0	11.7	10.9	2.3	6.7	9.1	8.6	3.4	0.0	2.9	0.0
2. Administrative and managerial	8.3	8.3	21.9	100.0	5.0	9.4	13.6	10.0	4.5	5.7	0.0	0.0	4.4	0.0
3. Clerical and related	18.3	22.9	6.3	0.0	10.0	15.6	6.8	6.7	0.0	11.4	0.0	0.0	5.9	9.1
4. Sales	8.3	6.3	9.4	0.0	13.3	17.2	45.5	6.7	9.1	2.9	0.0	0.0	3.7	9.1
5. Service	5.0	2.1	6.3	0.0	3.3	4.7	9.1	10.0	13.6	11.4	0.0	0.0	2.9	18.2
6. Agricultural	1.7	16.7	15.6	0.0	15.0	6.3	6.8	6.7	9.1	17.1	75.9	100.0	15.4	9.1
7. Production and related	35.0	29.2	40.6	0.0	41.7	35.9	15.9	53.3	54.5	42.9	20.7	0.0	64.7	54.5
Total	99.9	100.1	100.1	100.0	100.0	100.0	100.0	100.1	99.9	100.0	100.0	100.0	99.9	100.0
N	(67)	(37)	(36)	(1)	(67)	(50)	(49)	(23)	(24)	(27)	(32)	(2)	(151)	(9)

Northern Ireland

1. Professional and technical	26.2	20.5	16.7	0.0	2.8	11.4	4.4	10.0	0.0	3.6	0.0	0.0	1.4	3.8
2. Administrative and managerial	0.0	10.3	8.3	0.0	2.8	2.3	2.2	5.0	0.0	0.0	0.0	0.0	0.9	0.0
3. Clerical and related	11.9	0.0	0.0	0.0	13.9	11.4	0.0	5.0	0.0	1.4	1.4	0.0	7.5	5.7
4. Sales	14.3	15.4	8.3	66.7	5.6	13.6	24.4	25.0	9.5	5.5	1.4	0.0	2.8	5.7

aThe occupational classification is the major group International Standard Classification of Occupations (ISCO) (ILO 1969).

Appendix B Inflow (Recruitment) Distributions of Employed Men and Women (All Ages), in Seven Industrialized Countries (in percentages) (Cont.)

Country and occupation of father[a]	Occupation and sex of respondent[a]													
	Professional and technical		Administrative and managerial		Clerical and related		Sales		Service		Agricultural		Production	
	M	F	M	F	M	F	M	F	M	F	M	F	M	F
5. Service	4.8	5.1	0.0	0.0	5.6	9.1	6.7	0.0	4.8	3.6	0.0	0.0	4.7	5.7
6. Agricultural	14.3	23.1	8.3	0.0	13.9	18.2	35.6	15.0	42.9	36.4	90.1	75.0	22.5	22.6
7. Production and related	28.6	25.6	58.3	33.3	55.6	34.1	26.7	40.0	42.9	43.6	7.0	25.0	60.1	56.6
Total	100.1	100.0	99.9	100.0	100.2	100.1	100.0	100.0	100.1	100.0	99.9	100.0	99.9	100.1
N	(43)	(37)	(12)	(3)	(37)	(41)	(46)	(19)	(22)	(52)	(73)	(8)	(220)	(50)
United States														
1. Professional and technical	14.6	19.6	10.0	2.9	6.3	8.9	10.0	8.6	4.9	3.7	2.3	20.0	4.3	3.0
2. Administrative and managerial	15.0	15.6	21.2	25.7	10.8	10.4	16.0	14.8	8.1	5.5	2.3	40.0	4.6	4.8
3. Clerical and related	7.1	4.4	3.5	5.7	6.3	6.4	4.7	7.4	4.9	0.9	1.1	0.0	3.0	3.0
4. Sales	9.5	8.5	7.6	11.4	9.9	8.7	16.0	11.1	6.5	2.8	2.3	0.0	3.3	5.4
5. Service	3.7	5.2	5.3	2.9	4.5	6.9	2.0	6.2	15.4	5.0	1.1	0.0	4.2	3.6
6. Agricultural	11.6	17.0	13.5	17.1	15.3	13.9	14.0	14.8	17.9	29.8	72.7	40.0	23.2	31.5
7. Production and related	38.4	29.6	38.8	34.3	46.8	44.8	37.3	37.0	42.3	52.3	18.2	0.0	57.2	48.8
Total	99.9	99.9	99.9	100.0	99.9	100.0	100.0	99.9	100.0	100.0	100.0	100.0	99.8	100.1
N	(307)	(254)	(178)	(33)	(116)	(380)	(157)	(76)	(129)	(205)	(92)	(5)	(721)	(158)

[a]The occupational classification is the major group International Standard Classification of Occupations (ISCO) (ILO 1969).

Appendix C Outflow (Supply) Distributions of Employed Men and Women (All Ages), in Seven Industrialized Countries (in percentages)

Country and occupation of father[a]	Professional and technical		Administrative and managerial		Clerical and related		Sales		Service		Agricultural		Production		Total		N	
	M	F	M	F	M	F	M	F	M	F	M	F	M	F	M	F	M	F
Austria																		
1. Professional and technical	53.3	25.0	0.0	0.0	13.3	58.3	0.0	16.7	6.7	0.0	13.3	0.0	13.3	0.0	99.9	100.0	16	11
2. Administrative and managerial	20.0	20.0	30.0	10.0	30.0	40.0	0.0	10.0	10.0	20.0	0.0	0.0	10.0	0.0	100.0	100.0	11	9
3. Clerical and related	7.9	8.7	5.3	0.0	26.3	52.2	10.5	13.0	0.0	17.4	0.0	0.0	50.0	8.7	100.0	100.0	40	21
4. Sales	28.6	14.3	3.6	0.0	14.3	28.6	28.6	42.9	3.6	4.8	3.6	4.8	17.9	4.8	100.2	100.2	29	19
5. Service	4.2	12.5	4.2	0.0	8.3	31.2	12.5	12.5	20.8	31.2	0.0	6.3	50.0	6.3	100.0	100.0	25	15
6. Agricultural	2.5	1.0	0.0	0.0	7.0	5.8	2.5	1.9	5.1	14.4	51.0	62.5	31.8	14.4	99.9	100.0	165	96
7. Production and related	8.5	10.1	3.4	0.7	9.7	25.2	13.1	13.7	3.4	18.0	2.3	2.2	59.7	30.2	100.1	100.1	185	129
N																	(471)	(300)
Germany (Fed. Rep.)																		
1. Professional and technical	52.6	43.0	8.5	0.0	14.2	30.9	7.3	20.9	6.6	5.2	0.0	0.0	10.8	0.0	100.0	100.0	40	27
2. Administrative and managerial	21.6	23.4	51.2	0.0	16.5	38.6	0.0	38.0	10.6	0.0	0.0	0.0	0.0	0.0	99.9	100.0	9	5
3. Clerical and related	19.9	14.9	3.3	0.0	37.0	47.4	10.0	15.3	4.5	14.4	1.3	0.0	24.1	7.9	100.1	99.9	103	80
4. Sales	9.2	22.3	0.0	0.0	38.1	55.7	31.3	22.0	0.0	0.0	0.0	0.0	21.4	0.0	100.0	100.0	29	12
5. Service	9.7	27.3	4.3	0.0	21.9	46.3	12.0	0.0	24.6	14.8	0.0	0.0	27.5	11.6	100.0	100.0	33	17
6. Agricultural	8.9	13.0	0.0	0.0	17.1	42.9	4.0	8.6	5.2	10.7	25.0	16.4	39.7	8.3	99.9	99.9	121	40
7. Production and related	7.8	7.9	1.6	0.0	20.3	35.7	4.5	19.2	5.3	10.4	0.0	2.0	60.5	24.9	100.0	100.1	275	177
N																	(610)	(358)

[a] The occupational classification is the major group International Standard Classification of Occupations (ISCO) (ILO 1969).

Appendix C Outflow (Supply) Distributions of Employed Men and Women (All Ages), in Seven Industrialized Countries (in percentages) (Cont.)

Country and occupation of father[a]	Professional and technical		Administrative and managerial		Clerical and related		Sales		Service		Agricultural		Production		Total		N	
	M	F	M	F	M	F	M	F	M	F	M	F	M	F	M	F	M	F
Israel																		
1. Professional and technical	36.1	49.9	8.7	2.0	14.6	22.1	8.5	4.3	3.5	12.8	4.5	2.1	24.1	6.8	100.0	100.0	413	256
2. Administrative and managerial	25.9	47.0	16.8	0.6	18.7	30.4	5.2	8.8	3.5	6.8	3.4	0.0	26.4	6.5	99.9	100.1	248	183
3. Clerical and related	25.4	50.4	4.9	0.0	27.6	35.1	3.5	2.3	4.4	7.7	1.5	3.6	32.7	0.9	100.0	100.0	375	216
4. Sales	13.4	23.5	4.9	2.4	15.4	24.4	16.2	16.2	6.7	19.0	4.4	3.4	39.1	11.1	100.1	100.0	2074	902
5. Service	9.8	23.5	7.6	4.5	8.5	25.3	8.8	7.4	12.7	27.3	5.4	5.0	47.2	7.0	100.0	100.0	307	135
6. Agricultural	10.6	39.3	1.7	1.2	6.2	15.6	6.4	9.1	7.5	16.7	18.8	10.2	48.8	7.9	100.0	100.0	842	182
7. Production and related	11.6	29.5	3.1	0.0	10.4	26.9	7.1	8.4	8.4	20.0	4.0	2.7	55.5	12.5	100.1	100.0	2069	856
N																	(6328)	(2730)
Japan																		
1. Professional and technical	53.4	24.2	3.1	0.0	18.6	43.1	6.2	19.6	3.1	0.0	0.0	0.0	15.5	13.1	99.9	100.0	31	17
2. Administrative and managerial	0.0	20.0	12.6	0.0	23.3	60.0	0.0	0.0	0.0	0.0	12.6	20.0	51.6	0.0	100.1	100.0	15	5
3. Clerical and related	8.8	14.1	9.4	2.8	38.8	47.3	5.2	8.5	7.9	18.9	0.0	0.0	29.9	8.5	100.0	100.1	73	39
4. Sales	5.2	9.4	17.4	9.4	29.1	18.8	14.8	21.9	7.0	12.5	1.7	9.4	24.7	18.8	99.9	100.2	55	35
5. Service	7.7	7.2	7.7	0.0	23.1	29.0	15.4	7.2	15.4	34.8	0.0	0.0	30.8	21.7	100.1	99.9	12	15
6. Agricultural	3.6	6.0	5.7	0.0	10.1	6.1	9.0	7.8	2.9	8.5	37.4	56.3	31.3	15.3	100.0	100.0	266	218
7. Production and related	4.8	5.5	7.7	0.0	9.7	16.3	7.7	23.9	3.7	18.3	5.8	5.5	60.5	30.5	99.9	100.0	98	59
N																	(550)	(388)

Netherlands

	1	1	2	2	3	3	4	4	5	5	6	6	7	7	Total	Total	N	N
1. Professional and technical	48.3	36.8	0.0	0.0	24.1	36.8	3.4	10.5	6.9	15.8	3.4	0.0	13.8	0.0	99.9	99.9	32	15
2. Administrative and managerial	17.9	25.0	25.0	6.3	10.7	37.5	21.4	18.7	3.6	12.5	0.0	0.0	21.4	0.0	100.0	100.0	31	12
3. Clerical and related	36.7	39.3	6.7	0.0	20.0	35.7	10.0	7.1	0.0	14.3	0.0	0.0	26.7	3.6	100.1	100.0	33	22
4. Sales	11.6	16.7	7.0	0.0	18.6	61.1	46.5	11.1	4.7	5.6	0.0	0.0	11.6	5.6	100.0	100.1	48	14
5. Service	16.7	7.7	11.1	0.0	11.1	23.1	22.2	23.1	16.7	30.8	0.0	0.0	22.2	15.4	100.0	100.0	20	10
6. Agricultural	1.6	33.3	7.9	0.0	14.3	16.7	4.8	8.3	3.2	25.0	34.9	12.5	33.3	4.2	100.1	100.0	70	19
7. Production and related	12.2	18.9	7.6	0.0	14.5	31.1	4.1	21.6	7.0	20.3	3.5	0.0	51.2	8.1	100.1	100.0	191	58
N																	(425)	(150)

Northern Ireland

	1	1	2	2	3	3	4	4	5	5	6	6	7	7	Total	Total	N	N
1. Professional and technical	57.9	42.1	10.5	0.0	5.3	26.3	10.5	10.5	0.0	10.5	0.0	0.0	15.8	10.5	100.0	99.9	20	18
2. Administrative and managerial	0.0	66.7	20.0	0.0	20.0	16.7	20.0	16.7	0.0	0.0	0.0	0.0	40.0	0.0	100.0	100.1	5	6
3. Clerical and related	18.5	0.0	0.0	0.0	18.5	38.5	0.0	7.7	0.0	30.8	3.7	0.0	59.3	23.1	100.0	100.1	28	12
4. Sales	20.7	24.0	3.4	8.0	6.9	24.0	37.9	20.0	6.9	12.0	3.4	0.0	20.7	12.0	99.9	100.0	30	23
5. Service	11.1	18.2	0.0	0.0	11.1	36.4	16.7	0.0	5.6	18.2	0.0	0.0	55.6	27.3	100.1	100.1	19	10
6. Agricultural	4.0	15.5	0.7	0.0	3.4	13.8	10.7	10.7	6.0	34.5	43.0	10.3	32.2	20.7	100.0	100.0	154	54
7. Production and related	6.2	11.1	3.6	1.1	10.4	16.7	6.2	8.9	4.7	26.7	2.6	2.2	66.3	33.3	100.0	100.0	199	85
N																	(455)	(208)

a The occupational classification is the major group International Standard Classification of Occupations (ISCO) (ILO 1969).

Appendix C Outflow (Supply) Distributions of Employed Men and Women (All Ages), in Seven Industrialized Countries (in percentages) *(Cont.)*

Occupation and sex of respondent[a]

Country and occupation of father[a]	Professional and technical		Administrative and managerial		Clerical and related		Sales		Service		Agricultural		Production		Total		N	
	M	F	M	F	M	F	M	F	M	F	M	F	M	F	M	F	M	F
United States																		
1. Professional and technical	35.8	47.7	14.2	0.9	5.8	32.4	12.5	6.3	5.0	7.2	1.7	0.9	25.0	4.5	100.0	99.9	125	104
2. Administrative and managerial	27.5	33.1	22.5	7.1	7.5	33.1	15.0	9.4	6.3	9.4	1.3	1.6	20.0	6.3	100.1	100.0	167	119
3. Clerical and related	30.4	22.6	8.7	3.8	10.1	49.1	10.1	11.3	8.7	3.8	1.4	0.0	30.4	9.4	99.8	100.0	72	50
4. Sales	25.7	26.7	11.9	4.7	10.1	40.7	22.0	10.5	7.3	7.0	1.8	0.0	21.1	10.5	99.9	100.1	114	81
5. Service	14.3	21.5	11.7	1.5	6.5	43.1	3.9	7.7	24.7	16.9	1.3	0.0	37.7	9.2	100.1	99.9	80	61
6. Agricultural	10.0	19.2	6.7	2.5	5.0	23.3	6.2	5.0	6.5	27.1	18.8	0.8	46.9	22.1	100.1	100.0	356	225
7. Production and related	15.1	16.0	8.8	2.4	6.9	36.3	7.5	6.0	6.9	22.8	2.1	0.0	52.7	16.4	100.0	99.9	784	469
N																	(1698)	(1109)

[a] The occupational classification is the major group International Standard Classification of Occupations (ISCO) (ILO 1969).

Appendix D Log-Linear Analysis of Gender Differences in Occupational Mobility from Father's to Respondent's Current Occupation; Employed Men and Women (All Ages), in Seven Industrialized Countries[a]

Model (null hypothesis), by country	X^2_{LR}	df	p	Δ
Austria				
A. Full mobility matrix (7×7×2)				
1. $[O_F]$ $[O_R]$ $[S]$	530.26	84	<.001	32.73
2. $[O_FS]$ $[O_R]$	527.50	78	<.001	32.58
3. $[O_RS]$ $[O_F]$	450.67	78	<.001	28.29
4. $[O_FO_R]$ $[S]$	107.18	48	<.001	13.82
5. $[O_FS]$ $[O_RS]$	447.91	72	<.001	28.02
6. $[O_FO_R]$ $[O_FS]$	104.42	42	<.001	13.93
7. $[O_FO_R]$ $[O_RS]$	27.60	42	>.5	5.76
8. $[O_FO_R]$ $[O_RS]$ $[O_FS]$	21.88	36	>.5	4.55
B. Main diagonal blocked (movers)				
1. $[O_F]$ $[O_R]$ $[S]$	164.28	70	<.001	13.20
2. $[O_FS]$ $[O_R]$	143.33	64	<.001	11.88
3. $[O_RS]$ $[O_F]$	96.95	64	<.010	9.05
4. $[O_FO_R]$ $[S]$	89.11	41	<.001	9.51
5. $[O_FS]$ $[O_RS]$	89.87	58	<.005	8.30
6. $[O_FO_R]$ $[O_FS]$	68.15	35	<.001	8.29
7. $[O_FO_R]$ $[O_RS]$	21.78	35	>.5	3.92
8. $[O_FO_R]$ $[O_RS]$ $[O_FS]$	18.58	29	>.5	3.45
Germany (Fed. Rep.)				
A. Full mobility matrix (7×7×2)				
1. $[O_F]$ $[O_R]$ $[S]$	443.68	84	<.001	26.02
2. $[O_FS]$ $[O_R]$	427.37	78	<.001	25.62
3. $[O_RS]$ $[O_F]$	337.54	78	<.001	20.44
4. $[O_FO_R]$ $[S]$	157.02	48	<.001	15.87
5. $[O_FS]$ $[O_RS]$	321.23	72	<.001	19.87
6. $[O_FO_R]$ $[O_FS]$	140.71	42	<.001	15.26
7. $[O_FO_R]$ $[O_RS]$	50.88	42	<.250	6.59
8. $[O_FO_R]$ $[O_RS]$ $[O_FS]$	33.45	36	>.5	5.24
B. Main diagonal blocked (movers)				
1. $[O_F]$ $[O_R]$ $[S]$	160.02	70	<.001	11.34
2. $[O_FS]$ $[O_R]$	129.82	64	<.001	10.02
3. $[O_RS]$ $[O_F]$	84.21	64	<.050	7.90
4. $[O_FO_R]$ $[S]$	107.35	41	<.001	9.48
5. $[O_FS]$ $[O_RS]$	69.16	58	<.250	7.13
6. $[O_FO_R]$ $[O_FS]$	77.15	35	<.001	7.88
7. $[O_FO_R]$ $[O_RS]$	31.54	35	>.5	4.40
8. $[O_FO_R]$ $[O_RS]$ $[O_FS]$	24.67	29	>.5	3.76

[a]O_F = occupation of father; O_R = occupation of respondent; S = sex of respondent. Great Britain, Denmark, Finland, Norway, and Sweden are not included in the table because of limitations in the way father's occupation was measured in these countries.

Appendix D Log-Linear Analysis of Gender Differences in Occupational Mobility from Father's to Respondent's Current Occupation; Employed Men and Women (All Ages), in Seven Industrialized Countries[a] *(Cont.)*

Model (null hypothesis), by country	X^2_{LR}	df	p	Δ
Israel				
A. Full mobility matrix (7×7×2)				
1. $[O_F] [O_R] [S]$	2897.65	84	<.001	22.95
2. $[O_FS] [O_R]$	2753.01	78	<.001	22.74
3. $[O_RS] [O_F]$	1339.83	78	<.001	14.59
4. $[O_FO_R] [S]$	1725.87	48	<.001	17.36
5. $[O_FS] [O_RS]$	1195.19	72	<.001	13.60
6. $[O_FO_R] [O_FS]$	1581.24	42	<.001	16.36
7. $[O_FO_R] [O_RS]$	168.06	42	<.001	4.02
8. $[O_FO_R] [O_RS] [O_FS]$	114.10	36	<.001	3.25
B. Main diagonal blocked (movers)				
1. $[O_F] [O_R] [S]$	1664.95	70	<.001	13.93
2. $[O_FS] [O_R]$	1439.98	64	<.001	12.98
3. $[O_RS] [O_F]$	589.46	64	<.001	7.53
4. $[O_FO_R] [S]$	1221.90	41	<.001	12.44
5. $[O_FS] [O_RS]$	466.41	58	<.001	6.54
6. $[O_FO_R] [O_FS]$	996.94	35	<.001	10.80
7. $[O_FO_R] [O_RS]$	146.42	35	<.001	3.49
8. $[O_FO_R] [O_RS] [O_FS]$	97.26	29	<.001	2.70
Japan				
A. Full mobility matrix (7×7×2)				
1. $[O_F] [O_R] [S]$	497.10	84	<.001	27.22
2. $[O_FS] [O_R]$	487.60	78	<.001	27.48
3. $[O_RS] [O_F]$	414.90	78	<.001	25.22
4. $[O_FO_R] [S]$	115.26	48	<.001	13.97
5. $[O_FS] [O_RS]$	405.40	72	<.001	24.99
6. $[O_FO_R] [O_FS]$	105.77	42	<.001	13.52
7. $[O_FO_R] [O_RS]$	33.06	42	>.5	6.02
8. $[O_FO_R] [O_RS] [O_FS]$	29.61	36	>.5	5.83
B. Main diagonal blocked (movers)				
1. $[O_F] [O_R] [S]$	132.83	70	<.001	10.93
2. $[O_FS] [O_R]$	124.17	64	<.001	10.31
3. $[O_RS] [O_F]$	81.50	64	<.100	8.24
4. $[O_FO_R] [S]$	77.39	41	<.001	8.07
5. $[O_FS] [O_RS]$	76.65	58	<.100	7.89
6. $[O_FO_R] [O_FS]$	68.73	35	<.001	7.37
7. $[O_FO_R] [O_RS]$	26.05	35	>.5	4.62
8. $[O_FO_R] [O_RS] [O_FS]$	20.50	29	>.5	3.76

[a]O_F = occupation of father; O_R = occupation of respondent; S = sex of respondent. Great Britain, Denmark, Finland, Norway, and Sweden are not included in the table because of limitations in the way father's occupation was measured in these countries.

Appendix D Log-Linear Analysis of Gender Differences in Occupational Mobility from Father's to Respondent's Current Occupation; Employed Men and Women (All Ages), in Seven Industrialized Countries[a] *(Cont.)*

Model (null hypothesis), by country	X^2_{LR}	df	p	Δ
Netherlands				
A. Full mobility matrix (7×7×2)				
1. $[O_F]$ $[O_R]$ $[S]$	315.93	84	<.001	28.20
2. $[O_FS]$ $[O_R]$	304.37	78	<.001	27.77
3. $[O_RS]$ $[O_F]$	225.01	78	<.001	21.65
4. $[O_FO_R]$ $[S]$	137.67	48	<.001	17.79
5. $[O_FS]$ $[O_RS]$	213.45	72	<.001	21.16
6. $[O_FO_R]$ $[O_FS]$	126.11	42	<.001	16.54
7. $[O_FO_R]$ $[O_RS]$	46.75	42	<.500	8.49
8. $[O_FO_R]$ $[O_RS]$ $[O_FS]$	40.44	36	<.500	7.25
B. Main diagonal blocked (movers)				
1. $[O_F]$ $[O_R]$ $[S]$	113.28	70	<.001	12.42
2. $[O_FS]$ $[O_R]$	111.73	64	<.001	12.27
3. $[O_RS]$ $[O_F]$	69.17	64	<.500	9.56
4. $[O_FO_R]$ $[S]$	73.06	41	<.005	9.62
5. $[O_FS]$ $[O_RS]$	65.73	58	<.250	9.34
6. $[O_FO_R]$ $[O_FS]$	71.51	35	<.001	9.16
7. $[O_FO_R]$ $[O_RS]$	28.95	35	>.5	5.80
8. $[O_FO_R]$ $[O_RS]$ $[O_FS]$	27.10	29	>.5	5.26
Northern Ireland				
A. Full mobility matrix (7×7×2)				
1. $[O_F]$ $[O_R]$ $[S]$	387.50	84	<.001	29.68
2. $[O_FS]$ $[O_R]$	369.21	78	<.001	29.10
3. $[O_RS]$ $[O_F]$	275.63	78	<.001	24.29
4. $[O_FO_R]$ $[S]$	148.88	48	<.001	18.57
5. $[O_FS]$ $[O_RS]$	257.34	72	<.001	23.40
6. $[O_FO_R]$ $[O_FS]$	130.60	42	<.001	16.88
7. $[O_FO_R]$ $[O_RS]$	37.01	42	>.5	6.62
8. $[O_FO_R]$ $[O_RS]$ $[O_FS]$	30.27	36	>.5	6.06
B. Main diagonal blocked (movers)				
1. $[O_F]$ $[O_R]$ $[S]$	127.90	70	<.001	13.29
2. $[O_FS]$ $[O_R]$	117.96	64	<.001	12.46
3. $[O_RS]$ $[O_F]$	73.55	64	<.250	8.77
4. $[O_FO_R]$ $[S]$	84.91	41	<.001	10.53
5. $[O_FS]$ $[O_RS]$	64.13	58	<.500	8.31
6. $[O_FO_R]$ $[O_FS]$	74.97	35	<.001	10.00
7. $[O_FO_R]$ $[O_RS]$	30.56	35	>.5	5.27
8. $[O_FO_R]$ $[O_RS]$ $[O_FS]$	22.93	29	>.5	4.14

[a]O_F = occupation of father; O_R = occupation of respondent; S = sex of respondent. Great Britain, Denmark, Finland, Norway, and Sweden are not included in the table because of limitations in the way father's occupation was measured in these countries.

Appendix D   Log-Linear Analysis of Gender Differences in Occupational Mobility from Father's to Respondent's Current Occupation; Employed Men and Women (All Ages), in Seven Industrialized Countries[a] *(Cont.)*

Model (null hypothesis), by country	X^2_{LR}	df	p	Δ
United States				
A. Full mobility matrix $(7 \times 7 \times 2)$				
1. $[O_F] [O_R] [S]$	1121.91	84	<.001	26.67
2. $[O_F S] [O_R]$	1112.98	78	<.001	26.50
3. $[O_R S] [O_F]$	471.11	78	<.001	15.34
4. $[O_F O_R] [S]$	715.46	48	<.001	20.89
5. $[O_F S] [O_R S]$	462.18	72	<.001	15.35
6. $[O_F O_R] [O_F S]$	706.54	42	<.001	20.52
7. $[O_F O_R] [O_R S]$	64.66	42	<.025	4.62
8. $[O_F O_R] [O_R S] [O_F S]$	55.18	36	<.025	3.76
B. Main diagonal blocked (movers)				
1. $[O_F] [O_R] [S]$	610.38	70	<.001	16.46
2. $[O_F S] [O_R]$	589.51	64	<.001	16.30
3. $[O_R S] [O_F]$	195.12	64	<.001	8.66
4. $[O_F O_R] [S]$	455.05	41	<.001	14.52
5. $[O_F S] [O_R S]$	191.69	58	<.001	8.66
6. $[O_F O_R] [O_F S]$	434.18	35	<.001	14.09
7. $[O_F O_R] [O_R S]$	39.78	35	<.500	3.03
8. $[O_F O_R] [O_R S] [O_F S]$	31.54	29	<.500	2.48

[a]O_F = occupation of father; O_R = occupation of respondent; S = sex of respondent. Great Britain, Denmark, Finland, Norway, and Sweden are not included in the table because of limitations in the way father's occupation was measured in these countries.

Appendix E Correlations of All Variables in Occupation Models, for Employed Men and Women 20–64 in Twelve Industrialized Countries (males below the diagonal, females above)[a]

	Father's occupation-prestige	Father's occupation-wage-rate scale	Age	$(Age*)^2$	Marital status	Years of schooling	Respondent's occupation-prestige	Respondent's occupation-wage-rate scale
Austria								
Father's occupation-prestige		.825	.069	.074	.069	.261	.302	.215
Father's occupation-wage-rate scale	.826		.017	.074	.042	.416	.289	.336
Age	.028	−.009		−.004	−.273	−.095	−.019	−.050
$(Age*)^2$	.028	.018	.202		.236	.123	.085	.109
Marital status (Never married=1)	−.032	−.063	−.419	.256		.099	−.003	.022
Years of schooling	.262	.374	−.028	.032	.052		.432	.536
Respondent's occupation-prestige	.297	.372	.065	.007	−.076	.561		.864
Respondent's occupation-wage-rate scale	.282	.429	.077	−.007	−.100	.565	.867	
Denmark								
Father's occupation-prestige		.819	.003	.065	.201	.259	.194	.162
Father's occupation-wage-rate scale	.799		−.013	.032	.153	.367	.178	.209
Age	.085	−.009		.173	−.204	−.253	−.144	−.168
$(Age*)^2$	−.002	−.027	−.039		.147	.044	.062	.029

[a] To avoid multicollinearity, a constant equal to the mean age of the group was subtracted from the age variable (i.e., Age* = Age − mean of age). Means and standard deviations for all variables are provided in Table 5.1.

Appendix E Correlations of All Variables in Occupation Models, for Employed Men and Women 20-64 in Twelve Industrialized Countries (males below the diagonal, females above)[a] *(Cont.)*

	Father's occupation-prestige	Father's occupation-wage-rate scale	Age	$(Age^*)^2$	Marital status	Years of schooling	Respondent's occupation-prestige	Respondent's occupation-wage-rate scale
Denmark								
Marital status (Never married=1)	.033	−.039	−.250	.220		.266	.187	.150
Years of schooling	.273	.395	−.096	−.045	−.076		.592	.550
Respondent's occupation-prestige	.330	.346	.009	−.011	−.149	.669		.887
Respondent's occupation-wage-rate scale	.222	.339	.020	−.084	−.149	.661	.822	
Finland								
Father's occupation-prestige		.821	.056	−.073	−.007	.354	.360	.324
Father's occupation-wage-rate scale	.804		−.044	−.021	−.019	.442	.365	.386
Age	−.024	−.101		−.119	−.193	−.269	.038	−.021
$(Age^*)^2$	.098	.052	.331		.230	−.015	−.107	−.086
Marital status (Never married=1)	−.009	−.041	−.345	.119		.159	.062	.065
Years of schooling	.229	.338	−.198	−.098	−.064		.652	.704
Respondent's occupation-prestige	.250	.249	.145	.002	−.187	.431		.776
Respondent's occupation-wage-rate scale	.224	.343	.071	−.032	−.198	.565	.827	

Germany (Fed. Rep.)

	(1)	(2)	(3)	(4)	(5)	(6)	(7)
Father's occupation-prestige							
Father's occupation-wage-rate scale	.799						
Age	−.029	−.136					
(Age*)²	−.023	.021	−.112				
Marital status (Never married=1)	.030	.122	−.513	.439			
Years of schooling	.336	.373	−.079	.016	.005		
Respondent's occupation-prestige	.313	.326	.028	−.033	−.078	.610	
Respondent's occupation-wage-rate scale	.322	.417	−.003	−.028	−.058	.645	.815

Great Britain[b]

	(1)	(2)	(3)	(4)	(5)	(6)	(7)
Father's occupation-prestige							
Father's occupation-wage-rate scale	—						
Age	−.019	—					
(Age*)²	−.137	—	.240				
Marital status (Never married=1)	−.093	—	−.347	−.240			
Years of schooling	−.078	—	−.156	−.045	−.030		
Respondent's occupation-prestige	.151	—	−.181	−.048	−.052	.476	
Respondent's occupation-wage-rate scale	.135	—	−.364	−.083	−.057	.407	.943

[a] To avoid multicollinearity, a constant equal to the mean age of the group was subtracted from the age variable (i.e., Age* = Age − mean of age). Means and standard deviations for all variables are provided in Table 5.1.

[b] The father's occupational wage-rate variable could not be constructed for Great Britain, due to the way father's occupation was measured.

Appendix E Correlations of All Variables in Occupation Models, for Employed Men and Women 20-64 in Twelve Industrialized Countries (males below the diagonal, females above)[a] *(Cont.)*

Israel

	Father's occupation-prestige	Father's occupation-wage-rate scale	Age	$(Age^*)^2$	Marital status	Years of schooling	Respondent's occupation-prestige	Respondent's occupation-wage-rate scale
Father's occupation-prestige		.866	.101	.062	.009	.279	.211	.212
Father's occupation-wage-rate scale	.850		.166	.116	-.001	.205	.151	.137
Age	.154	.186		.605	-.520	-.248	-.170	-.178
$(Age^*)^2$	.055	.075	.168		-.076	-.166	-.176	-.184
Marital status (Never married=1)	.043	.041	-.475	.290		.060	-.023	-.020
Years of schooling	.273	.230	-.169	-.050	.041		.675	.654
Respondent's occupation-prestige	.250	.204	-.010	-.086	-.052	.587		.838
Respondent's occupation-wage-rate scale	.266	.245	.042	-.075	-.070	.560	.902	

Japan

	Father's occupation-prestige	Father's occupation-wage-rate scale	Age	$(Age^*)^2$	Marital status	Years of schooling	Respondent's occupation-prestige	Respondent's occupation-wage-rate scale
Father's occupation-prestige		.883	-.174	.065	.117	.330	.271	.261
Father's occupation-wage-rate scale	.909		-.194	.086	.172	.324	.281	.319
Age	-.040	-.098		.058	-.575	-.366	-.192	-.215
$(Age^*)^2$	-.017	-.070	.376		.402	-.089	-.023	-.041
Marital status (Never married=1)	.091	.128	-.506	.196		.189	.146	.190
Years of schooling	.330	.372	-.186	-.179	.062		.439	.434

Correlation matrix (continued)

	Father's occupation-prestige	Father's occupation-wage-rate scale	Age	(Age*)²	Marital status	Years of schooling	Respondent's occupation-prestige	Respondent's occupation-wage-rate scale
Respondent's occupation-prestige	.206	.217	.258	-.014	-.178	.380	.823	.922
Respondent's occupation-wage-rate scale	.215	.251	.145	-.045	-.118	.394		

Netherlands

	Father's occupation-prestige	Father's occupation-wage-rate scale	Age	(Age*)²	Marital status	Years of schooling	Respondent's occupation-prestige	Respondent's occupation-wage-rate scale
Father's occupation-prestige		.878	-.037	-.128	-.008	.322	.231	.232
Father's occupation-wage-rate scale	.878		-.042	-.102	.015	.336	.227	.247
Age	-.037	-.042		.299	.804	-.349	-.008	.013
(Age*)²	-.128	-.102	.299		-.447	-.239	.006	.021
Marital status (Never married=1)	-.008	.015	.804	-.447		-.173	.095	.096
Years of schooling	.322	.336	-.349	-.239	-.173		.513	.484
Respondent's occupation-prestige	.340	.351	.019	.176	.135	.106		.950
Respondent's occupation-wage-rate scale	.303	.361	.054	-.150	-.112	.483	.891	

Northern Ireland

	Father's occupation-prestige	Father's occupation-wage-rate scale	Age	(Age*)²	Marital status	Years of schooling	Respondent's occupation-prestige	Respondent's occupation-wage-rate scale
Father's occupation-prestige		.718	.060	.011	.104	.387	.318	.287
Father's occupation-wage-rate scale	.718		.023	-.001	.122	.389	.326	.316
Age	.060	.023		.079	-.321	-.181	-.039	-.030
(Age*)²	.011	-.001	.079		.137	.067	.016	.034
	.045	.020	.035	.177	.014			

[a] To avoid multicollinearity, a constant equal to the mean age of the group was subtracted from the age variable (i.e., Age* = Age − mean of age). Means and standard deviations for all variables are provided in Table 5.1.

Appendix E Correlations of All Variables in Occupation Models, for Employed Men and Women 20–64 in Twelve Industrialized Countries (males below the diagonal, females above)[a] *(Cont.)*

	Father's occupation-prestige	Father's occupation-wage-rate scale	Age	(Age*)²	Marital status	Years of schooling	Respondent's occupation-prestige	Respondent's occupation-wage-rate scale
Northern Ireland								
Marital status (Never married=1)	.074	.020	-.337	.229		.190	.107	.049
Years of schooling	.291	.356	-.244	-.050	.116		.611	.659
Respondent's occupation-prestige	.409	.311	.024	-.056	-.006	.477		.909
Respondent's occupation-wage-rate scale	.257	.366	-.057	-.048	-.034	.543	.780	
Norway								
Father's occupation-prestige		.902	.012	.032	.089	.434	.401	.354
Father's occupation-wage-rate scale	.876		-.052	.065	.097	.426	.366	.333
Age	-.073	-.163		-.017	.023	-.263	-.197	-.140
(Age*)²	-.017	-.006	-.033		.053	.060	.082	.080
Marital Status (Never married=1)	.036	.056	-.229	.232		.058	.121	.124
Years of schooling	.387	.438	-.254	-.039	.094		.711	.708
Respondent's occupation-prestige	.369	.369	-.156	-.080	.032	.674		.871
Respondent's occupation-wage-rate scale	.324	.402	-.162	-.059	-.029	.682	.810	

Sweden

	1	2	3	4	5	6	7	8
Father's occupation-prestige		.907	−.054	.116	.077	.489	.296	.284
Father's occupation-wage-rate scale	.852		−.092	.107	.069	.539	.392	.348
Age	−.031	−.085		.222	−.194	−.339	−.185	−.178
(Age*)²	.022	.036	−.112		.185	.004	−.009	−.015
Marital status (Never married=1)	.046	−.013	−.310	.219		.132	−.016	.005
Years of schooling	.435	.510	−.260	.037	−.023		.686	.608
Respondent's occupation-prestige	.327	.345	−.103	−.060	−.138	.644		.913
Respondent's occupation-wage-rate scale	.276	.351	−.019	−.060	−.217	.634	.839	

United States

	1	2	3	4	5	6	7	8
Father's occupation-prestige		.799	−.142	−.066	.044	.376	.293	.258
Father's occupation-wage-rate scale	.805		−.168	−.084	.047	.350	.267	.238
Age	−.057	−.088		.330	−.331	−.247	−.079	−.033
(Age*)²	−.008	.006	.229		.146	−.118	−.061	−.039
Marital status (Never married=1)	.086	.134	−.357	.192		.152	.092	.051
Years of schooling	.262	.286	−.194	−.127	.121		.564	.482
Respondent's occupation-prestige	.228	.239	.060	−.110	−.057	.582		.847
Respondent's occupation-wage-rate scale	.220	.259	.061	−.126	−.061	.507	.825	

[a] To avoid multicollinearity, a constant equal to the mean age of the group was subtracted from the age variable (i.e., Age* = Age − mean of age). Means and standard deviations for all variables are provided in Table 5.1.

Appendix F Coefficients of a Model of Occupational Prestige Attainment, for Currently Employed Men and Women 20–64, in Twelve Industrialized Countries[a]

		Father's occupational prestige	Age	$(Age^*)^2$	Marital status	Years of schooling	Intercept
				Metric coefficients			
Austria	Men	.179*	.045	−.000	−2.56	3.02*	1.31
	Women	.220*	−.016	.003	−1.93	2.63*	3.79
Denmark	Men	.191*	.028	.004	−3.83*	3.27*	4.79
	Women	.038	.001	.002	.688	3.22*	10.3
Finland	Men	.217*	.211*	−.003	−2.11	2.30*	4.74
	Women	.153*	.199*	−.006	.356	2.87*	1.02
Germany	Men	.135*	.050	−.001	−2.01	2.94*	4.16
(Fed. Rep.)	Women	.064	−.039	−.003	−1.67	2.40*	15.1
Great	Men	.062*	−.016	−.008*	−2.96	2.73*	10.3
Britain	Women	−.037	.050	−.002	2.74	3.38*	3.09
Israel	Men	.100*	.076*	−.006*	−.993	1.87*	16.2
	Women	.034*	−.002	−.005*	−2.08*	2.16*	19.1
Japan	Men	.114*	.343*	−.005	−.500	1.43*	9.43
	Women	.173*	.017	−.002	1.97	1.53*	14.1
Netherlands	Men	.176*	.141*	−.005	−3.00	2.40*	8.23
	Women	.013	.066	.006	1.97	2.95*	5.86
Northern	Men	.265*	.105*	−.004	−.962	2.86*	−3.39
Ireland	Women	.087	.085	−.004	.482	3.90*	−10.1
Norway	Men	.166*	.006	−.004	−.740	2.78*	11.4
	Women	.138	−.031	.003	2.67	3.12*	6.87
Sweden	Men	.085	.021	−.006	−3.96*	2.84*	13.2
	Women	−.067	.046	.000	−4.02	3.53*	9.98
United	Men	.104*	.178*	−.006*	−2.28*	2.36*	2.18
States	Women	.109*	.093*	−.002	1.43	2.63*	1.13

[a] Age* = Age − mean of age. Means and standard deviations for all variables are provided in Table 5.1 and correlations in Appendix E.
* Metric coefficient is twice its standard error.

Appendix F Coefficients of a Model of Occupational Prestige Attainment, for Currently Employed Men and Women 20–64, in Twelve Industrialized Countries[a] *(Cont.)*

		Father's occupational prestige	Age	$(Age^*)^2$	Marital status	Years of schooling	R^2
		Standardized coefficients					
Austria	Men	.156*	.043	−.003	−.080	.526*	.350
	Women	.206*	−.016	.040	−.069	.378*	.229
Denmark	Men	.161*	.030	.042	−.109*	.622*	.486
	Women	.039	.001	.031	.022	.575*	.354
Finland	Men	.160*	.219*	−.035	−.079	.430*	.272
	Women	.107*	.206*	−.067	.012	.667*	.489
Germany	Men	.124*	.046	−.008	−.058	.572*	.394
(Fed. Rep.)	Women	.064	−.042	−.040	−.060	.426*	.215
Great	Men	.108*	−.106	−.087*	−.079	.469*	.256
Britain	Women	−.063	.050	−.025	.081	.515*	.272
Israel	Men	.088*	.072*	−.066*	−.026	.572*	.364
	Women	.033*	−.002	−.072*	−.070*	.658*	.466
Japan	Men	.087*	.355*	−.070	−.017	.406*	.268
	Women	.141*	.022	−.033	.083	.381*	.214
Netherlands	Men	.166*	.131*	−.059	−.085	.530*	.367
	Women	.014	.060	.104	.073	.541*	.288
Northern	Men	.283*	.102*	−.039	−.032	.421*	.322
Ireland	Women	.089	.080	−.044	.017	.591*	.387
Norway	Men	.127*	.006	−.048	−.019	.627*	.472
	Women	.112	−.029	.036	.072	.648*	.523
Sweden	Men	.064	.020	−.058	−.108*	.621*	.437
	Women	−.058	.043	.004	−.101*	.742*	.486
United	Men	.087*	.171*	−.061*	−.063*	.592*	.384
States	Women	.099*	.090*	−.026	.039	.540*	.331

[a] Age* = Age − mean of age. Means and standard deviations for all variables are provided in Table 5.1 and correlations in Appendix E.
* Metric coefficient is twice its standard error.

Appendix G Occupational Distribution of Older Employed Women,[a] by Marital Status, for Twelve Industrialized Countries (in percentages)

Occupational Category[b]	Austria		Denmark		Finland		Germany (Fed. Rep.)		Great Britain		Israel	
	Ever married	Never married	Ever married	Never married	Ever married	Never married	Ever married	Never married	Ever married	Never married	Ever married	Never married
1. Professional and technical	6.0	15.1	14.0	33.3	13.4	25.0	14.3	21.0	12.7	34.3	31.4	33.7
2. Administrative and managerial	0.7	0.0	0.0	0.0	1.3	2.8	0.0	0.0	1.2	0.0	1.3	1.4
3. Clerical and related	20.9	26.4	26.3	27.8	15.1	25.0	38.4	39.7	26.1	37.3	23.6	28.9
4. Sales	12.4	9.4	10.8	5.6	11.6	0.0	16.0	19.8	13.4	7.5	10.8	7.6
5. Service	18.1	13.2	19.4	11.1	13.4	16.7	12.9	8.1	26.9	10.4	19.4	15.1
6. Agricultural	23.4	11.3	21.0	16.7	32.8	22.2	3.4	1.3	1.3	3.0	3.6	0.7
7. Production and related	18.4	24.5	8.6	5.6	12.5	8.3	15.0	10.1	18.4	7.5	10.0	12.5
Total	99.9	99.9	100.1	100.1	100.1	100.0	100.0	100.0	100.0	100.0	100.1	99.9
N	261	49	210	20	228	35	282	46	239	31	2784	367
Index of dissimilarity	20.7		20.8		26.4		11.8		34.5		10.3	

[a] "Older Employed Women" includes those women older than the average age at which women in the particular country first marry. See text for additional details.
[b] International Standard Classification of Occupations (ISCO) major groups (International Labour Office 1969).

Appendix G Occupational Distribution of Older Employed Women,[a] by Marital Status, for Twelve Industrialized Countries (in percentages) (Cont.)

Occupational Category[b]	Japan		Netherlands		Northern Ireland		Norway		Sweden		United States	
	Ever married	Never married	Ever married	Never married	Ever married	Never married	Ever married	Never married	Ever married	Never married	Ever married	Never married
1. Professional and technical	6.9	9.4	22.3	33.3	17.4	21.2	18.5	23.8	25.9	5.0	21.5	35.7
2. Administrative and managerial	1.0	4.7	1.0	0.0	1.4	0.0	1.6	9.5	0.5	0.0	3.5	1.3
3. Clerical and related	6.6	23.6	30.1	31.5	12.5	28.8	16.9	23.8	26.4	50.0	32.5	34.4
4. Sales	11.3	29.2	21.4	9.3	7.6	9.1	15.3	4.8	12.7	10.0	6.8	3.8
5. Service	11.0	9.4	17.5	20.4	32.6	13.6	16.9	28.6	25.0	30.0	19.2	15.9
6. Agricultural	46.2	4.7	3.9	0.0	2.8	6.1	21.8	9.5	1.4	0.0	0.5	0.0
7. Production and related	17.0	18.9	3.9	5.6	25.7	21.2	8.9	0.0	8.2	5.0	16.0	8.9
Total	100.0	99.9	100.1	100.1	100.0	100.0	99.9	100.0	100.1	100.0	100.0	100.0
N	343	23	80	42	135	62	112	19	240	22	1065	148
Index of dissimilarity	43.0		17.0		24.9		31.8		28.6		16.1	

[a] "Older Employed Women" includes those women older than the average age at which women in the particular country first marry. See text for additional details.

[b] International Standard Classification of Occupations (ISCO) major groups (International Labour Office 1969).

Notes

Chapter 1 notes

1. The analytic focus is on the economic role of women in industrial societies. A study of women's role in preindustrial societies is beyond the scope of the present analysis and is already well documented (see, for example, Boserup 1970; Friedl 1975; and Huber and Spitze 1983). Although such massive social changes as the Industrial Revolution unarguably affected the work women did, the modern data I rely on cannot address these issues.

2. The sample, stratified by urban and suburban location and selected family composition variables (for example, number and ages of children and age of wife), consisted of 1,296 households selected randomly from 50,000 husband-wife families in Syracuse, New York, and surrounding suburbs.

3. More recent data (collected in 1975 and 1976) show that while these overall patterns persist, the difference in the amount of time spent on family work by husbands and wives has narrowed somewhat. Using time diaries similar to those employed by Walker and Woods (1976), Pleck (1983:281) found that nonemployed wives spend 6.8 hours per day on family work compared to the 4 hours spent by employed wives. Husbands, in contrast, spend 1.8 hours per day on family work if their wives are not employed and 1.9 hours if their wives are employed.

4. The survey sites for the comparative analysis were drawn on a selective basis from medium-sized industrial cities. Fifteen survey sites from twelve different countries were chosen, including those from Western Europe (Belgium, France, and West Germany), Eastern Europe (Bulgaria, Czechoslovakia, East Germany, Hungary, Poland, the Soviet Union, and Yugoslavia), and the Western hemisphere (Peru and the United States).

Chapter 2 notes

1. It is somewhat of a misnomer to call the enumeration of unpaid family workers in developing societies an "overcount," since family workers in these societies do play a vital productive function. The problem of noncomparability comes about because countries differ in whether they count this segment of workers as part of the productive labor force.

2. Austria and Netherlands—1971 data (ILO 1977, Table 1); Great Britain—1973 data (United Nations 1974, Table 38); Denmark, Finland, West Germany, Norway, and Sweden—1970 data (ILO 1977, Table 1); Israel—1972 data (ILO 1977, Table 1); Japan—1969 data (ILO 1970, Table 1); Northern Ireland—1966 data (United Nations 1973, Table 8); United States—1976 data (U.S. Bureau of the Census 1977).

3. The categories include: (1) high-prestige professional and technical, (2) administrative and managerial, (3) high-prestige clerical and related, (4) high-prestige sales, (5) low-prestige professional and technical, (6) high-prestige agricultural, (7) high-prestige production and related, (8) high-prestige service, (9) medium-prestige production and related, (10) low-prestige clerical and related, (11) low-prestige sales, (12) low-prestige agricultural, (13) low-prestige service, and (14) low-prestige production and related (Treiman 1977, Table 9.1). Refer to Chapter 3 and Treiman (1977, Table 9.1 and Appendix A) for examples of occupations included within these major categories.

4. Recall that the fourteen-category classification described in note 3 is merely the seven-category ISCO classification with additional prestige distinctions.

5. Northern Ireland and Great Britain had no personal income variable and thus were not used in creating the occupational wage rate scale.

6. This formula was adapted from Nunnally (1967, 108).

7. The following formula was used for the transformation:

$$X' = \frac{100 \times (X - \text{minimum score})}{(\text{maximum score} - \text{minimum score})}$$

where, X' = transformed score,
X = original score.

Chapter 3 notes

1. Chapter 6 compares the participation and occupational composition patterns of ever- and never-married women.

2. Gaskin (1979) created a standard occupation classification by matching 1960–1961 census data for seven countries [she used the International Standard Classification of Occupations (ISCO) as the base classification (ILO 1969)]. The resulting scale had eighty-six occupational categories, a level of detail not available in previous investigations of gender differences in occupational placement.

3. The overrepresentation of women in medicine and other scientific/technical fields in the Soviet Union is expected to decrease since medical and other scientific schools currently favor men in their admissions policies

(Dodge 1971, 215). In addition, there is some indication that women's integration into male employment in the Soviet Union is due in large measure to the heavy male war losses suffered during World War II. Dodge (p. 208) estimated that in 1946, the sex ratio in the Soviet Union was only 74 males per 100 females, an imbalance that has yet to correct itself.

4. Because the patterns described in this section derive from cross-section data, they may be misleading in times of rapid change. From 1900 to 1960, for example, the United States pattern changed from an early peak to a double peak pattern (Oppenheimer 1970, 9). In addition, recent work by Kreps and Leaper (1976, Chart 1B) documented that cross-section data underestimate the extent to which the United States has recently shifted toward the single peak pattern. Data for five-year age cohorts indicate that the double peak pattern is no longer the norm among the youngest cohorts of United States women.

5. Note that Israeli men also have a much lower participation rate in the twenty- to twenty-four-year old age cohort, relative to the remaining countries.

6. Some of this differential is undoubtedly due to differences in how the economically active population was defined in the three countries. In the Scandinavian countries, the employed category includes those who worked full or part time during the preceding year, while in the United States the employed population includes only those employed "last week," a categorization that underestimates the total number of women who worked during the preceding year (see Chapter 2 for details).

7. As previously described, the higher proportions employed in the four Scandinavian data sets, relative to those in other countries, are due in part to the way the employment variable was constructed. See Chapter 2 for details.

8. For crosscultural descriptions of the history and current implementation of strategies for achieving equal employment opportunity for women, see Ratner (1979). Other discussions of the impact of social arrangements and legislative policy on women's employment can be found in OECD (1975, 1979), Haavio-Mannila (1975), Safilios-Rothschild (1975), Sullerot (1976), Leijon (1976), Jonung (1977, 1978a), Haavio-Mannila and Sokolowska (1978), Kamerman and Kahn (1978), Kamerman (1979), and Shaffer (1981).

9. Since the focus is on the occupational attainments of men and women, it makes little sense to include those who are not currently employed. This restriction is potentially more serious for females than for males since a selectivity bias may result from restricting the sample to working women. Although Fligstein and Wolf (1978) suggested that any such bias is minimal, at least in the United States, knowledge of this factor should be kept in mind in interpreting sex differences that do emerge.

10. The estimates of the proportions of Israeli men and women in agriculture may be slightly low since members of kibbutzim were not included in the sample.

11. These estimates of sex dissimilarity in occupational distribution are lower, for the most part, than those of Gross (1968) and Gaskin (1979) because they are based on only fourteen occupational categories.

12. Note that this transition from agricultural to clerical work is still occurring in other countries as well—Table 3.3 suggests that smaller proportions of the female labor force engaged in agricultural production are strongly associated with larger proportions of the female labor force in clerical work (the correlation is −.89, as calculated from Table 3.3).

13. Undoubtedly there are a few Norwegian women doing high-prestige production work, but none are included in the present sample.

14. "Occupations mainly held by women" are those occupational groups where women are overrepresented by 20 percent or more, given their representation in the labor force as a whole (based on data in the last column in Table 3.4). "Occupations mainly held by men" are those where women are underrepresented by 20 percent or more, given their representation in the labor force as a whole. Occupations not meeting either of these criteria are described as jobs where women are either over or underrepresented.

15. The average deviation for those cells differing from the row trend was derived by taking the mean of the underlined percentages in Table 3.4; the average deviation for those cells conforming to the row trend was obtained by calculating the mean for the remaining cells (bracketed percentages were omitted from both calculations).

16. An alternative explanation for the Northern Ireland finding is that the coding of teachers is not as precise as one might wish. The Northern Ireland data set has only two categories of teachers: "university teachers" and "teachers, not elsewhere classified." Well over two-thirds of the women in the high-prestige professional category in Northern Ireland are classified in the latter group, a category that presumably includes school principals, special education teachers, and high school teachers (high-prestige occupations in the classification I employ in this study), as well as elementary-school teachers (low-prestige occupations in my classification). It is possible to speculate that if a more detailed occupational classification had been available, specifically one that allowed greater distinctions between different kinds of teachers, fewer women would have been in the high-prestige professional category. The problem of coding will be discussed further in a subsequent section.

17. The other occupation groups with an overrepresentation of females, given their average proportion in the labor force, include low-prestige professional and technical (for example, junior high and primary teachers, nurses, librarians), high-prestige service (such as, beauticians, airline flight attendants), and low-prestige clerical and related (for example, cashiers, post office clerks, receptionists).

18. The other occupation groups with an underrepresentation of females, given their average proportion in the labor force, include high-prestige professional and technical (for example, chemists, engineers, physicians, high school teachers, the clergy), high-prestige sales (such as, working proprietors, traveling salesmen, insurance agents), high-prestige agricultural [for example, farmer, farm foreman (but also unpaid family farm workers)], low-prestige agricultural (for example, field crop workers, gardeners, fishermen), and low-prestige production (for example, paperhanger, longshoremen, porter, laborer).

19. Since 1939, when the first *Dictionary of Occupational Titles* (DOT) was published, the Division of Occupational Analysis of the Department of Labor has conducted on-site job analyses at establishments to define the characteristics of jobs in the United States economy. Now in its fourth edition, the DOT (U.S. Department of Labor 1977) provides definitions and occupational ratings for 12,099 specific occupations. Other industrial societies (notably Japan and Canada) have adopted or modified the DOT for use in their own programs of occupational research.

20. The upgrading of the complexity of women's jobs with respect to "things" was due to the abolition, between the third and fourth editions, of the "no significant relationship" rating in the DOT's worker function variables. For critical evaluations of the *Dictionary of Occupational Titles*, see Miller et al. (1980) and Cain and Treiman (1981).

21. This figure and those following were calculated from Table 3.4 (30 percent = 46−16).

22. The results of the summary analysis are:
Regression equation (unstandardized coefficients):
$$\hat{I} = -19.3 + 1.47E - .496P$$
Regression equation (standardized coefficients):
$$\hat{I} = .756E - .449P$$
where, I = average occupational earnings;

      E = average education of occupational category;

      P = average percent female of occupational category.

R^2 = .838; all coefficients are greater than twice their standard error.

Chapter 4 notes

1. One would not expect a similar overrepresentation of working- or lower-class sons in the male labor force, since men from all classes have traditionally been responsible for the financial security of their family.

2. To distinguish between these two traditions in the present study, I use *mobility* to refer to the mobility table tradition and *attainment* to refer to status attainment.

3. In the Great Britain survey, father's occupation was measured in such a way as to make its translation into the categorical classification impossible. Additionally, in the four Scandinavian countries (Denmark, Finland, Norway, and Sweden), the father's occupation variable did not include a category for service workers. Because of inadequacies in these data, the mobility analyses were performed in only seven of the twelve countries. Fortunately, Pöntinen (1980) performed a similar investigation of patterns of mobility of men and women in the four Scandinavian countries using the same data, although a different occupational classification. I use his results to supplement this discussion.

4. The occupational classification is the seven-category ISCO Classification (ILO 1969). Recall that this classification is a collapsed version of the fourteen-category variable used in Chapter 3. Some loss of precision occurred with collapsing, as evidenced by the decrease in the indexes of dissimilarity between the current occupations of men and women (compare the figures

in the second column of the "Total" row in Table 4.1 with the indexes of dissimilarity derived on the basis of the fourteen-category classification presented in Table 3.3; see also Table 6.4 for a comparison of the two classifications for all twelve countries). Table 4.1 and Appendixes B and C describe gender differences in the pattern of movement between occupational origins and destinations. Unfortunately, because most of the data sets have no information on the respondent's mother, it is only possible to consider intergenerational mobility from father to respondent, and the present analysis is thus limited in the ways suggested.

5. The supply figures in the second column of Table 4.1 are lower than those reported in Hauser et al. (1977, Table 8.1) because only employed men and women are included while Hauser's and his coauthors' estimates included "not in the labor force" as a separate category.

6. Pöntinen (1980) used the same Scandinavian data used in this study, but a different occupational classification. His has six categories: upper white collar, lower white collar, entrepreneur, skilled worker, unskilled worker, and farmer.

7. With one small exception, the United States findings are reassuringly similar to previous analyses using different data (Hauser et al. 1977; Dunton and Featherman 1979). Hauser and his coauthors found a significant sex difference in inheritance but no gender differences in the mobility process among movers, as the present analysis does, and as did Dunton and Featherman. However, in the present case, as in Dunton and Featherman, the sex difference in inheritance is sufficiently large to produce significance in the global test of gender differences in the relationship between father's and respondent's occupation (that is, pure mobility).

8. Bishop and her coauthors (1975, 329) proposed a different procedure for comparing chi-square values across samples with different N's. They suggested dividing each estimated chi-square by N, which produces an alternative estimate of the closeness of fit of the hypothesized values to the true values. This alternative statistic can then be compared across samples (or in the present case, countries) to measure the relative goodness of fit of specified models. An example will clarify the use of this statistic. In the present Israel-United States comparison, the results of Model 5 relative to Model 4 suggest that the "father's occupation-sex" interaction (the A5 vs. A4 comparison) significantly improves the fit of the model in Israel, but not in the United States. The interesting question is whether the significance of the Israeli interaction is attributable to the relatively larger Israeli sample or to a real difference in the mobility process of that country (compared with the United States). The estimated chi-square statistic for Israel's A5 vs. A4 comparison is 53.96, while the comparable statistic for the United States is a lower 9.48. If these statistics are compared, the incorrect generalization could be made that the "father's occupation-sex" interaction improves the model's goodness of fit better in Israel than in the United States. This generalization, however, is not appropriate, since the chi-square statistic is in part a function of sample size, increasing as N increases. Dividing each chi-square value by N produces figures of .006 in Israel and .003 in the United States, statistics now standardized for differences in sample size. On

the basis of these revised figures, it can be deduced that the specified interaction improves the model's fit about equally well in the two countries, providing additional evidence that the significance of the Israel interaction (relative to the nonsignificance of the United States interaction) is probably more a reflection of differences in sample size than true differences in the mobility process between the two countries.

9. The focus here is on the net effect of sex differences in social origins, since this study is most interested in determining whether such an interaction must be specified in addition to the mobility and "current occupation-sex" interactions. Some readers may wonder whether sex differences in social origins account for a significant portion of the total association if this interaction is entered prior to the other two-way interactions. To test this possibility, I calculated the gross effect of sex differences in social origins (by subtracting the chi-square value of Model A2 from Model A1 for each country in Appendix D and determining its significance). As before, Germany and Israel have significant gender differences in social origins. Additionally, significant sex differences in social origins exist in Northern Ireland (also an early peak country), a result that disappears when viewed as net of gender differences in composition. It should be noted that although sex differences in father's occupation are significant in three of the countries, they are still small relative to the mobility or "current occupation-sex" interactions.

Chapter 5 notes

1. The gender similarity in status derives from the way in which the SEI status scores were created. Blau and Duncan (1967, 125) described status scores as deriving from approximately equal weightings of the average education and income of occupational categories. As Oppenheimer (1968) and Treiman and Terrell (1975c) found, incumbents in women's occupations are highly educated but earn low salaries. Thus, the comparable status of women's and men's employment results in part from the high average education characteristic of women's employment and not from high average levels of earned income. The prestige similarity follows from the fact that, as Treiman (1977) has shown, prestige derives in part from education and income.

2. Refer to Chapter 2 for a more detailed discussion of data and measurement decisions.

3. It is unfortunate that mother's occupation is not available for inclusion, given Rosenfeld's (1978b) documentation of its relevance for women. Although perhaps less important historically, since so few married women worked outside the home, this factor is likely to increase in importance as more women engage in paid employment (see Chapter 1).

4. In Germany, although gender differences in social origins exist when occupation is measured by occupational categories, the sexes apparently do not differ significantly when one measures social origins by either the prestige or the wage-rate scale.

5. Results for the four Scandinavian data sets (not shown in Appendix C) are also in accord with this finding.

6. There are two exceptions: (1) a sex difference in prestige, but not in the wage-rate scale, exists in Norway, and (2) a sex difference in occupation emerges in the United States only when the wage-rate scale is employed.

7. The literature documenting these assertions is too voluminous to report on here and several empirical and theoretical reviews are already available (for example, Blau and Jusenius 1976; Blau 1977; Treiman and Hartmann 1981; Bielby and Baron 1984; Reskin and Hartmann 1985).

8. Because no interaction terms with other independent variables are included in the attainment equations, these analyses do not test for differences in the process of occupational attainment of ever-married and never-married women, but only for differences in the average occupational wage. Chapter 6 presents a more thorough discussion of these issues and further analyses of marital differences in the labor-force behavior and occupational attainment of women.

9. There is an alternative explanation for the cross-country variation in gender differences in rates of occupational return to educational investment. It may be that the relationship between occupational wage and education is curvilinear, with larger rates of return accruing to the highest education levels. If this were true, then the correct functional form would be curvilinear, and could be tested by estimating a quadratic equation including education and education-squared. Certainly the finding of this study that the countries with greater male coefficients are also those in which males have higher average education levels, and vice versa, is consistent with this possibility.

10. By sequentially ordering the independent variables, I am not implying that variables included first are logically prior to those included later. Although one's social origins can be considered logically prior to age, and both of these are prior to the last two variables, it could be argued that education should precede marital status. In the present case, I place years of schooling last in the sequential ordering because I am interested in its effect net of father' occupation, age, and marital status.

11. There are four countries in Panel A (Denmark, Great Britain, Norway, and Sweden) in which a significant gender difference in occupational wage attainment does not exist. Only Denmark and Great Britain show changes in the relative female wage rate after adjustment for compositional differences. In Norway, where the gender difference barely lacks significance, the greater female return to education and the slightly higher male average education combine to produce a 10.7 percent increase in the relative female wage rate. The lack of a gender difference in the wage-rate scale in Sweden may be due to offsetting social origin and education effects—substituting men's lower social origins into the female equation decreases the female relative wage rate while substituting men's slightly higher education increases it.

12. Although not significant, the male wage rates in Finland and Northern Ireland are also less than those of their female counterparts—the relative male wage rate is 94 percent in Finland and 97 percent in Northern Ireland. The decomposition of the mean occupational wage rates reveals that gender differences favoring women, in both Finland and Northern Ireland, are due entirely to the fact that women in these countries come from higher-status social origins and that they have on average more education. In fact, as

column 7 of Panel B indicates, if Finnish and Northern Ireland men had the higher female social origins and education, their relative wage rates would exceed those of women by 7 and 5 percent, respectively.

Chapter 6 notes

1. I do not, however, expect the attainments of never-married women to exactly approximate those of men, since most men have traditionally had the responsibility for assuring their family's as well as their own financial security, whereas single women usually need only be concerned with their own security. Although this male responsibility has been mitigated somewhat in recent years as more married women are working for pay outside the home, it is still the case that men on average contribute the larger share of the household income, if for no other reason than they are typically older than their wives and generally work in jobs that pay more than the jobs in which women work. Smith (1979, 12) estimated that working wives in the United States contribute on average one-quarter of their family's total income; the comparable figure for wives employed full time, year round is 38 percent. This is not to suggest that wives' income is not necessary for the family's financial security. To the contrary, Oppenheimer (1982) found that wives' economic role is an important one, especially when their husbands are in poorly paid occupations. Women's added earnings, according to Oppenheimer, are often a functional substitute for upward occupational mobility by the husband.

2. The average age at first marriage was based on 1974 or 1975 data (United Nations 1977). The ages were: Austria: 22.6; Denmark: 23.3; Finland: 23.1; Germany: 22.3; Great Britain (England and Wales): 22.3; Israel: 21.5; Japan: 24.5; Netherlands: 21.9; Northern Ireland: 22.6; Norway: 22.5; Sweden: 24.8; United States: 21.4.

3. A further simplifying assumption made in these analyses is that women's labor-force decisions depend only on their own background and personal characteristics, which, from previous analyses, is known to not be the case at all. Certainly, from a historical perspective, women's labor-force decisions depended to a considerable extent on their family's economic need (see Chapter 1). Moreover, economists (for example, Mincer 1962; Cain 1966; Bowen and Finegan 1969) and sociologists (for example, Oppenheimer 1982) have noted the connection between women's labor-force decisions and the characteristics of their husbands (for example, the negative correlation between wives' labor-force participation and their husbands' income). Unfortunately, lack of appropriate data precludes a consideration of these possibilities.

4. Sewell and his coauthors (1980) also found that most women work in clerical or service occupations regardless of their marital status.

5. Treiman and Terrell (1975b, 191) attributed the smaller marital difference for black women to the larger number of children black never-married women have relative to their white counterparts. Forty percent of never-married black women have children compared with 3 percent of their white counterparts. Among blacks in the United States, therefore, a larger proportion

of never-married women face dual responsibilities, perhaps one explanation for their low average occupational attainment.

6. The bases of these percentages include all employed women aged twenty to sixty-four; thus, any part-time workers and young women in the labor force prior to marriage are included in the sampled population.

7. Mention should be made of the three exceptions to the general finding—in Germany, Great Britain, and Northern Ireland, older never-married women are somewhat less likely to work than all never-married women.

8. Because the findings from Denmark, Norway, and Sweden are based on particularly small samples, results for these countries should be viewed as suggestive.

9. Even in Finland, the father's occupation coefficient loses significance when older women are compared.

Bibliography

Barrett, Nancy S. 1976. "Women in Industrial Society: An International Perspective." In *Economic Independence for Women: The Foundation for Equal Rights*, edited by Jane R. Chapman, 77–111. Beverly Hills, Ca.: Sage.

———. 1979. "Women in the Job Market: Occupations, Earnings, and Career Opportunities." In *The Subtle Revolution: Women at Work*, edited by Ralph E. Smith, 31–61. Washington, D.C.: Urban Institute.

Becker, Gary. 1981. *A Treatise on the Family.* Cambridge, Ma.: Harvard University Press.

Bianchi, Suzanne, and Nancy Rytina. 1984. "Occupational Change, 1970–80." Paper presented at the Annual Meetings of the Population Association of America, Minneapolis, Mn., May.

Bielby, William T., and James N. Baron. 1984. "A Woman's Place is With Other Women." In *Sex Segregation in the Workplace: Trends, Explanations, Remedies*, edited by Barbara F. Reskin, 27–55. Washington, D.C.: National Academy Press.

Bishop, Yvonne M. M., Stephen E. Fienberg, and Paul W. Holland. 1975. *Discrete Multivariate Analysis: Theory and Practice.* Boston, Ma.: MIT Press.

Blau, Francine D. 1977. *Equal Pay in the Office.* Lexington, Ma.: Lexington Books.

Blau, Francine D., and Wallace E. Hendricks. 1979. "Occupational Segregation by Sex: Trends and Prospects." *Journal of Human Resources* 14:197–210.

Blau, Francine D., and Carol L. Jusenius. 1976. "Economists' Approaches to Sex Segregation in the Labor Market: An Appraisal." In *Women and the Workplace: The Implications of Occupational Segregation*, edited by Martha Blaxall and Barbara Reagan, 181–99. Chicago, Il.: University of Chicago Press.

217

Blau, Peter M., and Otis Dudley Duncan. 1967. *The American Occupational Structure*. New York: Wiley.

Blaxall, Martha, and Barbara Reagan (eds.). 1976. *Women and the Workplace: The Implications of Occupational Segregation*. Chicago, Il.: University of Chicago Press.

Blekher, Feiga. 1979. *The Soviet Woman in the Family and in Society*. New York: Wiley.

Boserup, Ester. 1970. *Woman's Role in Economic Development*. London: George Allen and Unwin Ltd.

Boulding, Elise. 1976. "Familial Constraints on Women's Work Roles." In *Women and the Workplace: The Implications of Occupational Segregation*, edited by Martha Blaxall and Barbara Reagan, 95–117. Chicago, Il.: University of Chicago Press.

———. 1977. *Women in the Twentieth Century World*. New York: Wiley.

Bowen, William G., and T. Aldrich Finegan. 1969. *The Economics of Labor Force Participation*. Princeton, N.J.: Princeton University Press.

Boyd, Monica, and Hugh McRoberts. 1982. "Women, Men and Socioeconomic Indices: An Assessment." In *Measures of Socioeconomic Status: Current Issues*, edited by Mary G. Powers, 129–59. Boulder, Co: Westview Press.

Cain, Glen C. 1966. *Married Women in the Labor Force: An Economic Analysis*. Chicago, Il: University of Chicago Press.

Cain, Pamela S., and Donald J. Treiman. 1981. "The Dictionary of Occupational Titles as a Source of Occupational Data." *American Sociological Review* 46:253–78.

Carlsson, Gosta. 1958. *Social Mobility and Class Structure*. Sweden: CWK Gleirup.

Cook, Alice H. 1979. *The Working Mother: A Survey of Problems and Programs in Nine Countries*. Ithaca, N.Y.: New York State School of Industrial and Labor Relations.

Cook, Alice H., and Hiroko Hayashi. 1980. *Working Women in Japan: Discrimination, Resistance, and Reform*. Ithaca, N.Y.: New York State School of Industrial and Labor Relations.

Corcoran, Mary, and Greg J. Duncan. 1979. "Work History, Labor Force Attachment, and Earnings Differences Between the Races and Sexes." *Journal of Human Resources* 14:3–20.

Council of Economic Advisers. 1973. "The Economic Role of Women." In *Economic Report of the President*, 89–112. Washington, D.C.: U.S. Government Printing Office.

Cummings, William K., and Atsushi Naoi. 1972. "Education and Mobility: An International Comparison With Special Reference to Japan and the United States." Paper presented at the Annual Meeting of the American Sociological Association, New Orleans, August.

Degler, Carl N. 1980. *At Odds: Women and the Family in America from the Revolution to the Present*. New York: Oxford University Press.

DeJong, Peter Y., Milton J. Brawer, and Stanley S. Robin. 1971. "Patterns of Female Intergenerational Occupational Mobility: A Comparison with

Male Patterns of Intergenerational Occupational Mobility." *American Sociological Review* 36:1033–42.

Dodge, Norton. 1971. "Women in the Soviet Economy." In *The Professional Woman,* edited by Athena Theodore, 207–23. Cambridge, Ma.: Schenkman.

Doeringer, Peter G., and Michael J. Piore. 1971. *Internal Labor Markets and Manpower Analysis.* Lexington, Ma.: D.C. Heath.

Doescher, Tabitha A. 1980. "Fertility and Female Occupational Choice." Paper presented at the Annual Meeting of the Population Association of America, Denver, April.

Duncan, Otis Dudley. 1969. "Inheritance of Poverty or Inheritance of Race." In *On Understanding Poverty,* edited by Daniel P. Moynihan, 85–110. New York: Basic Books.

Duncan, Otis Dudley, David L. Featherman, and Beverly Duncan. 1972. *Socioeconomic Background and Achievement.* New York: Seminar Press.

Dunton, Nancy E., and David L. Featherman. 1979. "Gender Differences in Intergenerational and Intragenerational Occupational Mobility." Working Paper 79–36, Center for Demography and Ecology, University of Wisconsin, Madison.

Durand, John D. 1975. *The Labor Force in Economic Development: A Comparison of International Census Data, 1946–1966.* Princeton, N.J.: Princeton University Press.

England, Paula. 1979. "Women and Occupational Prestige: A Case of Vacuous Sex Equality." *Signs* 5:252–65.

Erikson, Robert. 1976. "Patterns of Social Mobility." In *Readings in the Swedish Class Structure,* edited by Richard Scase, 171–204. Elmsford, N.Y.: Pergamon Press.

Featherman, David L., and Robert M. Hauser. 1976. "Sexual Inequalities and Socioeconomic Achievement in the U.S., 1962–1973." *American Sociological Review* 41:462–83.

―――. 1978. *Opportunity and Change.* New York: Academic Press.

Feldberg, Roslyn L., and Evelyn N. Glenn. 1980. "Effects of Technological Change on Clerical Work: Review and Reassessment." Paper presented at the Annual Meeting of the American Sociological Association, New York, August.

Finland Central Statistical Office. 1975. *The Population of Finland.* Committee for International Coordination of National Research in Demography. CICRED series. Finland: Central Statistical Office.

Finn, Jeremy D., Loretta Dulberg, and Janet Reis. 1979. "Sex Differences in Educational Attainment." *Harvard Educational Review* 49:477–503.

Finn, Jeremy D., Janet Reis, and Loretta Dulberg. 1980. "Sex Differences in Educational Attainment: The Process." *Comparative Education Review* 24:533–52.

Fligstein, Neil D., and Wendy C. Wolf. 1978. "Sex Similarities in Occupational Status Attainment: Are the Results Due to the Restriction of the Sample to Employed Women?" *Social Science Research* 7:197–212.

Friedl, Ernestine. 1975. *Women and Men: An Anthropologist's View.* New York: Holt, Rinehart & Winston.

Galenson, Marjorie. 1973. *Women and Work: An International Comparison.* Ithaca, N.Y.: New York State School of Industrial and Labor Relations.

Gaskin, Katharine A. 1979. "Occupational Differentiation by Sex: An International Comparison." Ph.D. diss., University of Michigan.

Geerken, Michael, and Walter R. Gove. 1983. *At Home and At Work: The Family's Allocation of Labor.* Beverly Hills, Ca.: Sage.

German Federal Institute for Population Research. 1974. *The Population of the Federal Republic of Germany.* Committee for International Coordination of National Research in Demography. CICRED series. Wiesbaden, Germany: Federal Institute for Population Research.

Giele, Janet Z., and Audrey C. Smock (eds.). 1977. *Women: Roles and Status in Eight Countries.* New York: Wiley.

Glass, David. 1954. *Social Mobility in Britain.* London: Routledge & Kegan Paul.

Gross, Edward. 1968. "Plus Ca Change . . .? The Sexual Structure of Occupations Over Time." *Social Problems* 16:198–208.

Grossman, Allyson S. 1979. "Labor Force Patterns of Single Women." *Monthly Labor Review* 102:46–9.

Haavio-Mannila, Elina. 1975. "Convergence Between East and West: Tradition and Modernity in Sex Roles in Sweden, Finland, and the Soviet Union." In *Women and Achievement: Social and Motivational Analyses,* edited by Martha T.S. Mednick, Sandra S. Tangri, and Lois W. Hoffman, 71–84. New York: Wiley.

Haavio-Mannila, Elina, and Magdalena Sokolowska. 1978. "Social Position of Women." In *Social Structure and Change: Finland and Poland Comparative Perspective,* edited by Erik Allardt and Włodzimierz Wesołowski, 183–216. Warsaw: Polish Scientific Publishers.

Hareven, Tamara K. 1975. "Family Time and Industrial Time: Family and Work in a Planned Corporation Town, 1900–1924." *Journal of Urban History* 1:365–89.

Hartman, Harriet, and Moshe Hartman. 1981. "The Effect of Immigration on Women's Roles in Various Countries." Paper presented at the Annual Meeting of the Population Association of America, Washington, D.C., March.

Hartman, Moshe. 1980. "The Role of Ethnicity in Married Women's Economic Activity in Israel." *Ethnicity* 7:225–55.

Hauser, Robert M., and David L. Featherman. 1977. *The Process of Stratification: Trends and Analyses.* New York: Academic Press.

Hauser, Robert M., David L. Featherman, and Dennis P. Hogan. 1977. "Sex in the Structure of Occupational Mobility in the United States, 1962." In *The Process of Stratification: Trends and Analyses,* edited by Robert M. Hauser and David L. Featherman, 191–215. New York: Academic Press.

Havens, Elizabeth M., and Judy Corder Tully. 1972. "Female Intergenerational Occupational Mobility: Comparisons of Patterns?" *American Sociological Review* 37:774–7.

Huber, Joan, and Glenna Spitze. 1983. *Sex Stratification: Children, Housework, and Jobs.* New York: Academic Press.

Hudis, Paula M. 1976. "Commitment to Work and to Family: Marital-Status Differences in Women's Earnings." *Journal of Marriage and the Family* 38:267–78.

Iglitzin, Lynne B., and Ruth Ross (eds.). 1976. *Women in the World: A Comparative Study.* Santa Barbara, Ca.: Clio Books.

International Labour Office (ILO). 1950. *Equal Remuneration for Men and Women Workers for Work of Equal Value.* Report VII (1) of the 34th Session of the International Labour Conference. Geneva: International Labour Office.

———. 1969. *International Standard Classification of Occupations.* Revised edition. Geneva: International Labour Office.

———. 1970. *Yearbook of Labour Statistics.* Geneva: International Labour Office.

———. 1975a. *Equality of Opportunity and Treatment for Women Workers.* Report VIII, International Labour Conference, 60th Session. Geneva: International Labour Office.

———. 1975b. *Fighting Discrimination in Employment and Occupation: A Worker's Education Manual.* Geneva: International Labour Office.

———. 1975c. *Yearbook of Labour Statistics.* Geneva: International Labour Office.

———. 1976. *Women Workers and Society: International Perspectives.* Geneva: International Labour Office.

———. 1977. *Yearbook of Labour Statistics.* Geneva: International Labour Office.

———. 1979a. *Equal Opportunities and Equal Treatment for Men and Women Workers: Workers with Family Responsibilities.* Geneva: International Labour Office.

———. 1979b. *Yearbook of Labour Statistics.* Geneva: International Labour Office.

———. 1984. *World Labour Report: Employment, Incomes, Social Protection, New Information Technology.* Geneva: International Labour Office.

Israel Central Bureau of Statistics. 1975. *Statistical Abstract of Israel,* Volume 26. Tel Aviv: Israel Ministry of Education and Culture.

Iutaka, Sugiyama, and E. Wilbur Bock. 1973. "Determinants of Occupational Status in Brazil." In *Social Stratification and Career Mobility,* edited by Walter Müller and Karl Ulrich Mayer, 213–22. Paris: Mouton.

Jacobs, Jerry. 1981. "The Prestige of Men's and Women's Occupations: A Reassessment." Unpublished paper, Harvard University.

———. 1982. "On Comparing the Socio-economic Standing of Men and Women." Paper presented at the Annual Meeting of the Eastern Sociological Society, Philadelphia.

Jonung, Christina. 1977. "Occupational Segregation by Sex in Sweden: Problems and Policies." Nationalekonomiska Institutionen, Lunds Universitet, Lund, Sweden.

———. 1978a. "Policies of 'Positive Discrimination' in Scandinavia in Respect of Women's Employment." Paper presented at the International Symposium on Women and Industrial Relations, Vienna, September.

————. 1978b. "Sexual Equality in the Swedish Labor Market." *Monthly Labor Review* 101:31–5.

Kahne, Hilda, with Andrew Kohen. 1975. "Economic Perspectives on the Roles of Women in the American Economy." *Journal of Economic Literature* 13:1249–92.

Kamerman, Sheila B. 1979. "Work and Family in Industrialized Societies." *Signs* 4:632–50.

Kamerman, Sheila B., and Alfred J. Kahn (eds.). 1978. *Family Policy: Government and Families in Fourteen Countries*. New York: Columbia University Press.

Kanter, Rosabeth Moss. 1977. *Work and Family in the United States: A Critical Review and Agenda for Research and Policy*. New York: Russell Sage.

Kraus, Vered, and Donald J. Treiman. 1980. "Sex and the Process of Status Attainment in Israel." Unpublished paper, University of California, Los Angeles.

Kreps, Juanita M. (ed.). 1976. *Women and the American Economy: A Look to the 1980s*. Englewood Cliffs, N.J.: Prentice-Hall.

Kreps, Juanita M., and R. John Leaper. 1976. "Home Work, Market Work, and the Allocation of Time." In *Women and the American Economy: A Look to the 1980s*, edited by Juanita M. Kreps, 61–81. Englewood Cliffs, N.J.: Prentice-Hall.

Lebra, Joyce, Joy Paulson, and Elizabeth Powers. 1976. *Women in Changing Japan*. Boulder, Co.: Westview Press.

Leijon, Anna-Greta. 1976. "Sexual Equality in the Labour Market: Some Experiences and Views of the Nordic Countries." In *Women Workers and Society: International Perspectives*, edited by International Labour Office, 161–75. Geneva: International Labour Office.

Lloyd, Cynthia B. (ed.). 1975. *Sex, Discrimination, and the Division of Labour*. New York: Columbia University Press.

The Mainichi Newspapers. 1976. *Japan Almanac 1976*. Tokyo: The Mainichi Newspaper.

Marini, Margaret Mooney, and Mary C. Brinton. 1984. "Sex Typing in Occupational Socialization." In *Sex Segregation in the Workplace: Trends, Explanations, Remedies*, edited by Barbara F. Reskin, 192–232. Washington, D.C.: National Academy Press.

Martin, Linda G. 1980. "Labor Force Consequences of Slowing Population Growth in Japan." Paper presented at the Annual Meeting of the Population Association of America, Denver, April.

Mason, Karen O., Maris A. Vinovskis, and Tamara K. Hareven. 1978. "Women's Work and the Life Course in Essex County, Massachusetts, 1880." In *Transitions: The Family and the Life Course in Historical Perspective*, edited by Tamara K. Hareven, 187–216. New York: Academic Press.

Matras, Judah, and Dov Weintraub. 1976. "Ethnic and Other Primordial Differentials in Intergenerational Mobility in Israel." Paper presented at the International Sociological Association Seminar on Mobility and Social Stratification, Jerusalem, April.

McAuley, Alistair. 1981. *Women's Work and Wages in the Soviet Union*. Boston, Ma.: George Allen & Unwin.

McClendon, McKee J. 1976. "The Occupational Status Attainment Processes of Males and Females." *American Sociological Review* 41:52–64.

McLaughlin, Steven D. 1975. "Occupational Characteristics and the Male-Female Income Differential." Ph.D. diss., Washington State University.

Miller, Ann R., Donald J. Treiman, Pamela S. Cain, and Patricia A. Roos (eds.). 1980. *Work, Jobs, and Occupations: A Critical Review of the Dictionary of Occupational Titles.* Washington, D.C.: National Academy Press.

Mincer, Jacob. 1962. "Labor Force Participation of Married Women: A Study of Labor Supply." In *Aspects of Labor Economics,* edited by National Bureau of Economic Research, 63–97. Princeton, N.J.: Princeton University Press.

Mincer, Jacob, and Solomon Polachek. 1974. "Family Investments in Human Capital: Earnings of Women." *Journal of Political Economy* 82:Supplement 76–108.

Müller, Walter. 1973. "Family Background, Education, and Career Mobility." In *Social Stratification and Career Mobility,* edited by Walter Müller and Karl Ulrich Mayer, 223–55. Paris: Mouton.

Myrdal, Alva, and Viola Klein. 1968. *Women's Two Roles: Home and Work.* London: Routledge and Kegan Paul.

Nam, Charles B., and Mary G. Powers. 1983. *The Socioeconomic Approach to Status Measurement.* Houston, Tx.: Cap and Gown Press.

Newland, Kathleen. 1979. *The Sisterhood of Man.* New York: Norton.

———. 1980. *Women, Men, and the Division of Labor.* Worldwatch Paper 37. Washington, D.C.: Worldwatch Institute.

Nunnally, J. C. 1967. *Psychometric Theory.* New York: McGraw-Hill.

Oppenheimer, Valerie K. 1968. "The Sex-Labeling of Jobs." *Industrial Relations* 7:219–34.

———. 1970. *The Female Labor Force in the United States: Demographic and Economic Factors Governing its Growth and Changing Composition.* Westport, Ct.: Greenwood Press.

———. 1982. *Work and the Family: A Study in Social Demography.* New York: Academic Press.

Organisation for Economic Cooperation and Development (OECD). 1975. *The Role of Women in the Economy.* Paris: Organisation for Economic Cooperation and Development.

———. 1979. *Equal Opportunities for Women.* Paris: Organisation for Economic Cooperation and Development.

Pettman, Barrie O. (ed.). 1975. *Equal Pay for Women: Progress and Problems in Seven Countries.* England: MCB Books.

Piore, Michael J. 1971. "The Dual Labor Market: Theory and Implications." In *Problems in Political Economy: An Urban Perspective,* edited by David M. Gordon, 90–4. Lexington, Ma.: D.C. Heath.

Pleck, Joseph H. 1983. "Husband's Paid Work and Family Roles: Current Research Issues." In *Research in the Interweave of Social Roles: Jobs and Families,* edited by Helena Z. Lopata and Joseph H. Pleck, 251–333. Greenwich, Ct.: JAI Press.

Polachek, Solomon W. 1975. "Discontinuous Labor Force Participation and its Effect on Women's Market Earnings." In *Sex, Discrimination, and the Division of Labor*, edited by Cynthia B. Lloyd, 90–122. New York: Columbia University Press.

Pöntinen, Seppo. 1974. "Comparison of Social Mobility in the Scandinavian Countries." Paper presented at the Mathematical Social Science Board Conference, Toronto, August.

————. 1980. *On the Social Mobility of Women in the Scandinavian Countries.* Finland: Societas Scientiarum Fennica.

Przeworski, Adam, and Henry Teune. 1970. *The Logic of Comparative Social Inquiry.* New York: Wiley-Interscience.

Ratner, Ronnie S. 1979. "Labor Market Inequality and Equal Opportunity Policy for Women: A Cross-National Comparison." Paper prepared for Working Party No. 6 on the Role of Women in the Economy, Organisation for Economic Cooperation and Development.

Ratner, Ronnie S. (ed.). 1980. *Equal Employment Policy for Women: Strategies for Implementation in the United States, Canada, and Western Europe.* Philadelphia, Pa.: Temple University Press.

Reskin, Barbara F., and Heidi I. Hartmann (eds.). 1985. *Women's Work, Men's Work: Sex Segregation on the Job.* Washington, D.C.: National Academy Press.

Rindfuss, Ronald R., Larry L. Bumpass, and Craig St. John. 1980. "Education and Fertility: Implications for the Roles Women Occupy." *American Sociological Review* 45:431–47.

Rizza, Carolyn C. 1982. "Women's Status and Fertility in Finland." Paper presented at the 10th Anniversary Conference of the Michigan Women's Studies Association, Ann Arbor, Mi., April.

Robinson, John P., Philip E. Converse, and Alexander Szalai. 1972. "Everyday Life in Twelve Countries." In *The Use of Time: Daily Activities of Urban and Suburban Populations in Twelve Countries*, edited by Alexander Szalai, 113–44. The Hague: Mouton.

Rohrlich-Leavitt, Ruby (ed.). 1975. *Women Cross-Culturally: Change and Challenge.* Chicago, Il.: Aldine.

Roos, Patricia A. 1981. "Sex Stratification in the Workplace: Male-Female Differences in Economic Returns to Occupation." *Social Science Research* 10:195–224.

Roos, Patricia A., and Barbara F. Reskin. 1984. "Institutional Factors Contributing to Sex Segregation in the Workplace." In *Sex Segregation in the Workplace: Trends, Explanations, Remedies*, edited by Barbara F. Reskin, 235–60. Washington, D.C.: National Academy Press.

Rosenfeld, Rachel A. 1978a. "Women's Employment Patterns and Occupational Achievements." *Social Science Research* 7:61–80.

————. 1978b. "Women's Intergenerational Occupational Mobility." *American Sociological Review* 43:36–46.

————. 1979. "Women's Occupational Careers: Individual and Structural Explanations." *Sociology of Work and Occupations* 6:283–311.

————. 1980. "Race and Sex Differences in Career Dynamics." *American Sociological Review* 45:583–609.

Rosenfeld, Rachel A., and Aage B. Sørensen. 1979. "Sex Differences in Patterns of Career Mobility." *Demography* 16:89–101.

Ryder, Norman B. 1979. "The Future of American Fertility." *Social Problems* 26:359–70.

Safilios-Rothschild, Constantina. 1975. "A Cross-Cultural Examination of Women's Marital, Educational and Occupational Options." In *Women and Achievement: Social and Motivational Analyses*, edited by Martha T. S. Mednick, Sandra S. Tangri, and Lois W. Hoffman, 48–70. New York: Wiley.

Safilios-Rothschild, Constantina. 1976. "Dual Linkages Between the Occupational and Family Systems: A Macrosociological Analysis." In *Women and the Workplace: The Implications of Occupational Segregation*, edited by Martha Blaxall and Barbara Reagan, 51–60. Chicago, Il.: University of Chicago Press.

Sawhill, Isabel V. 1973. "The Economics of Discrimination Against Women: Some New Findings." *Journal of Human Resources* 8:383–96.

Semyonov, Moshe. 1980. "The Social Context of Women's Labor Force Participation: A Comparative Analysis." *American Journal of Sociology* 86:534–50.

Sewell, William H., Robert M. Hauser, and Wendy C. Wolf. 1980. "Sex, Schooling, and Occupational Status." *American Journal of Sociology* 86:551–83.

Shaffer, Harry G. 1981. *Women in the Two Germanies: A Comparative Study of a Socialist and a Non-Socialist Society*. Elmsford, N.Y.: Pergamon Press.

Singelmann, Joachim. 1978. "The Sectoral Transformation of the Labor Force in Seven Industrialized Countries." *American Journal of Sociology* 83:1224–34.

Smith, James P. 1972. "The Life Cycle Allocation of Time in a Family Context." Ph.D. diss., University of Chicago.

———. 1980. *Female Labor Supply: Theory and Estimation*. Princeton, N.J.: Princeton University Press.

Smith, Ralph E. 1979. "The Movement of Women into the Labor Force." In *The Subtle Revolution: Women at Work*, edited by Ralph E. Smith, 1–29. Washington, D.C.: The Urban Institute.

Smuts, Robert. 1959. *Women and Work in America*. New York: Columbia University Press.

Sokolowska, Magdalena. 1977. "Poland: Women's Experience Under Socialism." In *Women: Roles and Status in Eight Countries*, edited by Janet Z. Giele and Audrey C. Smock, 347–81. New York: Wiley.

Standing, Guy. 1978. *Labour Force Participation and Development*. Geneva: International Labour Office.

Sullerot, Evelyn. 1976. "Equality of Remuneration for Men and Women in the Member States of the EEC." In *Women Workers and Society: International Perspectives*, edited by International Labour Office, 89–110. Geneva: International Labour Office.

Suter, Larry E., and Herman P. Miller. 1973. "Income Differences between Men and Career Women." *American Journal of Sociology* 78:962–74.

Svalastoga, Kaare. 1959. *Prestige, Class and Mobility.* Copenhagen: Gyldendal.

Sweet, James A. 1975. "Recent Trends in the Employment of American Women." Working Paper 75–14, Center for Demography and Ecology, University of Wisconsin, Madison.

Szalai, Alexander (ed.). 1972. *The Use of Time: Daily Activities of Urban and Suburban Populations in Twelve Countries.* The Hague: Mouton.

Tilly, Louise A., and Joan W. Scott. 1978. *Women, Work, and Family.* New York: Holt, Rinehart and Winston.

Treiman, Donald J. 1977. *Occupational Prestige in Comparative Perspective.* New York: Academic Press.

Treiman, Donald J., and Heidi I. Hartmann. 1981. *Women, Work, and Wages: Equal Pay for Jobs of Equal Value.* Washington, D.C.: National Academy Press.

Treiman, Donald J., and Jonathan Kelley. 1974. *A Comparative Study of Status Attainment.* Grant proposal submitted to the National Institute of Mental Health. August.

———. 1978. *Extension of a Comparative Study of Status Attainment.* Grant proposal submitted to the National Institute of Mental Health. January.

Treiman, Donald J., and Kermit Terrell. 1975a. "The Process of Status Attainment in the United States and Great Britain." *American Journal of Sociology* 81:563–83.

———. 1975b. "Sex and the Process of Status Attainment: A Comparison of Working Women and Men." *American Sociological Review* 40:174–200.

———. 1975c. "Women, Work, and Wages: Trends in the Female Occupational Structure Since 1940." In *Social Indicator Models,* edited by Kenneth Land and Seymour Spilerman, 157–99. New York: Russell Sage Foundation.

Turchaninova, Svetlana. 1976. "Trends in Women's Employment in the USSR." In *Women Workers and Society: International Perspectives,* edited by International Labour Office, 149–60. Geneva: International Labour Office.

Tyree, Andrea, and Judith Treas. 1974. "The Occupational and Marital Mobility of Women." *American Sociological Review* 39:293–302.

United Nations. 1973. *Demographic Yearbook, 1972.* New York: United Nations.

———. 1974. *Demographic Yearbook, 1973.* New York: United Nations.

———. 1977. *Demographic Yearbook, 1976.* New York: United Nations.

United Nations Educational, Scientific, and Cultural Organization (UNESCO). 1966. *World Survey of Education.* Volume 4: Higher Education. New York: UNESCO Publications Center.

U.S. Bureau of the Census. 1974. *Population of the United States, Trends and Prospects: 1950–1990.* Current Population Reports, Series P-23, No. 49. Washington, D.C.: U.S. Government Printing Office.

———. 1977. *Population Profile of the United States: 1976.* Current Population Reports, Series P-20, No. 307. Washington, D.C.: U.S. Government Printing Office.

———. 1982. *Statistical Abstract of the United States, 1982–83.* Washington, D.C.: U.S. Government Printing Office.

————. 1983. *Population Profile of the United States.* Current Population Reports, Series P-23, No. 130. Washington, D.C.: U.S. Government Printing Office.

————. 1984. *Lifetime Work Experience and its Effect on Earnings: Retrospective Data from the 1979 Income Survey Development Program.* Washington, D.C.: U.S. Government Printing Office.

U.S. Commission on Civil Rights. 1978. *Social Indicators of Equality for Minorities and Women.* Washington, D.C.: U.S. Government Printing Office.

U.S. Department of Labor. 1977. *Dictionary of Occupational Titles.* 4th ed. Washington, D.C.: U.S. Government Printing Office.

Vogel, Eliane. 1976. "Some Suggestions for the Advancement of Working Women." In *Women Workers and Society: International Perspectives,* edited by International Labour Office, 11–25. Geneva: International Labour Office.

Volgyes, Ivan, and Nancy Volgyes. 1977. *The Liberated Female: Life, Work, and Sex in Socialist Hungary.* Boulder, Co.: Westview Press.

Wachter, Michael L. 1974. "Primary and Secondary Labor Markets: A Critique of the Dual Approach." Vol. 3 of *Brookings Papers on Economic Activity,* edited by Arthur M. Okun and George L. Perry. Washington, D.C.: Brookings Institution.

Waite, Linda J. 1976. "Working Wives: 1940–1960." *American Sociological Review* 41:65–80.

Waite, Linda J., and Ross M. Stolzenberg. 1976. "Intended Childbearing and Labor Force Participation of Young Women: Insights from Nonrecursive Models." *American Sociological Review* 41:235–52.

Waldman, Elizabeth, and Beverly McEaddy. 1974. "Where Women Work— An Analysis by Industry and Occupation." *Monthly Labor Review* 97:3–13.

Walker, Kathryn E., and Margaret E. Woods. 1976. *Time Use: A Measure of Household Production of Family Goods and Services.* Washington, D.C.: American Home Economics Association, Center for the Family.

Ward, Kathryn B., and Fred C. Pampel. 1983. "Structural Determinants of Female Labor Force Participation Rates in Developed Nations, 1950–1975." Paper presented at the Annual Meeting of the American Sociological Association, Detroit, August.

Westoff, Charles. 1978. "The Infertile Society." *Scientific American* 238:81.

Whitaker, Donald P. 1974. *Area Handbook for Japan.* Washington, D.C.: U.S. Government Printing Office.

Wolf, Wendy C. 1976. "Occupational Attainments of Married Women: Do Career Contingencies Matter?" Working Paper 76-3, Center for Demography and Ecology, University of Wisconsin, Madison.

Wolf, Wendy C., and Neil D. Fligstein. 1979. "Sex and Authority in the Workplace: The Causes of Sexual Inequality." *American Sociological Review* 44:235–52.

Wolf, Wendy C., and Rachel A. Rosenfeld. 1978. "Sex Structure of Occupational and Job Mobility." *Social Forces* 56:823–44.

Youssef, Nadia H. 1974. *Women and Work in Developing Societies.* Westport, Cn.: Greenwood Press.

Index